SONGS OF
LOVE AND DEATH

Recent Titles in
Contributions to the Study of Popular Culture

Seeking the Perfect Game: Baseball in American Literature
Cordelia Candelaria

Take One: The Control Room Insights of Ten TV Directors
Jack Kuney

A "Brand" New Language: Commercial Influences in Literature and Culture
Monroe Friedman

Out of the Woodpile: Black Characters in Crime and Detective Fiction
Frankie Y. Bailey

Freaks of Genius
Daniel Shealy, editor
Madeleine B. Stern and Joel Myerson, associate editors

Encounters with Filmmakers: Eight Career Studies
Jon Tuska

Master Space: Film Images of Capra, Lubitsch, Sternberg, and Wyler
Barbara Bowman

The Cosby Show: Audiences, Impact, and Implications
Linda K. Fuller

America's Musical Pulse: Popular Music in Twentieth-Century Society
Kenneth J. Bindas, editor

Not Just for Children: The Mexican Comic Book in the Late 1960s and 1970s
Harold E. Hinds, Jr., and Charles M. Tatum

Creating the Big Game: John W. Heisman and the Invention of American Football
Wiley Lee Umphlett

"Mr. B" Or Comforting Thoughts About the Bison: A Critical Biography of
Robert Benchley
Wes D. Gehring

Religion and Sport: The Meeting of Sacred and Profane
Charles S. Prebish

SONGS OF
LOVE AND DEATH

The Classical American
Horror Film of the 1930s

MICHAEL SEVASTAKIS

Contributions to the Study of Popular Culture, Number 37

GREENWOOD PRESS
Westport, Connecticut • London

Library of Congress Cataloging-in-Publication Data

Sevastakis, Michael.
    Songs of love and death : the classical American horror film of
the 1930s / Michael Sevastakis.
        p.   cm.—(Contributions to the study of popular culture,
ISSN 0198–9871 ; no. 37)
    Includes bibliographical references and index.
    ISBN 0–313–27949–7 (alk. paper)
    1. Horror films—United States—History and criticism. 2. Motion
pictures and literature—United States. 3. Gothic revival
(Literature)—United States. 4. Gothic revival (Literature)—
Europe. 5. Romanticism. I. Title. II. Series.
PN1995.9.H6S46   1993
791.43′616—dc20   92–32226

British Library Cataloguing in Publication Data is available.

Library of Congress Catalog Card Number: 92–32226
ISBN: 0–313–27949–7
ISSN: 0198–9871

First published in 1993

Greenwood Press, 88 Post Road West, Westport, CT 06881
An imprint of Greenwood Publishing Group, Inc.

Printed in the United States of America

∞™

The paper used in this book complies with the
Permanent Paper Standard issued by the National
Information Standards Organization (Z39.48–1984).

10 9 8 7 6 5 4 3 2 1

To Mom and Dad, the first teachers in my life,
and
Donald Staples and William K. Everson,
who made learning a joy

Contents

Acknowledgments

I sincerely wish to thank Turner Entertainment Company for permitting me to quote freely from the films *Mad Love*, *Dr. Jekyll and Mr. Hyde* and *The Devil Doll*. I am also indebted to the brothers of San Miguel Community for the facilities they provided for me to write this book and for their understanding and encouragement.

Introduction

What is our life but a succession of preludes to that unknown
song whose first solemn note is sounded by Death?
— Alphonse de Lamartine, *Meditations Poetiques*

The coming of sound in the United States literally recreated the horror film
from its staid origins in the silent period, where horror was of secondary
importance, to what is regarded as its golden age, beginning with Tod
Browning's *Dracula* and ending in the mid-thirties where the genre had,
by that time, been played out and with few exceptions continued its decline
in the 1940s. What is unique about the 1930s horror film in America is
that it was not overburdened with the social realism that it began to assume
in the following decades, but "carried the burden of the imaginative
tradition, the tradition of parable."[1]

This book centers its criticism on a group of noted American horror
films produced between 1931 and 1936 with origins in American and
European gothic fiction of late eighteenth through early twentieth-century
dealing with the supernatural and preternatural that "made a particular set
of conventions familiar and essential to conveying horror to the popular
audience. . . . " Even more importantly these films had to "work within
[the] conventions" to provide the predictability crucial to the genre.[2]

The approach is simple. Each chapter examines literature ranging from
Ann Radcliffe and Matthew Gregory Lewis in the eighteenth-century to
Maurice Renard and Abraham Merritt in the twentieth, depending on
applicable stylistic elements, themes and the source of the film's plot, and

then closely investigates the individual films by asking specific questions about each concerning the characters (especially the villain-hero), their blocking within the frame, dialogue, camera placement, and the *mise-en-scène* in order to illustrate how the conventions are employed by the filmmaker.

This strategy leads to the basis for division among the chapters which have been differentiated according to character types: (1) The Romantic as Necrophile: *Dracula*, *The Mummy*, *White Zombie*; (2) The Romantic as Modern Prometheus: *Frankenstein*, *Island of Lost Souls*, *The Bride of Frankenstein*; (3) The Romantic as Symbol of Destiny: *The Invisible Man*, *The Devil Doll*; and (4) The Romantic as Tormented Hero: *Dr. Jekyll and Mr. Hyde*, *Mad Love*, and *Dracula's Daughter*. These models are paradigmatic of the romantic villain-hero, the dominant character in the narrative, and are easily discerned in gothic literature. Mary Shelley's *Frankenstein*, for example, contains a wealth of detail to illustrate all four types. First, Victor Frankenstein, the novel's protagonist, can be likened to a necrophile with incestuous desires, spending "days and nights in the vaults and charnel-houses" and dreaming disconcerting dreams in which he kisses Elizabeth, his fiancée, only to see her lips become "livid with the hue of death." His fiancée turns into the corpse of his dead mother, whose shroud-enveloped form contains "grave-worms crawling in the folds of the flannel."[3] Second, Victor also embodies the myth of the fallen angel, Lucifer, and that of Prometheus, whom Zeus punished by having him chained to a mountain peak in the Caucasus. Speaking of his work, Victor says to a friend, Robert Walton: "I could not rank myself with the herd of common projectors. But this thought . . . now serves only to plunge me lower in the dust . . . and like the archangel who aspired to omnipotence, I am chained in an eternal hell. . . . I trod heaven in my thoughts . . . but how am I [now] sunk!"[4] Third, the Romantic hero is presented as a symbol of destiny: "Some destiny of the most horrible kind hangs over me," he tells his father, "and I must live to fulfill it." To Walton, Victor remonstrates, "You may give up your purpose, but mine is assigned to me by heaven, and I dare not." Fourth, as the embodiment of the tormented romantic, Victor, remarks:

I appeared rather like one doomed by slavery to toil in the mines, or any other unwholesome trade than an artist occupied by his favorite employment. . . . I became nervous to a most painful degree; the fall of a leaf startled me, and I shunned my fellow creatures as if I had been guilty of a crime. Sometimes I grew alarmed at the wreck I perceived that I had become. . . . Sometimes my pulse beat so quickly and hardly that I felt the palpitation of

every artery. . . . I nearly sank to the ground through languor and extreme
weakness . . . dreams that had been my food and pleasant rest for so long a
space were now become a hell to me.[5]

The psychological insight the character has of himself is exemplified
through a comparison of things of different classes, alike in one or more
particulars. In the above quote similies and physical actions are used
together with hyperbole to describe Victor's state of mind. The reader is
thus presented with poetic images that concretize complex psychological
conditions that are communicated in film through encoded styles of acting
to delineate character.

There are several reasons for these categories, all of which contribute
to the narrative structure of the genre. First, the supernatural in literature
and film depends upon indefiniteness—not vagueness—upon a revolt
against rationality, an obscuring of the antecedents of an event that may
be starkly clear.[6] For this reason, characterization is affected because
motivations are many times sketchy, causing literary and film characters
to fall into similar behavior patterns expressed through stylized description
(the gaze of the villain-hero, the timidity of the heroine). Second, and
contributing to the first, the dominant Hollywood cinema has its own
coding that also allows for a particular "reading" of a film in terms of signs
used as signifiers, that is, the manner in which the sign is expressed. These
signs have remained intact in the 1930s horror genre due to the degree of
stylistic conventions and demand for narrative closure. Likewise the
signifiers have been codified so that not only the object itself but the means
of presenting that object has been fixed to express a given idea. Cinematic
codes then control the "reading" of the characters, their actions, setting
and variances in the narrative as they do of their literary counterparts in
previous decades and centuries.

Aside from the technical aspects of analysis, it is always useful to make
some distinction in terminology for a group of films where "horror is an
essential ingredient, but not the only . . . one."[7] Poe might have designated
these films as "arabesque," where "horror in violent suspense" gives the
story its power. Poe's idea of horror finds a modern equivalent in the term
"shock," and it is the shock appeal of the gothic film and literature that
attracts a continuing audience of devotees to the genre[8] "because this is
the only way to play out these particular fantasies." The shudder originates
because "the wishes are tabooed and because we pay the price . . . for
transporting these wishes out of the subconscious, past the censor, and into
a text."[9] Of course, in considering an art that is a product of a particular
era, "shock" becomes a relative term and must be placed in a historical

context to deal with those films which, at one time, had that ability. More importantly, however, forgetting for a moment the historical perspective involved in viewing older films and concentrating on audience involvement instead, shock truly resides in a projection of ourselves "across the footlights." Film has actually penetrated the ancient past of magical belief that influenced the thinking of primitive man and fosters in us today a belief in the images on the screen.[10] But even if audiences did not possess a belief in the supernatural, there would be the desire to suspend disbelief (or to believe, if you will) to enjoy the aesthetic pleasures of horror and in effect be shocked regardless of the viewers' past movie conditioning.

Throughout the book I use "supernatural" to designate those movies that contain unusual occurrences, existing through some agency beyond the known forces of nature—like the vampire Count in *Dracula*—as opposed to "preternatural" which designates films containing phenomenological experiences exceeding the common order of nature but within the realm of possibility. "Gothic science fiction" films like *Frankenstein* fit into this group and are included here because any 1930s science fiction film properly belongs in the horror category, for the emphasis on the scientific is only apparent; fear of the unknown is the paramount factor.[11]

Finally, "Romanticism" in this book refers to imaginary tales characteristic of the remote and unfamiliar, or to the landscape of nature as opposed to the neoclassic landscape of the mind or of reason. When applying this term to characters in the films, "Romantic" deals with "sensibility" or "sensitiveness," and expresses a sense of wonder at the mystery of life as opposed to the eighteenth century notion of "common sense" or "wit." The horror film derives its characteristics from a Romanticism that originated in the late eighteenth century with the "graveyard" school of literature. Hollywood transformed this older literary gothic into a new and popular idiom of poetic expression that typified essential premises of the Romantic movement in its subject matter, attitude and form.

With the horror film of the 1930s the inauguration of neo-Romanticism began, and looking at the films selected for this book I am struck with their lyricism, their poetry born of an age when some of the best European and American artists worked in Hollywood to make a particular mark in the horror genre and where the German expressionism of the 1920s found a home within the American fantasy film of the 1930s. These films are lyrics where villain-heroes sing seductive songs of death: Dracula's love-death embrace, the mummy's search for love amid the tombs of the pharaohs, Hyde's sado-masochistic relationship with his mistress, the Frankenstein monster who loves the dead and hates the living, the living-dead state in which a zombie leader keeps the woman he loves, and an escaped convict disguised as an old woman who lures men into his deadly trap. On and on goes the list of films at war with the civilization science has evolved, standing for an unknown quantity of spiritual life because it presents the mysterious for the beauty of it, and the wildness for the glory of it.[12]

NOTES

1. R.H.W. Dillard, "Even a Man Who Is Pure at Heart" in *Man and the Movies* ed. by W. R. Robinson (Baton Rouge: Louisiana State University Press, 1967), p. 93.

2. Wayne A. Losano, *The Horror Film and the Gothic Narrative Tradition* [doctoral dissertation] (Troy, N.Y.: Rensselaer Polytechnic Institute, 1973), pp. 7–8. Also see: Russel Nye, *The Unembarrassed Muse: The Popular Arts in America* (New York: The Dial Press, 1970), p. 4; and Walter Kendrick, *The Thrill of Fear*, Chapt. 7, "Scream and Scream Again" (New York: Grove Weidenfeld, 1991).

3. Mary Shelley, *Frankenstein or the Modern Prometheus* (New York: New American Library, 1965), p. 57.

4. Shelley, pp. 200–01.

5. Shelley, pp. 54–55, 173, 205.

6. Robert H. West, "Supernatural," in *Dictionary of World Literature*, ed. by Joseph T. Shipley (New Jersey: Littlefield, Adams & Co., 1960), p. 402.

7. Ivan Butler, *Horror in the Cinema* (New York: A. S. Barnes and Co., Inc., 1970), p. 11.

8. See Robert D. Hume, "Gothic versus Romantic: A Revaluation of the Gothic Novel," in *PMLA*, (1969), p. 284.

9. James B. Twitchell, *Dreadful Pleasures: An Anatomy of Modern Horror* (New York: Oxford University Press, 1985), p. 78.

10. Parker Tyler, *Magic and Myth in the Movies* (New York: Simon and Schuster, 1970), pp. 76, 81, 83.

11. Roy Huss, "Almost Eve: The Creation Scene in *The Bride of Frankenstein*," in *Focus on the Horror Film* (Englewood Cliffs, N.J.: Prentice Hall, 1972), p. 75.

12. Vachel Lindsay, *The Art of the Moving Picture* (New York: Liveright Publishing Corporation, 1970), pp. 292, 293, 294.

PART I

THE ROMANTIC AS NECROPHILE

CHAPTER 1

Dracula: The Amorous Death

"This sepulchre seems to me Love's bower."
— Matthew Gregory Lewis, *The Monk*

Among the lesser-known vampire stories in literature is Charles Pigault-Lebrun's (1753–1835) *The Unholy Compact Abjured*. The vampires here are little more than demons with no individuality and conforming to the conventions dealing with vampires and victims which were to appear fully developed in Bram Stoker's *Dracula*: a young soldier, Sgt. Amand, takes refuge from a storm in a mysterious chateau and cannot escape; there he dreams. Upon awakening he meets a strange old man who tells him that if he wishes to be saved from the vampires he must give the old man the blood of a dove. The soldier promises and is immediately in the chamber of his beloved, Ninette. She is the dove that the vampire wants as a sacrifice.[1] The story is short and almost Caligariesque with dream and reality intermixed to the point that all seems true. In a further development of the vampire subgenre, John William Polidori, a close friend of Percy and Mary Shelley and doctor to Byron, wrote a story that was no doubt later imitated by Thomas Preskett Prest in *Varney the Vampyre or the Feast of Blood* (1847). Polidori's *The Vampyre* (1819) introduces Lord Ruthven, whose aloofness, nobility of rank, paleness of color, power in his glance and haughtiness in his manner characterize him as the archetypical Romantic villain-hero vampire, a precursor to Count Dracula.[2]

Like Polidori's Lord Ruthven, Alexis Tolstoy presents his vampire to the reader at a social gathering in a story also entitled *The Vampire* (1841).

The main character, Runevsky, first discovers an odd gentleman named Rybarenko, who tells him about vampires, or "oupyrs." His description is reminiscent of the vampire prototype: "a man who, though apparently young, was pale and almost entirely gray-haired."[3] Rybarenko's narrative of his trip to Italy and his dreamlike experiences which end as a living nightmare continue the conventions of Romantic literature's oneiric tradition.

Another type of vampire is the "vourdalak." In Tolstoy's *The Family of a Vourdalak*, the Marquis d'Urfe tells his audience of Grocha, the father of a family and a vourdalak himself, of his distaste for food and his pale complexion that point to his vampirism. The narrator then speaks about his own seduction by the vampire, Zdenka, daughter-in-law of Grocha, whose "features, though beautiful, were imprinted with death," whose eyes were glazed and whose smile was "convulsed with the agony of a condemned prisoner." In her presence the Marquis "sensed in the room a putrid odor like some half-opened tomb."[4]

Even before Polidori's novella there was John Stagg's ballad called "The Vampire" (1810). Emerging from "the dreary mansions of the tomb," Sigismund's cadaverous jaws "were besmear'd / With clotted carnage . . . / and all his horrid whole appear'd / Distent, and fill'd with human gore!" The next day, Sigismund's tomb is opened, and he is seen lying in it "still warm as life, and undecay'd / with blood his visage was distain'd / Ensanguin'd were his frightful eyes."[5] This rather grisly poem, included out of chronological order, is a good introduction to Thomas Preskett Prest's *Varney the Vampire*. The novel bears the almost mandatory "preface" which gives an air of realism to the story narrated by the author.

The first chapter, of this 220-chapter novel of almost 900 pages, describes with a wealth of sexual detail the attack by the vampire on a sleeping girl during a stormy night and concludes, four pages later, with a highly charged *Grand Guignol* finish: "With a plunge he seizes her neck in his fang-like teeth—a gush of blood, and a hideous sucking noise follows. The girl has swooned, and the vampyre is at his hideous repast."[6] This is repeated *ad infinitum* through the novel. But Prest is also interested in giving a rationale for the existence of the vampire, Sir Francis Varney. Dr. Chillingworth, a prototype of Van Helsing, tells Henry Bannerworth, whose sister is succumbing to the vampire's influence, of a French doctor's experiments in galvanism in resurrecting the dead. The curious story contains the eighteenth century's influence on rationalistic gothic horror and is similar to Victor Frankenstein's experiments in galvanism. Varney is created, like the Frankenstein monster, by such an experiment, and like the monster of the novel and film, is a figure to be pitied; he is tormented by his base cravings for blood and his desire not to injure those who love him. In the end rather than take the lives of others, he takes his own life by hurling himself into Mount Vesuvius. Compared to Stoker's novel, *Varney the Vampire* is absurd and tasteless, lacking all the refinements and believability of *Dracula*, but Margaret L. Carter, in a preface to *Varney*, shows how Stoker may have been influenced by Prest.[7]

These brief selections indicate the evolution of the vampire from the "fiend" of Pigault-Lebrun, to the "Byronic figure" of Polidori's young male vampire, to the more-rounded domestic female vampire of Tolstoy, and finally to the modern *angst* suffered by Prest's Varney. The above narratives contain characteristics of the vampire's cinematic equivalent and conventions that the vampire film would subsume: the dream vision and the gothic paraphernalia (bats, owls, cock crows at dawn) of *The Holy Compact Abjured*, the exotic locales and the strong sexual overtones connected with vampirism in Tolstoy's *The Vampire*, and the grotesque realism of Stagg's "Vampyre," a prelude to Prest's *Varney*, and to those films where vampirism is accepted by learned men. These conventions are, to varying degrees, contained in Tod Browning's *Dracula* and Lambert Hillyer's *Dracula's Daughter*.

Dracula (1931), as a film, incorporates the essential subject matter of the Romantic gothic tradition as illustrated above: the opening (by far the most visually exciting) is set in the remote Carpathian Mountains, and Castle Dracula is, itself, something from the national past suggesting moral as well as social decay. Even the atmosphere is charged with evil, the weather acting as an objective correlative (as it does in many of the films in this genre) to the palpable evil that surrounds the characters in the form of mists of the Borgo Pass on Walpurgis Night. The constant references to death, the ruins of the castle, the spider web as an image of entrapment and the graves inhabited by Dracula and his wives are all the trapping from the Horace Walpole–Ann Radcliffe school of horror. If the gothic trappings during the first half of the picture seem more to the point of the genre, *Dracula* becomes interesting thematically, although visually more stage bound, when the scene changes to civilized England.

In the novel Jonathan Harker's ride through the Carpathians is filled with the Romantic adjectives of the scenery: "growing twilight," "dark fancies," "ghost-like clouds."[8] The ruins of Castle Dracula suggested for the Victorians not only a portent of evil through the lack of symmetry in the castle's structure but the "collapse of the feudal period, . . . a revolt against the oppressive materialism of the time [and] . . . a complete reaction against the unpleasant murkiness of industrial civilization."[9] Chapter one of *Dracula* concludes with a view of "*a vast ruined castle,* from whose *tall black windows* came *no ray of light*, and whose *broken battlements* showed a *jagged line* against the moonlit sky."[10] In *The Mysteries of Udolpho* by Ann Radcliffe[11] Montoni's castle bears similar traces of ruin and decay harkening back to a collapsed feudal period: "the mossy walls of the ramparts . . . vast, ancient and dreary," the gateway "where now weaved long grass and wild plants, that had taken root among the moldering stones," and "the walls of the ramparts . . . whose shattered outline . . . told of the ravages of war." In Poe's *Ligeia* this physical decay takes on the aspect of beauty mirroring the melancholy of the man taken up in a rapturous bout of necrophilia for the Lady Ligeia:

> I . . . put in some repair, an abbey, . . . in one of the wildest and least frequented portions of fair England. The gloomy and dreary grandeur of the building, the almost savage aspect of the domain, the many melancholy and time-honored memories connected with both, had much in unison with the feelings of utter abandonment which had driven me into that remote and unsocial region of the country . . . [T]he external abbey, with its verdant decay . . . suffered but little alteration.[12]

The excerpt begins and ends with similar use of words in describing the abbey: the narrator puts it "in some repair," while at the close he mentions that the abbey "suffered but little alteration." These words recall the conversation in the film between Dracula and John Harker at the concert when John, on finding out that the Count has purchased Carfax Abbey, tells him that the abbey could become very attractive but that it would need a great deal of repair. Dracula retorts, "I shall do very little repairing. It reminds me of the broken battlements of my own castle in Transylvania," recalling the description just quoted in *Dracula* where decay is implicitly connected with vampirism. In *Ligeia*, semioxymoronic language is engaged to describe the abbey's "gloomy and dreary grandeur," and "verdant decay," linking "melancholy and time-honored" to the noun "memories." The landscape is depicted twice in similar phraseology, "savage aspect of the domain," and "remote and unsocial region." The paragraph is summed up in a self-reflexive response delineating the narrator's internal state of mind: "the many melancholy . . . memories connected with [the land and the abbey] . . . , had much in unison with the feelings of utter abandonment which had driven me into that remote and unsocial region." This sensibility becomes quite common in gothic literature and the 1930s horror films.[13]

These nightmarish gothic settings, once transposed to the screen, are inhabited by somnambulistic characters who are themselves fitting subjects that become one with the dreamlike *mise-en-scène*. In each of the horror films selected, the romantic leads imitate this somnambulism through their extreme passivity, a condition more prevalent in film characters such as Mina (Helen Chandler) and John (David Manners) in *Dracula* than in their literary equivalents. Passivity, for instance, is not an attribute of Stoker's characters. In the novel, Mina is an energetic heroine aiding Van Helsing to uncover the vampire. She is one of Stoker's most vivid characterizations, a foil to Lucy and unlike her counterpart in the film, strong and even virile in the face of danger. In the film, however, Mina's vitality emerges only under Dracula's influence, and this is, ironically, a sign of her spiritual and moral decline. In both the novel and the film, Mina's ensnarement by Dracula takes up most of the plot, yet, in the novel it is through Mina's positive heroic actions, rather than through verbalization, that the reader understands her spiritual qualities and virtue which matches those of the men. In the concluding "Note" of the novel, Jonathan Harker writes that his son "will some day know what a brave and gallant woman his mother is . . . [and] understand how some men so love her, that they did dare much for her sake."[14] In the film, however, Helen Chandler has "a fragile, wistful quality . . . gone completely was any hint of the New Woman of the novel; the character was now a complete milksop."[15] The change in the characters' behaviors has come about because the film version has veered considerably from the Stoker original. Browning, working during a period when adapting a stage success to the screen was common practice, based his film on the 1927 play by John L. Balderston and Hamilton Deane rather than on the 1897 novel which had more cinematic potential. Part of the problem was that when Louis Bromfield was replaced by Garrett Fort as scriptwriter, Bromfield's elaborate script, which was more closely in tune with the novel, was deemed too costly for Universal's budget. Browning, acting under Universal's mandate to save money, cut some of the most cinematic sequences including the chase back to Castle Dracula.[16] The result of this budget trimming was seen in a review by *Hollywood Filmograph*'s Harold Weight who stated that it did not seem that the first and later parts of the film were directed by the same man, and that had the rest of the film lived up to the first half the picture could have been a classic.[17]

When weighing these changes in characterization from the novel into film in horror pictures of the 1930s, it is not to the romantic leads that the viewer allies himself but to their alter ego, the villain-hero. The reason for this incongruity, if one considers the romantic assertion that man lives essentially by his subconscious nature and not by facts or reasons, is the *doppelganger* associated in fiction with Poe's *William Wilson* and in film with Henrik Galeen's *Student von Prag*. The *doppelganger* is equally applicable to Rouben Mamoulian's *Dr. Jekyll and Mr. Hyde*. Browning's *Dracula* has an analogous composite character, though not easily recognized because he is not a physical "double." John Harker, at one end of the pole, is an impotent lover (spiritually as well as physically in his inability to help Mina resist the advances of the Count). In the center is Dr. Van Helsing (Edward Van Sloan), representing the marriage of occult reasoning with science to aid human understanding, informs his colleagues: "The superstition of yesterday becomes the scientific reality of today." Dracula, at the opposite pole, is the ideal Romantic lover, the man of mystery, the outcast of society, the seer who knows far more than the mortals he encounters and brings life-in-death to all he touches.

John's (Jonathan in the novel) alter ego is the Count, who definitely exercises the erotic influence over Mina that John is unable to. In the horror films of the 1930s it is only after the villain is done away with that the hero comes to potency. In *Dracula* the sexually aggressive character is the vampire-lover, and only through his death (impotence in sexual terms) is the romantic lead, his other self, revitalized. Roger Dadoun goes so far as to observe that Dracula carries his body like an erect phallus with his stiff posture, long cape and quick appearances "like a bolt from the blue."[18]

Mina is the ultimate expression of the Romantic heroine in her somnambulistic state with obsessive dreams of being possessed by the dead, raped by a living corpse. The novel more explicitly states the sexual attraction of the vampire for the romantic leads. In his journal, Jonathan Harker, describing the "voluptuous lips" of three female vampires, reports their phallocentric description of him around his prostrate form: "he is young and strong; there are kisses for us all." Jonathan finds in one of the vampire women bending over him a "deliberate voluptuousness which was both thrilling and repulsive," and describes "the moisture shining on [her] scarlet lips and . . . red tongue." He describes the pleasure she gives him: "the hot breath on my neck, . . . the soft, shivering touch of the lips on . . . my throat, and the hard dents of two sharp teeth, just touching and pausing there." He relates this sensation as he closes his eyes "in a languorous ecstasy" while he waits "with beating heart."[19] In fact, from the above description Jonathan sounds more like a Victorian heroine in the arms of her lover than one of the male leads in the novel.

In the film, Mina, using erotic images, tells how she felt first the breath of Dracula on her face, then his lips, and how all life seemed to have been drained from her. Yet Mina, wishing to protect her vampire lover, does not want anyone to see the marks on her neck; she is entranced when Dracula comes into the room and acts peevishly when asked to leave the Count's presence. Even John becomes jealous when he sees the attention Dracula is paying her. Dr. Van Helsing alone is capable of saving Harker's fiancée, while the lover is unable to ascertain the danger they are being drawn into. Mina appears in white flowing garments suggestive not only of a sleep-walker but a bride on her wedding night. She is a virgin, and Dracula's seduction of her is paradoxically a nightmarish yet pleasurable experience: Mina longs for the Count's company and yet is deathly afraid of him, begging Van Helsing for aid. In fact, Dracula's possession first of Lucy and then of Mina takes place in an erotic atmosphere of the bedroom as they lie helpless. In another amorous-sadistic situation, Dracula, in the movie version, opens a vein in his arm and makes Mina drink in a blood wedding, which, while only reported, is strikingly presented in the novel as Dracula says: "you . . . are now to me, flesh of my flesh; blood of my blood; kin of my kin; my bountiful wine-press for awhile; and shall be later on my companion and my helper." Mina then recounts that with "his long sharp nails [he] opened a vein in his breast . . . seized my neck and pressed my mouth to the wound."[20] Stoker's description of the blood wedding, suggestive of the oral sex act and vampirism where "vital fluid [is] withdrawn through an exhausting love embrace," contains perverse overtones of sadism and hate. The sucking that takes place before the biting is connected with the love aspect and the biting the sadistic aspect connected with the element of hate. "The act of sucking has a sexual significance" and "can actually replace the vagina itself."[21] Furthermore, the references made by Dracula to Mina are biblical in tone and not only suggest the covenant of God with Israel but the amorous poem "The Song of Solomon," which has an overbearing sensuality. This erotic theme is carried through in other horror films of the period: the Frankenstein monster goes through the motions of raping the heroine on her bridal day; Imhotep begins to perform a ritualistic sacrifice over the semiclad and prostrate figure of Helen in *The Mummy*; and Yvonne in *Mad Love* finds herself the intended victim in a lust-murder. So closely is the erotic situation found between villain-hero and heroine that it leaves little room for the romantic lead who looks upon the heroine far differently than does the customary villain-hero: Frankenstein compares Elizabeth to a heavenly object, and in *The Mummy* Helen is likened by her lover to an Egyptian princess. Elevating the beloved is a typical convention of courtly love where it became a cult, and the lady a goddess, sometimes raised to the level of abstraction.[22] The romantics took this over but in gothic literature and the horror film the love is rendered perverse, reminding one of Poe's *Berenice* with its morbidly sick protagonist who violates his prematurely buried wife's grave with "a disfigured body enshrouded, yet still breathing—still palpitating—still alive."[23] In *Dracula*, Browning has presented a fantasy in which adults never copulate in the flesh, but rape each other's wills, at least as long as they are alive.24

In true romantic tradition then, the hero of the piece is Count Dracula, representing Harker's "id." Van Helsing is the symbol of Harker's "super-ego." Harker, himself, represents a very ineffectual "ego," so that while the hero is unable to cope with reality, the composite picture of the Count and the doctor complete the individuality of the "incomplete" lover.

This vampire-lover, however, who first introduces himself to Jonathan Harker is quite different from the one presented in the film: he is described as having an aquiline face with a "lofty domed forehead, and hair growing scantly round the temples but profusely elsewhere." His eyebrows meet over his nose, and his mouth with a heavy moustache is pictured as "fixed and rather cruel-looking, with peculiarly sharp white teeth" that "protruded over the lips." Dracula's ears are "extremely pointed," and he has "hairs in the centre of the palm" and nails "long and fine, and cut to a sharp point."25 The description contains a profusion of visual detail; it is the way Louis Bromfield had envisioned the Count in his screenplay, which was vastly different from Lugosi's drawing-room gentleman in evening clothes that he had popularized on the stage. The actor, in fact, had clashed with make-up artist, Jack Pierce, over the Count's appearance which, according to the directives in the script, would have required Lugosi to wear fangs.26

In relying on the stage version of the novel, Browning has structured his film in deep focus, imitating the stage conventions. In the film Romantic elements are constantly juxtaposed with realistic ones; in the first half of the film the two polarities are centered on the Count (the Byronic hero with transcendent powers) and Renfield (modern skeptic of the supernatural). The wayside inn in the Carpathians is set against the Romantic decay of the castle; the frenzied activity of the sailors on board the storm-tossed *Vesta* is juxtaposed to the coffin with the sleeping Count in the slip's hold; the noisy London streets at night are contrasted to the Romantic music at the concert; the bed chamber with the vampire who drains the victim's blood is replaced by the operating theater with its blood transfusions to preserve the victim's life. In the second half of the film Browning centers the realistic and Romantic poles on Seward's modern home and its rationalism and Dracula's medieval Carfax Abbey shrouded in supernatural mystery. As a nexus Browning uses the sanatorium with Renfield, who under the vampire's power, becomes a link between the natural and supernatural worlds. With this analog between the two halves, the film comes full circle so that Dracula's rising to life from the coffin in Transylvania at the opening parallels his death in the coffin at Carfax Abbey at the conclusion. Van Helsing's knowledge of the occult has triumphed, and this knowledge at the film's finale in the vaults under Carfax Abbey, far removed from the activity of city life, unites the romantic leads. The director is very careful to keep this delicate balance of the supernatural-Romantic world and the natural world together.

The opening sequence on the coach headed at a furious pace to the inn on Walpurgis Night serves as the film's preface and stresses four important and standard conventions for gothic horror: (1) The wildness of the countryside seen in the opening shot of the carriage surrounded by a glass shot of mountains,[27] the words of the young girl reading the book that tells of the ruggedness of the landscape, its anthropomorphic qualities ("peaks that frown down"), the degenerated state of the castle on the rugged terrain; (2) Fear of the vampire and superstitious beliefs that are closely linked to formal religion: the "gods" and the "virgin" are mentioned in the same breath by a passenger, while a peasant woman gives Renfield, a realtor, a crucifix to preserve him from harm; (3) The realtor who sees all the warnings as mere superstition, the embodiment of the rational world, the urban man; and (4) Sexual connotations associated with vampirism implied by the mention of Dracula's "wives." Romantic gothic fiction is permeated with sexual references that deal with perversity centering on necrophilia which the introduction to *Dracula*, resplendent in its gothic trappings, supplies.

The Transylvania segment of Browning's film with Karl Freund's expressive camera work and Universal Studio's Germanic set design is, perhaps, the most memorable within the film and might be divided into three distinct parts: Dracula's rise from the tomb, the carriage at Borgo Pass and Renfield's arrival at Castle Dracula.

Gothic conventions as well as Romantic motifs are amplified in the sequences that follow Renfield's arrival by coach at the inn. In the establishing shots of the Carpathian Mountains and the castle introducing the awakening of Dracula and his "wives" from their coffins, a high degree of stylization is attained which, although intended in 1931 to appear realistic, now assumes all the aspects of an idealized Romantic landscape. The formal pattern has been carried out further still in the phantomlike coach of Dracula, in the interior decor of the castle's one furnished room and in the ruinous grand hallway. There is no doubt that the action takes place in the early 1930s by the style of clothes, yet the director is at pains to keep to a nineteenth-century atmosphere. When Dracula makes his voyage to England aboard the *Vesta*, for example, it is in a picturesque schooner in full sail.

Once the establishing shots are concluded, the sequence begins in the vaults below the castle, and it is here that Browning creates the quintessential choreographed movements and editing associated with the vampire's emergence from the tomb. The viewer is brought into the scene by the dollying in of the camera to the coffin. When a hand begins to emerge from the slightly opened lid, the shot cuts to another closed coffin covered with cobwebs and inhabited by rats. This cutting between Dracula's coffin and the surroundings continues, thus thwarting the viewers' expectations of the casket's contents by expanding narrative time. Death and decay, evil and perversity associated with the vampire through shots of vermin and lower forms of animal life intrude upon the scene. The cutaways from Dracula emerging slowly from the coffin punctuate the movement by inserting, as tropes, loathsome creatures to enhance the impact of the mounting action. Browning has neatly orchestrated the activity within the sequence. As Dracula's hand emerges from the coffin, a rat scampers behind another coffin; as still another casket opens and hands are seen emerging, a large insect emerges from yet another vault; as a female vampire rises from one coffin, a rat runs into another one.

When the Count has fully emerged from his resting place with his three wives, a statue of an angel in profile pointed in their direction is seen to the right of the frame. The presence of the angel and the vampires establishes one of the film's dichotomies. Within this same shot, a spotlight from the right theatrically illuminates the screen. The light's rays spread out into a wide angle so that the viewer's eye is led from the women to the statue and from there to the source of the light. The eye moves from left to right since the women in the left of the frame are in motion and the viewer naturally follows their progression. Once the eye moves in this left-right direction, Dracula in the following shot completes the movement by walking to the right of the frame, thus ending the sequence.

With a dissolve this wordless, ritualistic sequence is joined to the "Borgo Pass sequence" with its swirling mist, hooded coachman and bewildered realtor. The central object is Dracula's carriage, which protrudes into the frame to create a tension of his unseen presence. The second important image is the Count's eyes with pinpoint lighting on them to magnify his malevolence. The sequence at the Borgo Pass is, like its predecessor, entirely visual with only a few words spoken by Renfield, who is angered at the speed of the coach.

The journey to the castle which, through editing, gives the impression of rapid action has, however, within individual shots, a baroque sense of motion in stasis. A bat hovers over horses whose heads, although moving rapidly, seem to glide. Only within the coach compartment where Renfield is tossed from side to side does the audience sense rapid movement. Browning relies on even-paced editing so that when a low-angle shot of the underbelly of the carriage is presented, one at least senses from a breathtaking perspective the furiousness (and unearthliness) of the speed of Dracula's coach.

The final Transylvanian sequence takes place within the castle, first in a gigantic hall with its immense staircase and then in a large furnished room prepared by the Count for Renfield. The establishing shot of the hall's interior is seen from a high angle that stresses its immensity, especially when Renfield emerges from the bottom of the frame only to appear dwarfed by the surroundings.

The descent of Dracula on the staircase is fragmented, as is his coming from the tomb. The staircase, used for dramatic impact, is Browning's method of conveying, through Karl Freund's camera work, emotional tension through spatial conflict involving height and distance. Usually Dracula and Renfield are never in the shot together, and because of their positioning on the staircase, Dracula is usually shown from a low angle looking down on Renfield, and the realtor is seen from a higher angle, foreshadowing the master-slave relationship that will be established later on in the film. Even the huge spider web covering the entire landing is employed as a distancing device to separate the Count and the realtor and becomes emblematic of the situation in which Renfield unknowingly finds himself. The motif of entrapment culminates with Dracula's cautionary bit of advice about the spider who spins a web for "the unwary fly," adding significantly to the already-confused realtor, "the blood is the life." The emphasis placed on the web is not solely for decorative effect; it becomes the threshold through which Renfield's transformation into Dracula's slave takes place. The rest of the quotation is taken from Deuteronomy in the Old Testament and is part of the inversion of religious motifs that scriptwriter Garrett Fort employs throughout the film. The scriptural passage (Deut. 12: 23) is an injunction by God to the Israelites to eat both clean and unclean animals for their nourishment, but not to "eat the blood," since this is to be offered to God in sacrifice: "for the blood is the life, and you shall not eat the life with the flesh." In short, drinking the blood is a sacrilege. Dracula, as Prince of Darkness, constantly reminds us of his reverse relationship to the deity. These religious overtones are reinforced in that "the high gothic architecture is ecclesiastical" and "Castle Dracula is religion in ruins, the castle's vaults . . . are places of death and resurrection, while Renfield is conducted to an altarlike table and offered a chalice."[28] Added to this is a Romantic sense of *langeur* conveyed through the *mise-en-scène* of decay, of broken gothic windows, of the melancholy sound of wolves[29] that Dracula in the film calls "music" and the noiseless flapping of bats' wings. Dracula's reference to the wolves as "children of the night" in the movie is a parody of Christ's injunction to his followers: "Live your lives while you have the light, so the darkness will not come upon you; because the one who lives in the dark does not know where he is going. Believe in the Light, then, while you have it, so that you will be the children of the light." Jesus is the Prince of Light; he asks his followers to believe in him while he is still with them on earth. Dracula is the Prince of Darkness or of the "night," and his followers are the wolves who do his bidding. To add to the *langeur* Lugosi speaks in a halting manner (due perhaps to his incomplete mastery of English or early recording difficulties requiring greater enunciation), gesticulates expressionistically with his hands and walks in a stilted manner.

Within the room Dracula has prepared for Renfield, the viewer can relish for its own sake the arch dialogue as it rolls from the tongue of Lugosi. His Hungarian accent, with its slow cadenced delivery of dramatic pauses, contributes to the vampire's sinister intentions, even when he pretends to be nonchalant. Renfield casually remarks that he has brought the labels for the Count's luggage. Dracula, reading the terms of the lease of Carfax Abbey, responds just as casually that he will be taking only three boxes, with a slight pause between "three" and "boxes." A little later Dracula offers his guest "very old wine" and Renfield, puzzled why his host does not drink it, is met with the reply by Dracula that he never drinks wine, and again a slight dramatic pause is inserted by the Count between "drink" and "wine." Reference to the departure by boat of Dracula and his guest in the "evening" is stressed by the vampire elongating the first vowel of "evening" to emphasize his nocturnal existence. The juxtaposition of Renfield's saying how inviting the bed looks with the Count's sudden discovery (by the quick dolly of the camera to Dracula) of the "inviting" blood on Renfield's fingertip sets up an immediate audio-visual double entendre.

The final shots at the castle are choreographed beautifully as Dracula's wives approach the camera from the background of the frame through the mists. While the women pause in the doorway, the realtor entering from the right of the frame and moving to the background, falls to the floor unconscious from the drugged wine. The women now enter from the left in precise and measured steps, as though moving to imperceptible sounds of a wedding march, and walk to the frame's background. At the same time, their activity is intercepted by Dracula as he walks about on the terrace signaling them back with his hand while the camera dollies forward to him and the prostrate Renfield. The whole balletic action reinforces the somnambulistic quality of the *mise-en-scène.*

Up to this point, *Dracula* is quite fluid cinematically and praised for its ability to set the mood, but once the story moves to London the picture becomes increasingly stilted.[30] The vampire's search for more victims that opens the London sequence, with its fog and heavy traffic, people walking quickly through the damp night and snatches of music from the concert hall, evokes in its own way the same sense of mystery as the start of the film. Dracula's slow stride is at odds with the rush of people to the scene of his first prey.

With the exception of the opening credits the only musical score that is heard comes from Schubert and Wagner. As Dracula enters the concert hall, the Schubert *Unfinished Symphony 8 in B Minor* is played (38 measures into the symphony) followed by a coda of the prelude to Wagner's *Die Meistersinger* as Dracula gets to his seat, and back again to the Schubert piece as the lights dim and Dracula tells Mina about worse things than death awaiting mankind. This illogical order suggests that the musical director of Universal, Heinz Roemheld, arranged the music in this static sequence with its emphasis on uniting the occupants within the theater box for dramatic effect.[31] Shots of them are presented in a rigidly balanced manner moving from the group to one that includes only Dracula and Dr. Seward, back to the composite shot and next to the individual members: Mina, then Lucy, followed by John and finally back to the entire party carefully blocked in the frame within the theater box. This classical balancing of one shot against another describes cinematically the social surroundings of the *mise-en-scène* and the propriety involved in the ritual of the formal introductions among the upper classes.

Lucy's reciting of an old toast connecting Carfax Abbey's bare walls with echoing laughter that reminds her of the presence of the dead foreshadows her own death ("Prof a cup to the dead already, a glass for the next to die") and unites Castle Dracula with the Count's newly purchased London residence into one menacing totality. Dracula's comment to this is strangely pathetic: "To die, to be really dead, that must be glorious." Mina begins to protest this when the Count interrupts with, "There are far worse things, waiting man, than death." To a certain degree the vampire is seen here not as a master of his destiny but a victim of his fate, an ambivalency that almost makes him human while he, at the same time, is contemplating his next victim. Several times during the course of the novel, Mina expresses pity for "any thing so haunted as the Count." And continuing in this vein, she writes: "That poor soul who has wrought all this misery is the saddest case of all. Just think what will be his joy when he, too, is destroyed in his worser part that his better part may have spiritual immortality."[32]

The scene after the concert opens with a shot of a music box in the form of a gilded cage on Lucy's vanity table, which extends the metaphor of the helpless and beautiful victim ensnared by the villain-hero, as the spider web was expressive of Renfield's entrapment. Lucy, typical of the Romantic heroine, is taken with the mystique of this "fascinating" Count, while Mina, still outside his influence, mockingly reflects the voice of reason in her desire for someone more normal like the dull but stolid John. This rational approach is later more pointedly reflected in John's and Seward's arguments with Van Helsing about the existence of vampires. The attack on Lucy by Dracula is as much of an attack as it is a sexual assault, ending in her death. In two shots with time spatially and temporally compressed, the love-death relationship is established. In one shot Lucy is seen in bed asleep while the camera moves from her to reveal Dracula, and as he starts to crouch down and steal toward her the camera pans with him and moves in once he reaches her face. There is a cut to a second shot of an operating table in a theater; men in white sit around the tiers as doctors bend over a body on the table. One doctor asks Seward when Miss Western had her last transfusion. The reply reveals that only four hours have elapsed. This shot of Lucy's corpse on an operating table is taken from an extremely high angle and reiterates those situations in literature where sexual intercourse and death are found.[33] The first shot, therefore, of the vampire-lover bending down over the somnambule is perfectly matched with startling unexpectancy in shot 2, for the scene has moved from the amatory death-embrace on the "nuptial" bed to that of the same woman as a corpse on an autopsy table.

Dracula's first seduction of Mina is more abbreviated but similar to the ravishing of Lucy, with repetitive shots depicting the passive recumbent victim as opposed to the aggressive *homme fatal*. This sequence, like that with Lucy, is completely silent. A bat comes through Mina's window, moving yet seemingly static, as though filmed with a telephoto lens. The final subjective shot (Mina's point of view) is even more sinister as Dracula's face, in close-up, looks down upon the victim-viewer and then protrudes out of the frame so that the attack is limited to the off-screen space.

A point must be made at this time about the presentation of the supernatural in *Dracula* and the other films of the 1930s that was markedly different from the films that preceded them. The best way to illustrate this is to look at the deleted concluding scene after Mina and John have walked up the stairs from the vaults of Carfax Abbey. There is a fade out and fade in to a medium shot of Van Helsing stepping up to the foreground of the proscenium arch with the motion-picture screen in the background. He addresses the audience directly saying on one hand that he hopes the film will not give them bad dreams but on the other hand tells them that when they are ready to retire and are fearful lest they see a face at the window to brace themselves and remember that vampires are real.[34] While much eighteenth- and nineteenth-century gothic fiction rationally explained away the supernatural, the films of the 1930s were usually at great pains to present it as real and yet, as part of the genre convention, retain one or more skeptical characters, symbols of European enlightenment. The rationalist's role is not to weaken the audience's belief in the supernatural but to confirm it and by confirming it help to work out the plot.[35] Since the visual image in film is more powerful than the verbal one, the scales are tilted on the side of the more fascinating characters, namely, the villain-hero and those who believe in the occult and its subsequent manifestations. In addition to this the dialogue given these characters is usually more persuasive or is uttered in a more-informed tone of voice. The short interplay between Van Helsing and Dr. Seward in the medical library at Whitby is characteristic of this conventional device. Seward staunchly tells Van Helsing that medical science does not acknowledge that such a creature exists, calling the vampire "pure myth." Van Helsing rebuts this with the now-famous line: "that the superstition of yesterday can become the scientific reality of today." Browning, however, in imitating the play's stage conventions for obvious cost-cutting reasons, did a disservice to the film by relying too heavily on the verbal images while minimizing the visual ones.

Mina's account to John of Dracula's first visit to her bedroom could have made good cinema, but unfortunately such a vivid description is simply quoted from the play. Mina speaks of getting drowsy and "dreams" of the room thick with mist while a "white livid face" and "two red eyes" stare at her. She then feels the vampire's breath on her face and lips and in the morning experiences weakness suggestive of sexual intercourse: "as if all the life had been drained out of me." Much of gothic fiction has this somnambulistic quality so that Mina in the novel also describes Dracula's visit in terms of a dream and speaks of his presence as a "pillar of cloud," the biblical symbol used in Exodus for God's saving power, and as a fire that seems to divide into "two red eyes," suggesting the coming of the Holy Spirit on Pentecost in the New Testament.[36] Stoker, like Browning, is again purposely inverting religious symbols in describing Dracula by employing the Judeo-Christian images familiar to his audience. In the novel Mina recalls her peculiar dream: "The mist . . . became concentrated into a sort of pillar of cloud in the room, . . . and through it all came the scriptural words, 'a pillar of cloud by day and of fire by night' . . . [A]s I looked, the fire divided, and seemed to shine on me through the fog like two red eyes . . . [and] a livid white face [bent] over me out of the mist."[37] Mina's oneiric-like account unites not only Jonathan Harker's description in the novel of the vampire women in Castle Dracula,[38] but also Renfield's depiction in the film of the Count's visit to him in the asylum.

There are other theatrical devices that could have been more appropriately employed through the visual medium rather than through dialogue. When Dracula leaves from the terrace door, after he has knocked the cigarette box out of Van Helsing's hand, John goes to the veranda and describes what is taking place off screen, the conversation playing upon the differences between John's rationalistic ideology and the professor's belief in the supernatural. Mina's description of meeting Lucy after her death could also have been a more visually interesting but a financially expensive addition to the film's gothicism. Lucy as vampire is associated with the dark side of existence as she comes out of the shadows to greet Mina and runs back into their concealing darkness. It becomes a moot point as to whether Mina's simile, "she looked like a hungry animal, a wolf" could be properly visualized, yet the use of filmic space as a place of emerging from darkness into light has not only superb chiaroscuro possibilities but allows for greater dramatic tension. Space is frequently used in gothic literature to create a *frisson* and is dealt with in the chapter on *White Zombie*. In the novel, Lucy, as a vampire bride, is transformed into a beautiful but degraded creature. The key word here is "transformed" which takes on Christian theological implications of a baptismal rite. In Lucy's new state she is described by Stoker as "voluptuous," "languorous," and "wanton"—characteristics of a Victorian harlot—with "hellfire" eyes that mirror her lost soul;[39] as a virgin, however, before her "nuptials," Stoker depicts her in terms of "sweetness" and "purity"—characteristics of the proper Victorian heroine but too spiritual and unsubstantial to be real. In the novel, as in the film, Lucy is never a rounded character, but as a vampire she is able to be described fully in erotic terms.

Renfield's temptation by Dracula again begs for pictorial presentation, especially since Dracula "promised [him] things not in words but by doing them." The vampire's pledge not only takes on the connotation of Christ's temptation by the Devil in the synoptic gospels,[40] but alludes to Pentecost ("a red mist spread over the law, coming on like a flame of fire, and he parted it"), and further hints at God's parting of the Red Sea for the Israelites, repeatedly, debasing biblical implications. These biblical references culminate in Van Helsing's questioning of Renfield's knowledge of Dracula, but the lunatic, outraged, denies knowing the Count, paralleling

Peter's denial of Christ.[41] Like Peter, Renfield repents, but out of fear of losing his soul.

Mina, also under Dracula's power, makes similar comments to those of Helen Grosvenor under Ardath Bey's influence in *The Mummy*. John's remark to Van Helsing as to what could have caused the wounds on Mina's throat and the maid's immediate announcement, "Count Dracula," is a classic example of timing and makes the vampire's off-screen presence felt. The Count enters the room and greets Mina but is interrupted by Van Helsing, who directs Seward to send his daughter to her room. Mina answers Van Helsing testily by informing him that the situation is not as important as he believes it is but finally agrees to leave only when Dracula suggests that she do as her father advises. This scene becomes a play on appearance and reality. Count Dracula comes to Seward's home to inquire about Mina's health, when in reality he is responsible for her worsening condition. In the mirror of the cigarette box Dracula's real essence is confirmed by Van Helsing; the Count casts no reflection and is immediately recognized as a vampire. The mirror, a symbolic device for reflected truth to nature, cannot deceive Van Helsing or the viewer, and the camera focuses on it at least three times to show the conspicuous absence of the Count, who is present in the room.

The "blood wedding" between Dracula and Mina becomes another baptism where, according to Christian theology, the individual is transformed, dedicated and marked as a member of the "body of Christ." Dracula tells Van Helsing: "My blood now flows through her veins. She will live through the centuries to come as I have lived." Mina's change toward John is quite apparent. As he enters the terrace off her bedroom, he is amazed to see her in a negligee radiantly and strangely beautiful and in love with the night. She confesses to John the truth about the "blood wedding," when Dracula opened a vein in his arm and made Mina drink from it. This too would have made an exciting visual climax to Dracula's seduction of Mina but instead it is shown in a long shot on the lawn as Mina is enfolded in Dracula's cape.

At the film's conclusion Van Helsing, off screen, has been left to drive the stake through the vampire's heart, freeing the heroine and reinstating the conquest of virtue over the vampire's corruption as John and Mina, in her white dressing gown, walk up a staircase from the vaults of the abbey with the first rays of sunlight streaming through the windows. This is to the accompaniment of bells and music that suggest, with the other signs, their forthcoming union.

I have waited to the end of this chapter to comment more fully on the differences and similarities between the play and Browning's film. Their affinity rests in the themes of blood letting, blood marriage, and the efficacy of young blood. Seward speaks of Harker's love for Lucy: "You love her with the warm blood of youth."[42] In the play it is Lucy who has the major part and Mina who, by the play's opening, is dead while the demented Renfield is already under Dracula's influence. Lucy, attacked by Dracula, resists John's wish to kiss her, but after her blood wedding to Dracula, she literally "vamps" Harker for his blood. The frigid heroine of the play, like in the film and novel, is transformed into the voluptuous creature of the night: "You've always thought me cold, but I've blood in my veins, hot blood, . . . I love you, I want you."[43] At this point in the play Lucy's mouth seeks John's throat and the professor runs in with a crucifix in his hand as he does in the Browning version. Contrasts continue to abound throughout the play. Lucy's dreams of Dracula's red eyes staring at her parallel those of her film counterpart, but Van Helsing strikes a contemporary note from Browning's characters when he talks about the superstitions of today becoming scientific facts of tomorrow, adding that modern science can now change the electron into energy. Nevertheless, Van Helsing returns to the supernatural when he equates the changing of matter into energy with those who practiced the dematerialization of matter centuries ago in India.[44] Like his film counterpart, he allows the audience to see how man's deductive mind works. Another reference to the play's late 1920s ambiance is the airplane by which Dracula arrives in England; the Fort film script substitutes a schooner which returns to the ambiance of the novel for its inspiration.

The Count is described in the play through the typical conventions given to the Byronic hero with his "satanic pride and contempt."[45] However, when he is seemingly trapped by Van Helsing, Harker and Seward, unlike the film, he arouses pity from both Lucy and the men. Van Helsing says, "We are not your judges—we know not how this curse may have come upon you."[46]

The climactic scene in the play where the vampire casts no reflection in the mirror is performed solely between Van Helsing and Dracula, unlike the film version where Mina, John and Dr. Seward are present; the play, also like the film version, initiates a cat-and-mouse game between Van Helsing and Dracula, but some of the vampire's actions and dialogue are only found in the play and harken back to the Stoker novel. The violent confrontation and dramatic action of the novel, however, have been substituted in the play and film versions for one more appropriate to drawing-room melodrama. Harker in the novel is amazed that he cannot see the Count's reflection in his shaving mirror at his room in Castle Dracula and being startled, cuts himself slightly: "[the Count's] eyes blazed with a sort of demoniac fury, and he suddenly made a grab at my throat." At this point the Count accidentally touches Jonathan's crucifix, and his fury quickly abates much to Harker's astonishment. Dracula warns him: "Take care . . . how you cut yourself. It is more dangerous than you think in this country." He then takes the mirror and throws it out the window shattering it to pieces in the courtyard below.[47]

In the play (as in the film), Van Helsing purposely uses the mirror to test Dracula's reaction while the stage directions read: "[Dracula] Turns to mirror . . . , face convulsed by fury, picks up small vase with flowers from stand, smashes mirror, pieces of mirror and vase tumbling to floor. Van Helsing steps back; looks at Dracula with loathing and terror." Dracula's ironically cautionary remark in the novel about Harker's health is turned into an equally moralistic observation in the play: "Forgive me, I dislike mirrors. They are the playthings of man's vanity."[48] In the play, unlike the film, the "game" between the two is increased in intensity. Van Helsing purposely gashes his finger on a knife that he uses cutting the string of a parcel and holds the bleeding finger right up to Dracula's face; Dracula "makes a sudden snap at finger" and Van Helsing quickly turns away and fastens a handkerchief around it. Oddly enough this drollery is part of the actions and dialogue of the main characters while the film leaves the humorous roles to the servants and asylum attendants. In the play, Dracula, after the incident above, regains his composure and replies, "The cut is not deep—I—looked." When Van Helsing next holds up wolfsbane to Dracula's face, the stage directions indicate that "Dracula leaps back, face distorted with rage and distress, shielding himself with a cloak," while Van Helsing inquires of Dracula, "Do you not care for the smell?" More evidence of this "camp" humor occurs when Van Helsing finally takes out of his arsenal a consecrated Host. Dracula becomes convulsed with terror and retreats with the word "sacrilege," Van Helsing laconically replying, "I have a dispensation."[49] Hollywood did not have such a dispensation, however, and the 1930 Code would have prohibited the use of such a sacred object, even in the hands of Van Helsing, and besides, the crucifix that was substituted is a more universal symbol.

Probably the most interesting bit of theater is the moment when all three men have Dracula at bay: Van Helsing with the Host and Seward and Harker with crucifixes. The counterpointing of characters sets up conflicts leading to the climax. First the boastful manner of the seemingly defeated Dracula is pitted against the ostensible smugness of those holding the balance of power. Then there is the constant reiteration by the three men to the time ticking away until dawn, functioning as a refrain that punctuates their warnings to Dracula. Van Helsing alerts the Count: "[W]e have each sworn to keep you here . . . for two minutes and a half, when you must collapse."[50] Since the spatial plane in the theater is limited and does not extend outside the proscenium as does screen space, constant references to time, without the aid of editing which film can employ, increase the viewer's awareness of the play's tempo and its immediate denouement. Unlike the film, there is an on-stage death of the vampire by a stake through the heart and the disintegration of the corpse.

If the play proved to be Lugosi's steppingstone to prominence on the silver screen, the film version of the play "marked the beginning and end of Lugosi's Hollywood career," for with the *Dracula* contract the king of vampires proved his services could be obtained cheaply and he never rose to the prestige he sought as a motion picture actor.[51]

Dracula was "reincarnated" in Universal's 1932 production of Karl Freund's *The Mummy* which bore a striking resemblance to it both in its narrative style and characterizations, but without the staginess that marred the Browning film. The author of its screenplay, John L. Balderston, was the coauthor of the stage version of *Dracula*.

NOTES

1. Charles Pigault-Lebrun, *The Unholy Compact Abjured*, in *Gothic Tales of Terror*, ed. by Peter Haining, Vol. II (Baltimore: Penguin Books, Inc., 1973), pp. 268–88.

2. John William Polidori, *The Vampyre*, in *Gothic Tales of Terror*, ed. by Peter Haining, Vol. I (Baltimore: Penguin Books, Inc., 1972), p. 287.

3. Alexis Tolstoy, *The Vampire*, in *Vampires: Stories of the Supernatural*, trans. by Fedor Nikanov (New York: Hawthorn Books, Inc., 1969), p. 9.

4. Tolstoy, *The Family of a Vourdalak*, in *Vampires: Stories of the Supernatural*, trans. by Fedor Nikanov (New York: Hawthorn Books, Inc., 1969), p. 122.

5. John Stagg, "The Vampyre" in "The Vampire in Legend, Lore and Literature," by Devendra P. Varma in the introduction to Thomas Preskett Prest's *Varney the Vampire or the Feast of Blood*, Vol. 1 (New York: Arno Press, 1970), pp. xxiii–xxiv.

6. Thomas Preskett Prest, *Varney the Vampyre or The Feast of Blood*, p. 4.

7. Margaret L. Carter, "A Preface from Polidori to Prest," in *Varney the Vampire*, pp. xxxvii–xxxix.

8. Bram Stoker, *Dracula* (New York: New American Library, 1960), p. 18.

9. Devendra P. Varma, *The Gothic Flame* (New York: Russell and Russell, 1966), p. 218.

10. Stoker, *Dracula*, p. 37. The italicized words illustrate Varma's idea of the "Gothic motif of the ruin."

11. Ann Radcliffe, *The Mysteries of Udolpho* (London: Oxford University Press, 1966), p. 227.

12. Edgar Allen Poe, *Ligeia*, in *American Poetry and Prose* 4th ed., ed. by Norman Foerster (Boston: Houghton Mifflin Company, 1962), p. 403.

13. See Mary Shelley, *The Heir of Mondolfo*, in *Seven Masterpieces of Gothic Horror*, ed. by Robert Donald Spector (New York: Bantam Books, 1971), pp. 343–44, and Sheridan LeFanu, *Sir Dominic Sarsfield*, in *Classic Ghost Stories* (New York: Dover Publications, 1975), pp. 1–2.

14. Stoker, p. 382.

15. David J. Skal, *Hollywood Gothic* (New York: W. W. Norton and Company, Inc. 1990), p. 126.

16. Skal, pp. 122, 139.

17. Harold Weight, *Hollywood Filmograph*, April 4, 1931.

18. Roger Dadoun, "Fetishism in the Horror Film," in *Fantasy and the Cinema* ed. by James Donald (London: British Film Institute Press, 1989), p. 54.

19. Stoker, pp. 46–47.

20. Stoker, pp. 293–94.

21. Ernest Jones, "On the Nightmare of Bloodsucking," in *Focus on the Horror Film*, ed. by Roy Huss and T. J. Ross (New Jersey: Prentice-Hall, Inc., 1972), p. 60.

22. Kathleen T. Butler, *A History of French Literature* Vol. 1 (New York: E. P. Dutton and Co., Inc., 1923), p. 50.

23. Edgar Allen Poe, *Berenice* in *Collected Works of Edgar Allan Poe*, ed. by Thomas Ollive Mabbott (Cambridge: Belknap Press, 1978), p. 218.

24. Leslie Fiedler, *Love and Death in the American Novel* (New York: Dell Publishing Co., Inc., 1967), p. 416.

25. Stoker, pp. 25, 27–28.

26. Gregory William Mank, *It's Alive!: The Classic Cinema Saga of Frankenstein* (New York: A. S. Barnes and Co., Inc., 1981), p. 14.

27. See Calvin Thomas Beck, *Heroes of the Horrors* (New York: Collier Books, 1975), chapter on "Bela Lugosi," pp. 56–70. The chapter shows how the special affects in *Dracula* were produced.

28. Skal, pp. 242–43. Losano sees the world itself depicted by the gothic horror film as an inversion of the familiar romantic world, saying that even if the standard romantic elements of characterization are present, the landscape is nevertheless, that of the demonic. See Wayne A. Losano, *The Horror Film and the Gothic Narrative Tradition* (Ph.D. dissertation, Troy: Rensselaer Polytechnic Institute, 1973), pp. 126–27.

29. See Stoker, p. 21–23.

30. Ivan Butler, *Horror in the Cinema* (New York: A. S. Barnes and Co., 1970), p. 40; Clarens, *An Illustrated History of the Horror Film* (New York: Capricorn Books, 1968), p. 61; Drake Douglas, *Horror* (New York: Collier Books, 1969), p. 44.

31. Philip J. Riley, editor, *Dracula* [original 1931 shooting script], (Atlantic City: MagicImage Filmbooks, 1990), p. 70.

32. Stoker, pp. 235, 314.

33. Intense concern with sexual pleasure and death is linked to the moral ambiguities in Matthew Gregory Lewis's *The Monk* (1975). Matthew G. Lewis, *The Monk* (New York: Grove Press, 1959), pp. 265–66.

34. Garrett Fort, *Dracula* [The Original 1931 Shooting Script] (Atlantic City: MagicImage Filmbooks, 1990), H–59.

35. Noel Carrol, *The Philosophy of Horror or Paradoxes of the Heart* (New York: Routledge, 1990), p. 108.

36. *Acts of the Apostles* 2: 1–4.

37. Stoker, pp. 264–65.

38. Stoker, pp. 45–49.

39. Stoker, pp. 217–18.

40. See *Gospel of St. Matthew* 4: 1–10; *Gospel of St. Mark* 1: 12–13; *Gospel of St. Luke* 4: 1–13.

41. See *Gospel of St. Mark* 14: 66–67; *Gospel of St. Matthew* 26: 69–75; *Gospel of St. Luke* 22: 56–62; *Gospel of St. John* 18: 25–27.

42. Hamilton Deane and John L. Balderston, *Dracula* (New York: Samuel French, 1960), p. 8.

43. Deane and Balderston, p. 63.

44. Deane and Balderston, pp. 25–26.

45. Deane and Balderston, p. 42.

46. Deane and Balderston, p. 168.

47. Stoker, pp. 34–35.

48. Deane and Balderston, p. 48.

49. Deane and Balderston, pp. 48–50.

50. Deane and Balderston, p. 69.

51. Skal, p. 184.

CHAPTER 2

The Mummy: Through Centuries of Love

He stood a stranger in this breathing world,
An erring spirit from another hurl'd;
A thing of dark imaginings.

—Lord Byron, "Lara"

Kenneth Clark maintained that the gothic was exotic and, if not remote in space like *chinoiserie*, it was remote in time.[1] Romantic literature, interesting itself in the exotic, with its richly colored backgrounds and strong undertones of eroticism was introduced early in the eighteenth century through Galland's French translation of the *Arabian Nights*, mixing humor with a weirdness that captivated Europeans.[2]

Of comparable extravagance to the *Arabian Nights* is William Beckford's novella, *Vathek: An Arabian Tale* (1781), beginning like a legendary oriental fable filled with sensuality, but concluding on a note of gothic horror with necrophilia, sadism and Faustian nightmares. On a lighter note, Poe's short story *The Thousand-And-Second Tale of Scheherazade* (1844) parodied the exotic descriptions contained in the others by depicting roofs of palaces on which hung "myriads of gems, like diamonds, but larger than men" and "immense rivers as black as ebony . . . swarming with fish that had no eyes" together with "a lofty mountain, down whose sides . . . streamed torrents of melted metal . . . twelve miles wide and sixty miles long."[3]

The influence on the English Romantic poets who employed similar oriental exoticism can be seen in Thomas Moore's *Lalla Rookh* (1817), four Eastern stories about an Indian princess journeying to her lover. Byron had written about the unfaithful concubine of Caliph Hassan in "The Giaour" (1813) and in the same year his poem "The Bride of Abydos" recounted the trials of Zuleika, daughter of a pasha. In *Hebrew Melodies* (1815) Byron wrote the "Vision of Belshazzar," which reveals the king sitting on his throne with satraps about him as he watched: "A thousand bright lamps / . . . O'er that high festival. / A thousand cups of gold, / In Judah deem'd divine— / Jehovah's vessels hold / The godless Heathen's wine" (ll. 3–8). Shelley penned "The Revolt of Islam" in 1818, and James Justinian Morier wrote a picaresque novel set in a Persian locale in *The Adventures of Hajji Baba of Ispahan* (1824).

The Victorians continued this convention of employing Eastern locales in their literature. G.W.M. Reynolds in *Wagner, The Wehr-Wolf* (1846–47) makes it a point to have his characters act out their roles in Constantinople. Alessandro, a major character in *Wagner*, finds himself, as Florentine Envoy, in the splendor of an oriental palace "elegantly furnished in the most luxurious . . . fashion" with "ottomans so conducive to the enjoyment of a voluptuous indolence" and "a carpet so thick that the feet sank into the silky texture, as into newly fallen snow."[4]

At the same time, in France, Eugene Sue in *The Wandering Jew* (1845) made one of his characters an East Indian whose apartment and person are described in a loving and lingering investigation into the room's "perfumed lamps," and a "tall chimney of oriental porphyry." The chamber is "impregnated with sweet odors and the aromatic vapor of Persian tobacco," and a man wearing a "robe of magnificent cashmere, with a border of a thousand hues . . . fastened . . . by the large folds of an orange colored shawl" kneels "upon a magnificent Turkey carpet, filling the golden bowl of a hookah."[5] Lastly, there is Edward Fitzgerald's rendering of Omar Khayyám's *Rubáiyát* (1868), which deals with the exotic East, and yet in the true Victorian spirit of the times, reacts against religious orthodoxy.

The exoticism that characterized Romantic literature makes Karl Freund's *The Mummy* (1932) even more riveting by introducing on three planes of action the intrigue of 1930s Cairo, the mysticism of ancient Egypt (in flashback), and a fascinating restructuring of Egyptian history in the Cairo Museum. According to Robin Wood, these strange locales act as an audience "disavowal" mechanism so that the horror is made acceptable to moviegoers by instilling confidence in them that these places and events are far removed from their ordinary way of life.[6]

The prelude to the film is a sequence which takes place eleven years earlier in 1921, the discovery of the tomb of Imhotep (Boris Karloff). It opens with a crane shot gliding over the pyramids, tombs and sphinx of ancient Egypt while oriental music is heard. This exoticism blends with Imhotep's erotic designs (the embodiment of life-in-death) on an English-Egyptian woman, Helen Grosvenor (Zita Johann), who is the reincarnation of the High Priest's love.

The film bears a striking resemblance to *Dracula* not only because two of its main characters are played by the same actors (Manners and Van Sloan) who have similar roles to the ones in Browning's film, but because the action and tone are similar in the film's leisurely pacing. This can partially be accounted for because *The Mummy*'s final rewrite was by John Balderston, upon whose play Browning based his version of *Dracula*. Helen, in the Freund film, is placed in a somnambulistic state (like Mina in *Dracula*) by the reincarnated mummy, Imhotep, posing as Ardath Bey (Karloff) who longs to possess her. She, like Mina, has a love-fear relationship with her demon-lover. Under his spell, she experiences strong impulses to go to him. She, too, like most somnambules, is dressed in white flowing garments or appears in the fantastic costume of an ancient Egyptian princess. Bey incorporates in himself the Romantic exoticist and mystic. As a mystic, he projects himself outside the visible world into a transcendental atmosphere where he unites himself with the deities of ancient Egypt; as an exoticist he transports himself and Helen, in imagination, outside the actualities of time and space seeing in this the ideal atmosphere for the contentment of his own senses.[7] Bey conjures up the remote past of Egypt from the images within his brain and materializes them for Helen in the pool of his atriumlike chamber, desiring to be united with her, his reincarnated princess, by hypnotizing and seducing her into his dream world. But to become his for eternity, Helen, like Mina, must pass through death to a new life.

Frank, her fiancé (David Manners), is quite a neutral neutered character, relying on help from a wiser, older man (Dr. Muller) played by Edward Van Sloan, who alone knows who Ardath Bey really is and possesses the knowledge to destroy the creature. However, it is not even the believer in the occult who is able to save Helen directly, although the professor is instrumental in bringing about a climactic confrontation with Bey. With the help of Helen, who summons in her trance the goddess Isis, Bey is returned to permanent decay while Muller tells Frank to call after Helen so that her soul will come back over the centuries. Human love proves stronger only after the immediate danger is past. In the same way, Mina returns to the love of John only after Van Helsing has put a stake through the vampire's heart and Henry and Elizabeth marry only after the Frankenstein monster is destroyed.

Without doubt the stronger of the two men, in the Freund film, is the mummy, but because Imhotep/Bey has transgressed the laws of nature by attempting to bring to life the dead princess, he is punished even in the present, and those who defy him must do so on his own terms (the Christian symbols to combat the vampire give way to the pagan ones of Isis and Anubis). Just as *Frankenstein* is the reworking of the Prometheus myth, so *The Mummy* is a reworking of the myth of Isis and Osiris with the roles reversed; instead of the beloved reviving the lover, in Freund's film it is the lover reviving the beloved from death. In this final death-resurrection sequence all three locales, ancient Egypt (Imhotep), present-day Egypt (Helen, who is part Egyptian) and Egypt reconstructed (the museum) meet.

What greater Romantic hero is there than Imhotep, a rebel against society and religion who seeks the princess beloved after three thousand years? Spatially he is made to stand out from the rest of the characters by appearing several times framed in doorways, and this is further enhanced by Helen's remark that his room is like ancient Egypt, where nothing is alive. Imhotep also dislikes to be touched, as though he was a god risen from the dead (the archetype being Jesus's words to Mary Magdalene: "Do not touch me because I have not yet gone back up to the Father" [John 20: 17]). His eyes glow much like the Count's in *Dracula*, and his nubian servant is in his power the same way Renfield is in the Count's power.

As in *Dracula*, and to a degree *Frankenstein*, the romantic lead (Manners) is not so much a complete individual as a composite of psychic attitudes found in Ardath Bey and Professor Muller. His attempts to save the girl he loves are ineffectual. Beauty is at the mercy of the monster who is, however, not totally unsympathetic. His temptation is as eternal as is his bondage to evil but in Imhotep, as well as in Dracula and Frankenstein's creature, some suffering can be sensed in his search for human love. The Romantic heroes of these horror films are, therefore, creatures, neither completely human nor completely other-worldly, offering to their brides an eternal Grand Guignol elysium.

Until now, the one Romantic convention that has been stressed in relation to *The Mummy* is the exotic sensualism that the East held for the nineteenth century. The other convention is "necrophilia," which appears frequently in fiction pertaining to Egyptology.

H. Rider Haggard's *She* (1887) is about a female "mummy," Ayesha, an empress who lives among the dead bones of those whom she knew centuries ago. Leo Vincey is a reincarnation of the Egyptian priest Kallikarates who fled with a royal princess and broke his vows of celibacy. This is so reminiscent of Freund's Imhotep that it is possible the screenplay, written by John L. Balderston and based on a treatment and script by

Nina Wilcox Putnam and Richard Schayer, was influenced by the Haggard novel.

When Horace Holly and his ward, Leo, start to open the Egyptian casket one is reminded of the unlocking of the casket in *The Mummy* containing the Scroll of Thoth, which Dr. Muller warns Sir Joseph Whemple against on pain of death.[8] There are other similarities to *The Mummy*. Ayesha, like Imhotep, waits for her five-thousand-year-old lover to return to her.[9] And like Imhotep, Ayesha has a magic pool in which she can see what takes place. Like Imhotep, she wishes to revive the body of her dead lover, Kallikarates, and decides not to do so when his reincarnated likeness appears.[10] When Ayesha discovers that Leo is this reincarnation, she then, as does Imhotep, decomposes the body of her mummified lover whom she has kept with her over the centuries. She seduces Vincey over the corpse of Ustane, a woman whom he has loved and whom Ayesha has just murdered: "and thus, with the corpse of his dead love for an altar, did Leo Vincey plight his troth . . . for ever and a day."[11] *She* rather vigorously and emphatically emphasizes its necrophilia and contains that splendid decadence to which *fin de siècle* literature aspired. And Ayesha, like Imhotep, is the perfect embodiment of the Romantic figure in yet another aspect of the convention: she lives in torment and even her smile seems to say, "memory haunts me . . . evil have I done, and with sorrow have I made acquaintance from age to age, . . . till my redemption comes."[12]

The second reference that bears relationship to *The Mummy* is Burton Stevenson's *A King in Babylon* (1917). Fictional works dealing with Egyptology do not predominate before the discovery of the tomb of Tutankhamen in 1922, although some exceptions exist.[13] As in *She*, *A King in Babylon* takes a modern twist on metempsychosis peculiar to the twentieth century. During the filming on location at Luxor of a story about reincarnation, the director, Warren Creel, asks the technical advisor and archaeologist, Davis, about the reasons for burying individuals alive. The scene parallels Imhotep's reason for being buried alive in *The Mummy*, namely, an act of blasphemy committed by opening Anck-es-en Amon's tomb to raise her to life. The genders in *A King in Babylon* are reversed: "It was the usual punishment for certain crimes." Davis remarks, "This woman probably committed blasphemy. . . . That is the reason mummies of this sort are considered unclean." The parallel to *The Mummy* can be extended. Like Freund's resurrected mummy and his reincarnated princess, Anck-es-en Amon, Stevenson's king and his slave girl lover are both reincarnated, and the mummified bodies of both women are exhumed almost 4,000 years later. Creel describes the script of the film to Davis, a script which unfolds in reality while filming:

[The pharaoh] had himself buried out there in the desert beside the place where he had walled up the woman. . . . And then, four thousand years later, reincarnated as a young and handsome Egyptologist . . . some mysterious influence draws him to this spot—and he digs up the mummy of his 4,000-years-old love.[14]

Again, the parallel of the discovery of Imhotep's tomb in *The Mummy* corresponds with the discovery of the tomb of the pharaoh Sekenyen-Re in the novel. Both are bare of ornamentation, Imhotep being punished in this world as well as in the next by having inscriptions and images defaced on his tomb so that his spirit can find no peace; the pharaoh in the Stevenson novel has his tomb unadorned as a penance for killing, rather than resuscitating, the woman he loved. Davis tells Creel, in *A King in Babylon*: "A man buried in a bare tomb like this would . . . be in hell—a place of ceaseless torment . . . which the Egyptian dreaded most of all."[15] Where Helen Grosvenor resembles the dead princess in *The Mummy*, the painted face on the sarcophagus of the pharaoh is exactly like that of Jimmy Allen, the male lead in Creel's film. Eventually fantasy and reality become one for Jimmy, and he does indeed become the Pharaoh, reliving the events of deeds long past. There is a possibility that Stevenson's novel might be another source for Putnam and Schayer's initial script of *The Mummy*, for Balderston had crafted the final shooting script from their own rewrites.

In January 1933 James Whitlatch wrote a story for *Mystery Magazine* based on the third revised Putnam-Schayer script. The story is told through an anonymous first-person narrator who is close to the main characters of the film. The first two chapters take place in the Cairo Museum, the third and fourth in the home of Sir Joseph Whemple, and the conclusion back at the museum. The major differences from the film are that the prologue of the film is missing from the short story and that Ardath Bey/Imhotep can kill by a simple touch. As the narrator investigates the death of a museum guard, he accidentally puts more weight on the dead man's chest than he intended and "the whole structure of the man . . . caved in like pie-crust under my touch."[16] The scene between Ardath Bey and Helen in Dr. Whemple's study is only reported and it is brief. The reason for Imhotep's being buried alive has also been made explicit in the story. Both he and a vestal virgin, Anck-es-en Amon, have been executed simultaneously "for the sin of loving under the veil" with the result that the resurrected mummy now wishes "with an ardor which will halt at nothing to bring back the vestal of Karnak."[17]

The question now is how was Freund able to combine the various elements of Romanticism just spoken about into such a memorable directorial debut? Let's proceed to the film's prologue, which has been alluded to in the opening section of *The Mummy*. The camera slowly dollies in (music from Tchaikovsky's *Swan Lake*) to the Scroll of Thoth which contains superimposed over the picture the words by which Isis raised the god Osiris from the dead. There is a dissolve to the same scroll with a prayer to Amon-Ra, again superimposed over the image stating the Egyptian tenet in reincarnation. This post-credit inscription sets the tone for the film, and is not unlike the notion of vampirism in *Dracula*, perpetuating the myth of the eternal return. The Scroll of Thoth, however, postulates the basis of immortality on a far more ancient myth, that of the rising of Osiris from the dead.

A mood of exoticism is set not only by the music but also by the camera movement in the prologue of the film. After providing an establishing shot of an excavation site, the camera moves to an inscription above the door of an archeological expedition hut: "Field Expedition, Season 1921, British Museum." This is accompanied by a series of dissolves, but the shots are not distinctly connected to one another and it is difficult to ascertain the location of the hut in relation to the excavation complex. Freund also frequently dollies back from a photographed object, which in itself creates an aura of mystery until the entire scene is revealed. In one shot at the excavation hut, for example, the sound of a typewriter suggests the off-screen presence of one character until the dollying back of the camera encompasses both a young man who is typing (Bramwell Fletcher) and Sir Joseph, the head of the expedition. While they carry on a conversation, the camera continues to pull back further within the hut's interior to reveal another man in the background of the frame with his back to the camera, quietly examining a mummy in an open coffin which has been placed upright against the wall. Within this sequence the dialogue next directs the audience's attention to the off-screen presence of the casket that contains the Scroll of Toth. The viewer is introduced to Dr. Muller whose back was previously seen. For a time the discussion relating to the box is dropped and interest in the mummy is generated. Finally, the viewer sees the mummy. The coffin's interior is shown, and the inscription revealed suggests the mummy's tomb in Stevenson's novel. The young man asks Dr. Muller about the defacing of the coffin. Muller responds that it is probably a crime of sacrilege since the sacred spells protecting the departed soul on its journey to the underworld have been chipped off the coffin. Once the mummy has been inadvertently resuscitated by the young man, who goes insane, the story cuts to another expedition eleven years later. It is here that Imhotep (known as Ardath Bey) introduces himself to Frank Whemple and Professor Pearson (Leonard Mudie), and gives the clue to the tomb of the Princess Anck-es-en Amon. The speech of Ardath Bey seems as mannered as that of Count Dracula, retaining that halting quality punctuated by pauses full of meaning.

The insert shots at the opening of the next sequence, which precede the establishing shots of the exterior and interior of the Cairo Museum, are meant not only to reinforce the connection with the previous sequence, that is, the discovery of the princess's tomb, but to inform the viewer what is to follow. There is an insert of the newspaper, *The Egyptian Mail*. Heavy, slow-paced martial music with a distinct funereal air is played throughout the sequence.[18] The shot dissolves to another insert of the newspaper article. This one recounts the find and announces the return of the museum curator, Sir Joseph Whemple, to London to supervise the discovery. The article contains two photographs showing a sarcophagus and the head of the princess. Following the establishing shots of the Cairo Museum, there is a dissolve to another insert describing the funerary equipment of the princess. This insert prepares the viewer for the camera's investigation of the perimeters of the museum room and the lingering shot of the ancient funerary artifacts. The necrophilic desires of Bey are made quite clear as he gazes rapturously at the mummy's sarcophagus, while the connection between Princess Anck-es-en Amon and the beautiful Helen Grosvenor is made just as clear with a swish pan that bridges the space between the museum and a hotel dance floor in the modern section of Cairo. During the pan the somber background music in the museum changes to the livelier music of the dance. Yet Helen is far removed from the mundane affairs of the dance in progress. The hotel dance becomes the focal point for the entire sequence in which Bey's attempts to resurrect the mummified princess with the words from the Scroll of Toth results in Helen's subsequent somnambulistic state as she seeks to enter the museum after closing time, which leads to the meeting of Ardath Bey with Helen. The swish pan that unites the desert pyramids and the dance floor in modern Egypt seems incongruous and yet it illustrates the dichotomies at work in the struggle of the heroine against the mummy; ancient and modern Egypt are yoked together in two shots. That Helen herself is part of the dichotomy is further amplified by a man at the hotel who remarks to another that while her father was English and a governor of the Sudan, her mother was from an old Egyptian family with a long pedigree.

For Helen, the pyramids, the tombs of ancient Egypt, are the "real Egypt" while the city of Cairo is "dreadful" and "modern." The woman's somnambulistic state is foreshadowed by the doctor's words that Helen's thoughts are far away from the dancing in progress at the hotel. After the remarks made by the man in the hotel there is an immediate cut to the museum's exterior, and once again the film comes full circle to the figure of Bey looking at the mummified princess. When Bey leaves the exhibit room with Sir Joseph, the camera tilts down on the embalmed remains of the princess, reinforcing the motif of necrophilia.

At this point in *The Mummy* the main conflict ensues. Ardath Bey draws Helen Grosvenor toward him, for in reality she is the reincarnation of Princess Anck-es-en Amon. In the story based on the third rewrite of the script Bey simply meets Helen at a dinner dance in the museum to honor Sir Joseph; Freund in the film ingeniously joins the two through intense parallel cutting with an unusual amount of contrapuntal sound and voice-over between Bey in the darkened museum and Helen on the dance floor. Not only has a swish pan linked Helen to the mummified princess, but now the voice of Bey intoning the name of Anck-es-en Amon and the sound-over of the dance music augment the connection. Freund now concentrates on shots of the mesmerized Helen, observed by Sir Joseph and Frank, attempting to get into the closed museum.

Helen makes the perfect somnambule; sexually passive and yet seductive, the black-haired heroine represents the libido and the old, dark side of Egypt. The dialogue is appropriately Romantic in its stylization and poetry as well as in its melodramatic delivery. For example, when Sir Joseph is asked by Frank what Helen was saying in her trance, he replies: "The language of ancient Egypt, not heard on earth for 2,000 years, and the name of a man unspoken of since before the siege of Troy." The structured balance in this sentence suggests the character of the deeply methodical archaeologist who utters it with perfect cadence. Furthermore, the sentence contains two implied independent compound clauses: "The language [is that] of ancient Egypt," and "the name [is that] of a man." These are modified by two implied dependent adjectival clauses mainly in iambic rhythm, "not heard on earth for 2,000 years," and "unspoken of since before the siege of Troy." The scene between Helen and Frank in Sir Joseph's house after the museum incident contains perverse overtones of necrophilia as Frank ecstatically speaks about his entrance into the princess's tomb, and his unwrapping the mummy himself and falling in love with her beauty. Helen's response is also poetical; the prose rhythm of which is attributable to a combination of anapestic, iambic and spondaic meters with skillful alliteration and assonance: "Do you have to open graves to find girls to fall in love with?" It might read like: "Do you have . . . to open graves . . . to find girls . . . to fall in love with?" There is repetition of alliterative words beginning with letters *t*, *g* and *f*, and the assonance of related vowel sounds of *u* and *a*. This quasi-poetic sentence is a good illustration of the necrophilic desires of the romantic lead which connect him to the villain-hero. At this moment Frank sees Helen's resemblance to the dead princess as Bey does, which immediately establishes the final link between Helen and the mummy.

When Ardath Bey first meets Helen at Sir Joseph's home, she is seductively reclining on a sofa in an evening dress, asleep. But in the presence of her living-dead "lover," Helen is never more alert. When Muller asks Frank to take Helen home, suspecting Bey is the reincarnated mummy who has her under his control, she says that she does not want to leave, and although she admits that she was tired, she now claims that she has "never felt so alive before." As Mina under Dracula's influence acts testily, so does Helen under the influence of Bey. In the short story based on an earlier script, the change is even more apparent: "The girl's innocent flower-like face was demoniacally transformed. The expression implanted on the familiar lovely features was one of wild and reckless fanaticism. And the large, up-slanted eyes were narrowed to slits . . . alight with a devilish joy."[19] Just as John Harker is jealous of the Count, Frank Whemple is jealous of Bey. Moreover, Dr. Muller (father surrogate to Helen) and the curator of the museum attempt to appease Helen as Dr. Seward (Mina's father) and Van Helsing (father surrogate to Mina) attempt to do with Mina. These father surrogates are the ones to whom the romantic leads must defer because they become, to a point, the ones in control of the action. Roy Huss explains:

> The "Oedipal" victory of the *juvenis* over the *senex* for the favors of the maiden . . . is, in the horror film, ironically reversed. Not that the authority-father figure gets or even wants the young girl, but it is his mentality representing the wisdom of the past rather than the instinctual vigor of youth that is triumphant.[20]

Likewise the confrontation between Van Helsing and Dracula with the mirror is repeated with a photograph of the mummy which reflects Bey's likeness and links him to the creature provoking Bey to threaten them with death.

Throughout this long sequence there is much play on light and dark: between the darkened museum room and the lighted hotel, between Sir Joseph's brightly lit living room and the Scroll of Thoth lit only by an oil lamp. This study in lightness and darkness is emblematic of the polarities of the spiritual good represented by the archeologists and the evil of the undead. Bey, for example, stands in the darkness before the open door of Sir Joseph's home, and Helen is presented in that twilight existence (both physical and symbolic) between the world of the dead and that of the living, both in her moonlight ride to the museum and as she sleeps on the couch in the curator's home. She is at her most vulnerable in these situations and almost invites the lustful desires of Bey. The burning of the scroll will release Helen from Bey's power, just as the driving of the stake through Dracula's heart will release Mina from the Count.

When Dr. Muller asks Frank to wear the image of Isis (the goddess of Life) around his neck to protect him from the mummy, the reason given is not far removed from when Van Helsing proffers the crucifix to John Harker. According to the doctor, Helen's soul is in danger, not her life, and the amulet is to protect her against the power of Bey. The soul for the ancient as well as Christian philosophers is far more important than the body, and for this reason too, Mina, in *Dracula*, pleads with Van Helsing to kill her as he did Lucy, should Dracula make Mina a vampire like himself. The professor has warned Dracula that he can free Mina's soul, if not her body, from the Count's domination by driving a stake through her heart. Likewise, human love, as opposed to the demonic, is the force that will fight Imhotep. The shot following the talk between Frank and Muller contains a close-up of Imhotep's cadaverous face briefly superimposed over the long shot of Helen dragging her dog to the house of Ardath Bey. Once inside Bey's strange house with its pool surrounded by numerous cushions, Helen, echoing what she had said in the hotel ballroom, is enthralled with the atmosphere of ancient Egypt that permeates the apartment. Bey utters, "You will not remember what I show you now, and yet I shall awaken memories of love and crime and death." These words contain prose rhythms that border on versification with their stress on iambic and dactylic feet. The movement of the camera as it cranes up, and, then from a direct overhead angle, peers into the misty waters adds to the somnambulistic atmosphere. A tableau of ancient Egypt is seen within the pool. The sequence concerns the attempt of Imhotep to raise the princess beloved to life. His punishment, being buried alive, is juxtaposed to the burial of the princess so that the perverse contrast which has been depicted by Bey is a foreshadowing of what is to happen to Helen. After the tableau has been presented, Bey turns to look at Helen and says

My love has lasted longer than the temples of our gods. No man ever suffered as I did for you. But the rest you may not know, not until you are about to pass through the great night of terror and triumph, until you are ready to face moments of horror for an eternity of love, until I send back your spirit that has wandered through so many forms and so many ages, but before then, Bast must again send forth death . . . death to that boy for whom

love is creeping into your heart . . . love that would keep you from myself,
love that might bring sickness and even death to you.

The prosody continues in this concluding speech of Bey, with its employment of alliteration, implied metaphor that equates sex and religion and
anaphora ("until . . . "), ending in a series of clauses that emphasize "love"
while uniting it with "death."

Helen's reaction to Frank's questioning where she went while she was
under Bey's spell is again petulant. She angrily tells Frank that she cannot
be confined in a stuffy room and that she does not like to be spied upon.
Yet Helen's injunction to Frank is akin to Mina's feelings about Dracula's
power over her. Helen begs Frank to stop her if she attempts to go to Bey
because she realizes that it means death for her and that within her she is
fighting for life. Helen, confessing her love for the young man and willing
to die rather than lose him, puts on her negligee to attract Frank, and at the
same time to counteract the evil force of Bey. Mina puts on an evening
dress for the opposite purpose: to seduce John and thus to drain him of his
blood. Both heroines, however, under the influence of the villain-hero
profess to hate or dislike those whose care they are under: Helen's dislike
for the attending physician and Mina's for Van Helsing. After all else has
failed, Dr. Muller employs Helen to locate Bey, as Van Helsing uses Mina
to find the Count.

The parallel that exists between Helen on the chaise longue beside Frank
and Helen as princess on the ancient Egyptian couch beside Bey is
skillfully designed to counterpoise images of life against those of death.
Even the positioning of the characters has been reversed: Helen reclines
her head to frame left and Frank is to screen right, while in the museum
Helen reclines to screen right and Imhotep is on the left. The pathetic
quality of Helen's lines that no man has suffered as much for a woman as
Bey has suffered for her might, in other circumstances turn to bathos if it
were not for the previous love scene between Helen and Frank. When Bey
brings Helen to the coffin of the dead princess, he attempts to persuade
her to be born again, similar in concept to the "blood wedding" of Dracula
with Mina, telling Helen that he could raise the lifeless form of the
mummified princess, but that it would be a living body without a soul,
animated by his power. He breaks the glass case enclosing the mummy
and burns it while Helen looks on wistfully. He then continues in a
melancholy fashion tinged with expectation to reveal that he not only loved
her body but her entire being, her soul. All that she has to do is to taste
death for a few moments and then rise as he has risen. Bey impassionately
presenting the notion of the union of body and soul, where sexuality and

spirituality are fused, is in effect voicing the Romantic concept of the transcendental in which natural objects possess a correspondence with the spiritual world.

When Imhotep brings Helen into the embalming room she rejects his promise of eternal life. To his request that he perform the ancient rites over her body and once again read the spell by which Isis brought Osiris back from the dead so that she will rise anew, Helen counters with an earnest plea that she loved him once but that he belongs with the dead. In similar words spoken to Frank earlier on that express the duality within her, Helen repeats to Imhotep that she knows she is Anch-es-en Amon but also realizes she is someone else too who wants to live, even if it is in a world different from the one she knew in ancient Egypt. Helen's words link the mummy in an uncanny way to the romantic lead. In the 1935 *The Bride of Frankenstein*, it is the monster who tells Pretorius and the "bride" that "we belong with the dead," while he allows Henry and Elizabeth to escape. Helen, in reality, accepts a depression-ridden world in preference to the exotic past which involves perversion in the natural order of the life-death process. Imhotep and his bride "belong with the dead." The dialogue continues in the same vein when Imhotep says to his princess: "For thy sake I was buried alive. I ask of thee only a moment of agony, only so can we be united." Emphasis is placed on the word "only" by its position in the sentence, while the "temporality" it suggests is juxtaposed to the visual image of the nubian slave's shadow as he stirs the embalming fluid which will preserve Helen. Bruce Kawin views this love much more disparagingly, calling Imhotep "a walking repetition compulsion, determined to complete his frustrated sacrilege and consummate his romance," which is nothing more than the "insatiability of unconscious drives . . . often involved in fantasies of eternal romance."[21]

As Imhotep is about to put the dagger into the supine figure of Helen on the altar of Anubis, he says: "You shall rest from life like the setting sun in the West, but you shall dawn anew in the East as the first rays of Amon-Ra dispel the shadow." Both the simile, "like the setting sun in the West," and the metaphor, "you shall dawn anew," present the anti-mechanistic philosophy of the Romantic poetic imagination and a reaction to the urbanity of eighteenth-century materialism. The Romantic positivism of the dialogue equates man with nature while stressing that through nature, man comes in contact with divinity. The polarities in Freund concentrate themselves in phrases like "setting sun" and "the first rays of Amon-Ra": the alpha and omega of the symbol of Christ, who, as Son of the Father, is reunited to the Godhead through his death and resurrection. The scroll is destroyed through the intervention of the goddess Isis, to whom Helen prays, and Imhotep returns to dust. As Helen slowly revives through Frank's calling her back, there is a close-up of the Scroll of Thoth burning and the decomposed remains of Imhotep.

Northrop Frye in *Anatomy of Criticism* presents a theory of fiction classified according to the hero's "power of action." Frye's classification includes five types of literature which have evolved in European fiction during the past fifteen centuries and which can be appropriated to the villain-heroes of the films in this book:

1. Superior in kind to other men and to the environment of other men: the hero is a divine being and the story about him a myth.

2. Superior in degree to other men and to his environment: this hero is identified as a human being of a romance containing marvelous actions.

3. Superior in degree to other men but not to his natural environment: the hero is a leader; his authority and powers of expression are far greater than ours but he is subject to social criticism and the order of nature.

4. Neither superior to other men nor to his environment: the hero is one of us; we respond to a sense of his common humanity.

5. Inferior in power and intelligence to ourselves: we have a sense of looking down on a scene of bondage, frustration, or absurdity.[22]

In most of the Romantic villain-heroes this progressive "degeneration" can be traced. The villain-heroes of the first two pictures, for example, may either be seen as supernatural creatures and, therefore, as part of a myth or as part of a romance: Dracula and Imhotep, human in outward appearance, are part of the first category, capable of bestowing eternal life on mortals. They move in a world in which the ordinary laws of human nature are suspended. They are superior in kind and in degree to other men and to man's environment. Yet if superior in degree, they soon cease to become superior to man's environment as the film unfolds. Dracula must live by night; Imhotep retains the dried skin of a mummy and cannot be touched. But these creatures also exhibit human feelings: Dracula wishes that he could taste death like other human beings; the mummy needs the love of a woman like ordinary mortals. In these cases both become similar to us and we respond to this sense of common humanity. Finally they reach the level of being inferior in power or intelligence to ourselves so that we have the sense of looking down on a scene of frustration, or even absurdity. Dracula, for all his immortality, can die and so can the mummy.

To bring the horror film to a satisfactory conclusion where romantic leads are united, the villain-hero must slowly divest himself of that claim of being superior in any degree, and awaken something akin to pity in the audience. Thus, we, the audience, are fascinated with the romantic protagonist who is basically evil, not only because of his tragic descent to the level of becoming one of us, but because we assume that the reversal of the situation is also possible, that is, that common humanity can aspire to the level of divinity. This is the case of biblical literature based on eschatology, as well as the myths of death and resurrection which the horror film continually stresses, whether it be the freeing of one's inner self as in *Dr. Jekyll and Mr. Hyde*, the return from the dead as in *The Mummy* or the creation of lower forms of life into human beings as in *The Island of Lost Souls*. These works, whether literary or filmic, are Romances which aspire to myths and yet move toward tragedy, and finally to lower mimetic modes of realistic fiction. In these cases the villain-hero is stripped not only of his "divinity," his romanticism, his power to command, but he becomes "merely human," subject to the laws of nature which inevitably bring about his destruction. More will be said of this in the chapter on *Dracula's Daughter*.

Many of these gothic villain-heroes lust after passive, pale heroines, somnambules who are as sexually attractive as they are vulnerable. In the next film, *White Zombie*, the villain-hero is superior to other men and his environment which he controls through voodoo until his passion for a woman whom he makes into a zombie causes his undoing.

NOTES

1. Kenneth Clark quoted in Varma, *The Gothic Flame* (New York: Russell and Russell, 1966), p. 18.

2. Howard Phillips Lovecraft, *Supernatural Horror in Literature* (New York: Dover Publications, 1973), p. 36.

3. Edgar Allan Poe, *The Thousand-and-Second Tale of Scheherazade*, in *The Complete Works* (New York: Desmond Publishing Company, 1908), pp. 24–25.

4. G.W.M. Reynolds, *Wagner, the Wehr-Wolf* (New York: Dover Publications, 1975), p. 79.

5. Eugene Sue, *The Wandering Jew*, vol. II (New York: The Modern Library, 1940), p. 123.

6. Robin Wood, "An Introduction to the American Horror Film" in *Movies and Methods Vol. II*, ed. by Bill Nichols (Berkeley: University of California Press, 1985), p. 209.

7. Mario Praz, *The Romantic Agony*, trans. by Angus Davidson (New York: Oxford University Press, 1970), p. 200.

8. H. Rider Haggard, *She* (New York: Dover Publications, 1951), p. 20.

9. Haggard, p. 114.

10. Haggard, pp. 115, 126.

11. Haggard, p. 173.

12. Haggard, p. 118.

13. There are notable exceptions: Bram Stoker's 1903 novel, *The Jewel of Seven Stars* (London: Jarrolds Publishers, 1966), deals with the spirit of a dead Egyptian princess who takes vengeance on the desecrators of her tomb and a group of Englishmen who attempt to bring her back from the dead. Arno Press has published more fiction in this area: Guy Boothby's *Pharos, The Egyptian* (1899), George Griffith's *The Mummy and Miss Nitocris: A Phantasy of the Fourth Dimension* (1906), Mrs. Cambell Praed's *The Brother of the Shadow: A Mystery of Today* (1886), and a shorter work by Maris Herrington Billings called *An Egyptian Love Spell* (1914).

14. Burton E. Stevenson, *A King in Babylon* (Boston: Small, Maynard and Co., 1917), pp. 160–62.

15. Stevenson, p. 215.

16. James Whitlatch, "The Mummy" in *The Mummy* [original shooting script], ed. by Philip J. Riley (Atlantic City: MagicImage Filmbooks, 1989), p. 47.

17. Whitlatch, p. 49.

18. The music here comes from the original score of Heinz Roemheld for *The White Hell of Pitz Palu* (1928) directed by Pabst and Dr. Arnold Fanck and occurs in the torchlight rescue sequence of the mountain climbers.

19. Whitlatch, p. 49.

20. Roy Huss, "Vampire's Progress: Dracula from Novel to Film via Broadway," in *Focus on the Horror Film* (Englewood Cliffs, N.J.: Prentice-Hall, 1972), p. 56.

21. Bruce Kawin, "The Mummy's Pool" in *Planks of Reason: Essays on the Horror Film* ed. by Barry Keith Grant (Metuchen, N.J.: Scarecrow Press, Inc., 1984), p. 13.

22. Northrop Frye, *Anatomy of Criticism* (Princeton: Princeton University Press, 1973), pp. 33–34.

CHAPTER 3

White Zombie: "Death and Love Together Mated"

Make a little man of straw and nail it . . . to some tree; the person imaginatively represented . . . should die thereafter in fearful agony.
—Lafcadio Hearn, *Kwaidan*, "Of a Mirror and a Bell"

White Zombie (1932) is a beautifully atmospheric film, highly stylized by Arthur Martinelli's photography and writer Garnett Weston's melodramatic dialogue, coupled with silent passages that solely rely on music and motion.[1] The film's interest, like *Dracula* and *The Mummy*, is centered on necrophilia and the power of the necromancer, Murder Legendre (Lugosi), to assume complete control of the heroine, Madeline (Madge Bellamy), for obvious sexual purposes. William Seabrook's 1929 ethnographic work in novel-like form, *The Magic Island*, describing the author's experiences with Haitian voodooism inspired both the film and a play, *Zombie*, by Kenneth Webb, which opened in Los Angeles in early 1932.[2] One of Seabrook's chapters, entitled " . . . Dead Men Working in the Cane Fields," is where the major idea for the film was derived. That zombies exist in fact is attested to by Article 249 of Haiti's Criminal Code, which states that qualified as attempted murder is "the employment . . . against any person with substances which, without causing actual death, produce a lethargic coma more or less prolonged. If . . . the person has been buried, the act shall be considered murder no matter what result follows."[3]

Victor Halperin's film sensationalizes the findings in *The Magic Island*, sensually relishing the exploration of the symbiotic relationship between love and death: Legendre wants Madeline to be his zombie bride, and Neil (John Harron), her husband, is faced with the tragedy of having married a "corpse," as Madeline "dies" at their wedding banquet. Half mad, he searches for her in the Beaumont mausoleum, after attempting in his delirium to embrace a vision of his deceased love. Charles Beaumont (Robert Frazer), jealously in love with Madeline, himself, has already stolen her away in the night from her coffin with the aid of Legendre, only to discover that she is a "zombie."[4]

To amplify these statements five sequences have been selected: (1) The night ride of Madeline and Neil to the Beaumont estate, and the meeting with Legendre; (2) The wedding banquet and Legendre's voodoo ritual to hold Madeline in his spell; (3) Neil's intoxicated hallucinations as he pictures his dead bride in a cafe; (4) The cemetery where Madeline's body is removed; and (5) Neil's quest in search of Madeline.

During the opening credits an assemblage of Haitians chant and dig in the roadway at night. In *The Magic Island*, Polynice, the author's friend, asks, "Why, so often, do you see a tomb or grave set close beside a busy road or footpath where people are always passing?" In the credits scene the answer is visually provided to Polynice's explanation: "It is to assure the poor unhappy dead such protection as we can" from having their graves plundered and the bodies resuscitated to work cheaply for the Haitian-American Sugar Company. The author, confronted with the zombies, receives a shock. "The eyes were the worst . . . like the eyes of a dead man . . . staring, unfocused, unseeing. The whole face . . . was vacant, as if there was nothing behind it. It seemed . . . incapable of expression."[5]

After the last credit appears the two main characters, Neil and his fiancée, Madeline, are seen riding in a horse-driven coach to Neil's new employer, Beaumont, whose estate is in the West Indies. Halperin immediately begins to generate suspense by creating a space devoid of temporality (as in the "fairy tale" of which Halperin's film is a gothic counterpart) through the movement of the carriage. For example, two long shots of the exterior of the coach traveling along a country roadway (separated by 15 other shots), although temporarily and spatially distinct, are visually the same shot repeated as if to deny the spatial-temporal continuum in which the characters move. As in a dream, the landscape of *White Zombie* has the unearthliness of a scene projected with negative stock with its continual reminders of death: the burial of the corpse on the roadway, the zombies and the cemetery. Contrasted to the long shots of the countryside and the people that inhabit it are a series of claustrophobic shots of the lovers which suggest their vulnerability. At times Madeline is further isolated by appearing without Neil in the frame. This spatial detachment is additionally enhanced by the scarcity of dialogue which is just enough to set the mood.

A second variation on the theme of death are the zombies whom Legendre controls through his penetrating eyes, which in true Romantic fashion become a means of defining his diabolic nature. They are seen superimposed over the carriage and in extreme close-ups throughout the film. In sexual terms, Legendre's piercing glance may be taken quite literally as an "effective way of displacing the phallic sign."[6] Villains' eyes, which are horrible to behold, glare for similar purposes in gothic fiction. Rosalina in Mary-Anne Radcliffe's *Manfrone* sees a stranger in the court of the castello and describes his "large and expressive eyes" as "dark and gloomy," and when "fixed on her . . . an unaccountable emotion made her draw back."[7] Likewise, the probing glance also suggests supernatural power. In Charles Robert Maturin's novel, *Melmoth the Wanderer* (1820), Alonzo speaks of the villain-hero in these terms: "I had never beheld such eyes blazing in a mortal face,—in the darkness of my prison, I held up my hand to shield myself from their preternatural glare."[8] It would not be difficult to cite many more references to inform the reader that through the eyes the soul of the character is laid bare, and Romantic gothic writers make much use of them.[9]

The movement of the zombies with Legendre from the background of the frame toward Madeline and Neil's coach (out of frame) places actors and viewers alike in the uncomfortable position of having their presence invaded by a palpable menace. The crosscutting between the people inside the carriage and the zombies outside gives the impression of the immediacy of the danger in relation to the couple. It also intensifies the presence of that evil even after the coach has moved on and Madeline has escaped near strangulation when Legendre steals the scarf around her throat. This fearful journey becomes the prelude to the young couple's wedding night.

When Beaumont, as best man, walks the bride down the stairs of his mansion for the wedding, he attempts to win Madeline from Neil, his sole reason for inviting them to his plantation and giving Neil a business position. His impassioned speech has a Romantic strain. Spoken while the organ is playing Mendelssohn's *Wedding March*, the plea brings together the cosmic polarities of heaven and hell, and suggests Lucifer's fall from grace. For Beaumont, Madeline is a goddess. He possesses everything to make a man happy but her. Her love means salvation; her rejection is his damnation ("Heaven or Hell lies in store for me. You can raise me up to paradise or you can blast my world into nothingness"). Beaumont, like Lucifer, risks all for a chance to aspire to this divinity called Madeline. She, by her disdain, causes him to fall from the flower-bedecked "paradise" created for her wedding day. After her "death," Beaumont lives with Legendre in a state of torment, slowly losing his senses to the necromancer's power. Thus the myth of Satan's fall has been transmuted to one of courtly love in which the woman replaces the divine principal of munificence. Madeline remains aloof, and with the stately, measured steps of the march, appears like a somnambule foreshadowing the state into which she is to be transformed once the drug-impregnated rose that she smells and Legendre's necromancy begin to take effect.

As the wedding ceremony takes place there is a dissolve to the outside of the house, and in a wordless passage filled with menacing chords of music, Legendre takes a candle and begins to carve an image, placing Madeline's scarf around the wax figure, while his "familiar," a vulture, shrieks from its perch on a stone wall. The scene cuts to the wedding banquet with a wealth of purple prose. Beaumont, in response to the dramatic irony in Neil's remark, "This night of nights, if I should live to be a thousand it will never happen again," rises from his seat and replies, "A toast to the bride, to Beauty's Queen!" Neil continues in this courtly vein with "Gladly, my Lord [then looking to Madeline off screen]. Leave but a kiss within the glass [giving her a champagne glass]. Fair gypsy, read my fortune?" Madeline, in a dreamy voice, answers, "I see happiness. I see love, far more than you deserve. I see [a close-up of the inside of the champagne glass with Legendre's face, his eyes glowing] . . . I see . . . death." Neil walks around the table quickly to her side to ask what is wrong, and there is a cut to Legendre burning the wax figure in a lamp outside the estate, then a cut to the banquet where Madeline extends her arms as if to ward off an approaching evil and falls into a dead faint in Neil's arms. A close-up of Legendre's glowing eyes is followed by a cut to Madeline's face as her eyes open staring blankly then begin to close. The final cut is to Legendre, looking at the camera and walking directly to it until his eyes alone fill up the frame.

The intercutting between the inside of the house and the outside is divided neatly into two parts: the marriage ceremony counterpointed to the making of the wax figure and the banquet to the figure's destruction. The leitmotif of the luminosity of the necromancer's eyes is repeated, a symbol of his dedication to total evil. At the conclusion of the banquet sequence, there is a quick fade-out on Legendre's face and a fade-in to a wreath of flowers with the inscription "Love, Neil." The bridal bouquet, seen previously, is now contrasted to the funeral wreath, and the nuptial bed, as in *Dracula*, becomes a coffin. The ambiance is charged with necrophilic overtones. Neil will later confess to Dr. Bruner that he kissed his wife's cold lips as she reposed in her coffin.

References to necrophilia and concomitant morbid emotions proliferate in gothic literature. In Ann Radcliffe's *The Italian*, the marriage ceremony that the bride, Ellena, is to participate in is equated with "mournful cypresses" that she sees as "funereal mementos."[10] W. Harrison Ainsworth (1805–82) in the short story, "The Spectre Bride," has his characters united in a graveyard where "the priest will be death, thy parents the moldering skeletons that rot in heaps around; and the witnesses our union, the lazy worms that revel on the carious bones of the dead."[11] LeFanu's mystery, *The Room in the Dragon Volant* (1872), has a song which begins with these lyrics: "Death and Love, together mated, / Watch and wait in ambuscade; / At early morn, or else belated, / They meet and mark the man or maid."[12] The stanza is emblematic of the relationships between the heroines and the villain-heroes in this group of films and is most appropriate for *White Zombie*. In a ballad by Gottfried August Burger (1749–97), translated by Walter Scott as "William and Helen" (1796), the heroine, Lenore, is carried off on horseback by the spectre of her lover after his death and is married to him at his grave's side. In Thomas Percy's *Reliques of Ancient English Poetry* (1765) is a ballad titled "Sweet William's Ghost." At the ballad's climax, the lover says: "Thou'se nevir get / Of me shalt nevir win, / Till thou take me to youn kirk yard, / And wed me with a ring" (ll. 29–32). In Scott's "William and Helen," the dead lover carries Helen to his grave for their nuptials: "The eyes desert the naked skull, / The mouldering flesh the bone, / Till Helen's lily arms entwine / A ghastly skeleton" (ll. 249–52).[13] Johann Ludwig Tieck's (1773–1853) short story *The Bride of the Grave* is similar to Poe's *Ligeia* in theme. The protagonist, Walter, is enamored of his dead wife Brunhilda and longs for her company. This unnatural love leads to vampirism, while Walter spends less time with his second wife, Swanhilda, whom he married because she resembled his first love: "Whenever she beheld some innocent child, whose lovely face denoted . . . infantine health and vigour, she would entice it . . . with fond caresses into her most secret apartment, where, lulling it to sleep in her arms, she would suck from its bosom the warm, purple tide of life."[14] It is reminiscent of Lucy Western in both the film and novel *Dracula* who, now a vampire like Brunhilda, entices children to her and drains them of their blood. In an anonymous Austrian work (1814) entitled "Louise or the Living Spectre," a brother falls in love with his sister and when she dies he marries a *doppelganger* of the reincarnation of the dead Louise.[15] Washington Irving (1783–1859) in the *Adventure of the German Student* has Gottfried Wolfgang unknowingly marry the reanimated spirit of a guillotined woman who dies again on their wedding night when her head rolls to the floor. The husband expires in a madhouse.[16] Macabre emotions proliferate in other works such as LeFanu's novella, *The Mysterious Lodger* (1850), where a father is wont to say about his dead son that "few things appear so beautiful as a very young child in its shroud."[17] And in Collins' *Mad Monkton*, the son, Alfred, keeps in his bedroom a coffin for his deceased uncle to remind him of his quest to discover where the body of his relative is hidden.[18] Marie Corelli's *The Sorrows of Satan* (1895) has the fascinated protagonist, Geoffrey Tempest, look upon his future mother-in-law, Lady Elton, as a living corpse whose "couch . . . suggested a black sarcophagus in bulk and outline. . . . The extended figure of the paralyzed Countess herself presented a death-like rigidity."[19] Yet no one can outdo the descriptions of Gilles de Rais in Huysmans' *La-Bas*:

> He . . . becomes a lover of the dead . . . kiss[ing] with cries of enthusiasm, the well-made limbs of his victims. He establishes sepulchral beauty contests, and whichever of the truncated heads receives the prize he raises by the hair and passionately kisses the cold lips. . . . He pollutes dead children . . . [and] even goes so far—one day when his supply of children is exhausted—as to disembowel a pregnant woman and sport with the foetus.[20]

These are some of the numerous references regarding love and death in Romantic fiction.

The chiaroscuro expressionism of the cafe scene in *White Zombie*, where Neil has gone to drown his sorrow after Madeline's death, contains these necrophilic qualities. Spatially, Neil remains isolated, for although there are music and people, the viewer only hears the former and sees shadows of the latter as they dance or converse at tables. From these shapes on the cafe walls emerges the figure of the "dead" Madeline, dressed in her bridal gown (which ironically becomes her shroud); she beckons to Neil. The shadows not only seem phantasmagorical because the people are not directly seen on the screen but combine with the image of the "dead" Madeline to create the nightmarish world of Neil's distraught mind. Also these silhouettes, which inhabit a space that is never defined, are the representations of real images like those in the cave in Plato's *Republic* (book VII). The music and noise suggest a fairly large group thus increasing the sense of isolation of the space in which Neil is framed. The shadows further tend to neutralize any depth of field, making the two dimensionality of the screen seem even less real and more dreamlike. Neil's seeing the apparition of his wife in the cafe and hearing her imploring tones drive him in a frenzy to the Beaumont family vaults. His action hints at Poe's *The Fall of the House of Usher* where Roderick realizes what he has done to his sister, Madeline: "Oh, pity me, miserable wretch that I am! . . . We have put her living in the tomb!"[21]

J. P. Telotte, quoting Owen Barfield, says that since we assist in the creation of collective representations from which our world is made, those images we see should be "of the same nature as the perceiving self," and not "objects wholly extrinsic to man." The horror film, he asserts, depends poignantly on "such an evocation of audience participation." To create such audience involvement, Halperin, in the exhumation of Madeline's body, puts into play the spatial dynamics of depth of field so that the viewers, aware of isolated figures moving toward or away from them, are left in the darkness of the theater space which, serving as an extension of the darkness of the cemetery, weakens their contact with actuality thereby threatening their own space.[22] In a long shot (taken from behind the niche where the coffin is placed) Beaumont and Legendre are seen standing in the background on the steps leading down to the vault. The zombies file in on either side of the two. The arch of the burial niche in the foreground serves as one framing device while the doorway to the vault in the background acts as a second means of creating depth as the zombies move toward the casket. Once the casket is removed, the audience experiences the spatial confines more acutely since the camera (and therefore the spectator) is placed behind the niche in the wall, creating a tunneling effect once the coffin is removed. The six zombies carry the coffin to the two men waiting in the background and place it on the steps. One opens the upper portion of the casket, revealing Madeline resting on her silk bed. Beaumont calls softly yet imploringly to her, but Legendre signals him to stop. Beaumont and Legendre pass along the road followed by the zombies carrying the open coffin and exit at the bottom of the frame. In the meantime the camera tracks with Neil as he staggers through the cemetery to Madeline's vault, stands by the open door apprehensively, walks in, and in a delayed reaction his wail is heard offscreen as he discovers the coffin is missing.

Neil enlists the aid of the minister, Dr. Bruner (Joseph Cawthorn), who married him and whom the natives consider a "magician." The scene between the doctor and Neil, the most wordy passage in the film, marks the film's midpoint. The dialogue is replete with allusions to necrophilia in Neil's love for his "deceased" wife, the visionary theories of a "mad" doctor, and the mysterious rites involving a life-in-death state older than Egypt itself. There is also a reference made by Bruner to the penal law of Haiti's Article 249 presented at the beginning of this chapter. Bruner speaks of people who, having been declared dead, have returned to life, living on for years, and the doctor reasons that if nature can fool human beings, human beings can also fool nature by creating a zombielike state. Dr. Bruner is a Van Helsing type, but more eccentrically humorous and more folksy in his discourse. In fact, he provides the only form of mild humor in the film, interrupting his narrative several times, much to the impatience of Neil, to ask for a light for his pipe. He even interrupts Neil and Madeline's embrace at the film's conclusion to ask for a match. But Bruner is calm and determined; he is a perfect foil for the overwrought Neil, just as Van Helsing is perfect for the equally overwrought and powerless John Harker. He rationally attempts to discover Legendre's mystical powers by which he directs his revenants. There are hints here of premature burial recalling not only Lewton's *Isle of the Dead* but Poe's own short story. Van Helsing in *Dracula* tries to prove that superstitions of today may prove to be scientific facts tomorrow while Bruner attempts to separate fact from fiction.

The unfolding of the second half of *White Zombie* is wrapped up in the Romantic quest which "may uncover sins that even the devil would be ashamed of." The quest is secularized in gothic literature and centers on the destruction of evil and the winning of the beautiful woman. Madeline is the "sleeping beauty" rescued from the diabolic enchanter. But Neil and Madeline are represented as asexual beings so that not even an on-screen kiss is vouchsafed them.

Among some gothic romances dealing with the "quest" for the beautiful heroine are two stories that are part of the German *Schauerroman*. The anonymous short story entitled *The Spectre Barber* (1807) is a tale about Francis, a young man who must undergo various experiences on his journey to seek a fortune in order to win his love, Meta, including passing the night at a castle whose host flagellates all visitors, spending time in a debtor's prison and lodging at a castle with a ghostly barber. Alois Wilhelm Schreiber's (1763–1841) *The Devil's Ladder* deals with a young knight, Ruthelm, who must attempt to scale the impregnable Redrich mountain to win the hand of the beautiful Garlinda, kidnaped by gnomes. He must awaken this sleeping beauty from her bed of flowers and make her his bride.[23] The villain-hero of M. G. Lewis's *The Bravo of Venice* (1804) attempts to free Venice from the menace of hired assassins to win the reward, Rosabella's love. He begins his quest with the invocation: "Arduous is the task before me.—Ah! should that task be gone through with success, and Rosabella be the reward of my labours. . . . Yet though 'tis impossible to attain, the striving to attain such an end is glorious!"[24] Lastly in Radcliffe's novel *Manfrone*, the hero, Romellino, tells of this quest for the imprisoned Angelica, a slave in captivity near Algiers. Virtually each paragraph takes leaps in time and place with a wealth of topographical minutia as the hero makes the journey.25

In *White Zombie* the quest for the captive Madeline has the fantastic quality of those in gothic fiction. The castle of the sorcerer, Legendre, is on a mountaintop with the sea below, similar to the castle in Arnold Becklin's drawing, "Isle of the Dead." Many passages in this final sequence are without dialogue, but have a continuous musical score that contributes to accelerating the tempo of the action.

In this setting, Madeline, bereft of her senses, is seen at a grand piano playing Liszt's "Liebestraum," while Beaumont's amatory advances prove useless against the somnambulist. The music, the perfect correlative for the sexually charged atmosphere, is enhanced by the fact that Madeline appears seductive and at the same time pitiable in her lethargic state. Beaumont and Legendre desire her, but she is incapable of exercising her power to either repel or entice their advances. She is a sleeper waiting to be awakened. Beaumont, while Madeline is playing, gives her a necklace, saying,

> Foolish things [the jewels], they can't bring the light back to those eyes. . . . I thought that beauty alone would satisfy. But the soul is gone. I can't bear those empty staring eyes. Oh, forgive me, Madeline . . . [She rises from the piano, heedless of what he is saying] . . . I must take you back.

Legendre, coming down the huge staircase, says sarcastically, "Back to the grave, monsieur?" Beaumont pleads with the man he thought was doing his bidding, "No, you must put the life back into her eyes and bring laughter to her lips. She must be happy again." The necromancer tells the distraught Beaumont, "You paint a charming picture, monsieur. One that I should like to see myself." His victim pleads, "You must bring her back! . . . Better to see hatred in [her eyes] than that dreadful emptiness." Legendre has other plans for Beaumont and has drugged the wine that will put the plantation owner under his control. He seems to go along with Beaumont by saying, "Perhaps, you're right. It would be a pity to destroy such a lovely flower. Let's drink to the future of this flower."

Emphasis in *White Zombie* is placed on the eyes as "mirrors of the soul." Certainly a great deal of emphasis is placed on Legendre's eyes. Madeline's are contrasted to his: hers are without light or life, "empty staring eyes," filled with "dreadful emptiness." Beaumont's speech is Romantic. He is in love with a "living corpse," and Legendre supplies the logical and cynical answer in the suggestion of taking Madeline back to the grave. The use of alliteration by Beaumont, "life," "laughter," "lips," increases this overcharged rhetoric. Interspersed in the dialogue comes the refrain in the form of a petition: "I must take you back," "You must put the life back," "You must bring her back," and "Foolish things, they can't bring back." Madeline is metaphorically called a "flower," comparing in Romantic fashion the beauty of nature to that of the human form with its comparable frailness and the tender care both require.

The quest for Madeline leads Neil and Bruner to the base of Legendre's castle, known to the natives and spoken of by the tribal witch doctor, Pierre, as "the land of the Living Dead." The means by which space is articulated in this quest to create conflict is to address the heart of the matter. In *White Zombie* suspense is increased by a disjunctive use of noncontiguous narrative space that isolates the individual actor in ill-defined areas. For example, on Neil and Dr. Bruner's quest to find Madeline, there are three separate shots. One, a long shot, shows the two men on horseback through the countryside surrounded by dense foliage so that the space is not clearly defined. Bruner remarks that he knows where to find the witch doctor who is familiar with everything that happens in the region. The second shot is an elaborate wipe which introduces the witch doctor, Pierre, on horseback with the other two. Pierre tells Bruner that his age prevents him from going the distance to where the evil sorcerer named "Murder" presides. This scene is shot again in the countryside but with less-dense foliage and, therefore, much more space as they proceed from the interior of the island to the shore. Neil is sick with fever and Bruner, realizing the difficult journey before them, recommends he lie down and take a little rest, referring to an off-screen space. Neil moves out of the frame. As Pierre informs Bruner about Legendre, there is an immediate diagonal wipe, to the castle, which is seen with Bruner in extreme long shot at the bottom of the frame looking up. Neil is resting at the base of a rocky incline. What needs to be pointed out here is that although there are constant verbal references to time lapses, it takes only three separate location shots to bring them to the castle fortress, leaving the viewer to invest the narrative with his own spatio-temporal continuum. In each of these locations the foliage becomes less dense, and by the third scene the viewer is in a rocky and barren landscape which communicates symbolically the nature of the place. Even with this air of topographical reality, the many stages of the journey, which have been compressed, pass rapidly as if in a dream. This dreamlike quality of *White Zombie* reinforces the dichotomy between verbal and visual referents, between what is spoken about (the distance) and the means used to speak of it (narrative space). The three spaces of the three scenes are not visually contiguous. The disjunction also takes place on a personal level between Neil and Madeline by suspensefully prolonging their union and resolves itself only when they occupy the same space. On a narrative level the denouement must wait until Legendre is destroyed.

As if by telepathy, Madeline in her trancelike state senses Neil's presence and he in turn, close to delirium with fever, senses hers. During this segment the spiritual "Listen to the Lambs" is hummed by a chorus intimating Neil and Madeline's telepathic union. With a split screen (a diagonal line dividing the frame in two), Madeline is seen dressed in a flowing medieval gown. She stares out on a terrace of the castle, while Neil on the right side of the frame feebly rises from his blanket by the outdoor fire. In a horizontal wipe Neil is seen throwing off his covers and smiling as if Madeline were before him. In another diagonal wipe Neil gets up from his improvised bed and calls her name. Madeline returns to the chamber and Neil makes his way to the castle.

Neil begins to search, and in a series of disjunctive shots he is seen (1) climbing up an exterior staircase of the castle, and (2) walking through a ruined courtyard with a sunken pool that runs out to the sea. These two shots are interspersed with those of Madeline getting up to return to the balcony, and shots of the confrontation between Legendre and Beaumont, who is now almost completely in the magician's power. There is a return to (3) Neil as he walks through undefined passages in the castle. Key lighting is used to cast shadows and bring out harsh contrasts in white and black as he descends a stone staircase and finds himself in the spacious gallery where Beaumont and Legendre sit.

Causing Neil to faint, Legendre summons the somnambulistic Madeline from her bed, and she too, clothed in white flowing garments, traverses the mazelike corridors of the castle while doors open without human contrivance for her. These seemingly repetitive incursions into the undefined and uncontiguous space act as a correlative to certain dream states or quasi-surrealistic situations where the exploration of spaces produces its known terror. The use of staircases, for instance, creates a dramatic distancing between the known and unknown, the known being at the foot of the stairs, the unknown at the head. Neil, for example, is mysteriously overcome at the head of the stairs by the psychic power of Legendre, and Madeline under the necromancer's influence attempts to murder her husband at the stair's head, but a hand from behind a curtain arrests the dagger she wields. Staircases also serve another dramaturgical function as places where the attitudes of the characters are illustrated: Madeline drifts down the stairs wraithlike; Legendre sinisterly and quietly proceeds down them; Neil rushes down them in determination; the zombies march down them like "angels of death." Staircases also provide a focus for the actors' words and gestures to be created; dialogue and gesticulation require space, allowing Legendre's dynamism to assert itself by emphasizing his psychological superiority[26] and the menacing aspect of his nature (as seen in *Dracula*).

The use of space is evident in Romantic literature and typical of this is a passage from Mary-Anne Radcliffe's *Manfrone or the One-Handed Monk*, where the heroine, Rosalina, is pursued through the castle by Prince de Manfrone. In literature, such space is elaborated upon more fully than that articulated in film, but the comparison is justified:

> A moment's consideration made her determine . . . to continue along some of the numerous passages, amongst whose intricate windings she doubted not she should soon escape her pursuer. . . . After waiting some time, . . . she began to be more composed, and to turn her steps toward her own apartments. This however was a matter of more difficulty than she imagined, for unacquainted with the part of the castello she was in, the more she wandered about, the more she was perplexed to find her right road.[27]

In paying tribute to Ann Radcliffe, LeFanu in *Uncle Silas* has his heroine, Maude Ruthyn, walk through a maze of corridors in the old mansion of Bartram-Haugh:

> I lighted upon a door at the end of a long gallery; . . . I pulled the door and it opened quite easily. I . . . [found] myself . . . at the entrance of a gallery, which diverged at right angles from that through which I had just passed; it . . . ended in total darkness . . . But I took heart . . . I opened a side door, and entered a large room, where were . . . some rusty and cobwebbed bird-cages. . . . I opened a door at its farther end, and entered another chamber . . . equally dismal. The door through which I had entered made a little accidental creak. . . . But . . . fighting against my cowardly nerves, . . . I walked to the door, and looking up and down the dismal passage, was reassured. . . . [O]ne room more—just that whose deep-set front door fronted me, with a melancholy frown, at the opposite end of the chamber. So to it I glided, shoved it open, . . . [28]

The opening of doors throughout *Uncle Silas* and in *White Zombie* operates not only as a means of further illumination on the part of the reader/viewer/protagonist but likewise is a way of extending spatial boundaries to increase off-screen tension. In Ann Radcliffe's *The Italian or the Confessional of the Black Penitents* (1796), Vivaldi, the hero, is in the dungeons of the Inquisition. An effective spatial and auditory play is evident:

the door was partly opened by a person whom Vivaldi could not distinguish in the gloom beyond . . . ; after which the door was closed. Several minutes had elapsed, when tones of deep voices aroused the attention of Vivaldi. . . . The voices drew nearer, and the door again unfolding, two figures stood before Vivaldi, . . . Vivaldi was delivered into their hands, and in the same moment heard the iron door shut, which enclosed him with them in a narrow passage. . . . They walked in silence . . . and came to a second door, which admitted them instantly into another passage. A third door, at a short distance, admitted them to a third avenue, at the end of which one of his mysterious guides struck upon a gate. . . . The gate was, at length, opened . . . and two other doors of iron placed very near each other, [were] also unlocked.[29]

This spatial distancing is achieved in *White Zombie* to create an ambiance of terror, ambiguity and uncertainty just as it does in these novels.

As has been mentioned, the stairs in *White Zombie* play an important part and in the concluding sequence act as a stage upon which the drama moves to its inevitable completion. On one occasion Legendre first, and then Madeline, is framed by the clover-leaf design on the balustrade as each comes down the stairs. From the staircase within, Madeline in a trance glides to the staircase outside the castle and Neil follows in haste. On one of these landings, which is perched above the sea, she almost falls to her death through a breach in the terrace wall. As Neil attempts to revive her, Legendre's legs are seen at the top of the frame walking slowly down until he is with the frame. The zombies are summoned and come down the stairs toward Neil. After Legendre is hit on the head by Bruner, the zombies fall to their death from the terrace, and while Neil and Bruner attempt to restore Madeline to life, Legendre retreats up the stairs, barring the way of Neil and Bruner with a gas pellet. Beaumont with the last of his strength is seen first in shadow coming down the steps. The shadow becomes a sign of Legendre's own destiny, an "angel of death" for him. He pushes Legendre over and in the process falls to his own death. As Madeline recovers she slowly says, "Neil, I dreamed." They are the last words heard from her and are emblematic of the somnambulistic quality of the characters who inhabit this fantasy world. Neil has recovered from his torpor and so has Madeline, but only at the death of the necromancer. The two lovers are powerless against Legendre, and even Bruner is only partially able to overcome him as Dr. Muller is with the mummy. Help comes from the unexpected source: in *The Mummy* it is the goddess Isis, in *White Zombie* the almost totally defenseless Beaumont who regains his strength long enough to kill Legendre. Once again, the potency of love can only operate when the strength of evil has been nullified. In gothic literature the characters undergo a rite of passage to attain wisdom and self-awareness, and when the heroine returns to the "diurnal world, she is wiser, stronger, and more mature," not succumbing to the evil to which she has been exposed.[30] One can only presume in the case of the gothic film heroine, whose passivity leaves little room to conjecture, whether or not she has developed into a more fully integrated person. For the most part these heroines are content to rest in the arms of the romantic lead and, it would seem, leave the rigors of the daylight world to him. Unfortunately, he too is as powerless as she and the closure to many of these films seems precarious at best.

The next group of films deal with the men who aspire, while mortal, to be gods, through the act of creation. But as Elizabeth, Henry's wife, observes in *The Bride of Frankenstein*: "It's death, not life that's in it all and at the end of it all."

The first of the films is James Whale's *Frankenstein*. It comes to a conclusion with the death of the monster and, as Whale had envisioned, the death of Henry Frankenstein. Universal created an epilogue showing the scientist's recovery. It prepared the way for Universal's own recovery with a $5,000,000 gross in its first release.[31]

NOTES

1. Much of the music is a pastiche of classical pieces arranged by Abe Meyer. One such piece is a paraphrase of Brahms's *Rhapsody in B Minor*.

2. Richard Bojarski, *The Films of Bela Lugosi* (Secaucus, N.J.: Citadel Press, 1980), pp. 74–75.

3. W. B. Seabrook, *The Magic Island* (New York: Harcourt, Brace and Company, 1929), p. 335.

4. Each of the men wishes to possess Madeline in what Lowry and deCordova call the "possessor/possessed" paradigm: from Neil to Beaumont to Legendre and then to Neil again to complete the film's circularity and its resolution. See Edward Lowry and Richard deCordova, "Enunciation and the Production of Horror in *White Zombie* in *Planks of Reason*, edited by Barry Keith Grant (Metuchen, N.J.: Scarecrow Press, Inc., 1984), p. 351.

5. Seabrook, pp. 94, 101.

6. Roger Dadoun, "Fetishism in the Horror Film," in *Fantasy and the Cinema*, edited by James Donald (London: British Film Institute Press, 1989), p. 55.

7. Mary-Anne Radcliffe, *Manfrone or the One-Handed Monk*, Vol. 1 (New York: Arno Press, 1972), pp. 19–20.

8. Charles Robert Maturin, *Melmoth the Wanderer* (Lincoln: University of Nebraska Press,1972), p. 176.

9. Charles Brockden Brown, *Wieland, or the Transformation* (New York: Harcourt, Brace and World, Inc., 1926), p. 167. Also see: G.W.M. Reynolds, *Wagner, the Wehr-Wolf*, p. 6; Matthew Gregory Lewis, *Mistrust or Blanche and Osbright*, in *Seven Masterpieces of Gothic Horror*, edited by Robert Donald Spector (New York: Bantam, 1971), p. 286; Sir Edward Bulwer-Lytton, *The Haunted and the Haunters*, in *Classic Ghost Stories* (New York: Dover Publications, 1975), pp. 309–10. In Samuel Taylor Coleridge's "The Rime of the Ancient Mariner," the mariner's eyes are referred to as "glittering" and "bright" (ll. 1–40, 618).

10. Ann Radcliffe, *The Italian or the Confessional of the Black Penitents* (New York: Oxford University Press, 1971), p. 184.

11. W. Harrison Ainsworth, "The Spectre Bride," in *Gothic Tales of Terror*, Vol. 1, edited by Peter Haining (Baltimore, Maryland: Penguin Books Inc., 1973), p. 368.

12. J. S. LeFanu, *The Room in the Dragon Volant*, in *Ghost Stories and Mysteries*, ed. by E. F. Bleiler (New York: Dover Publications, 1975), p. 9.

13. Thomas Percy, *Reliques of Ancient English Poetry* (Philadelphia: Porter and Coates, 1890), p. 361; Sir Walter Scott, *The Complete Poetical Works of Sir Walter Scott* (New York: Houghton, Mifflin and Company, 1900), pp. 2–3.

14. Johann Ludwig Tieck, *The Bride of the Grave*, in *Gothic Tales of Terror*, Vol. 2, pp. 106–07.

15. *Louise or the Living Spectre*, in *Gothic Tales of Terror*, Vol. 2, pp. 304–16.

16. Washington Irving, *Adventure of the German Student, Gothic Tales of Terror*, Vol. 2, pp. 424–30.

17. LeFanu, *The Mysterious Lodger*, in *Ghost Stories and Mysteries*, p. 356.

18. Wilkie Collins, *Mad Monkton*, in *Tales of Terror and the Supernatural*, ed. by Herbert van Thal (New York: Dover Publications, 1972), p. 225.

19. Marie Corelli, *The Sorrows of Satan* (Illinois: Palmer Publications, Spring, 1965, Issue No. D-2), p. 82.

20. J. K. Huysmans, *La-Bas*, trans. by Keene Wallace (New York: Dover Publications, 1972), p. 159.

21. Edgar Allan Poe, *Fall of the House of Usher* in *The Fall of the House of Usher and Other Tales* (New York: New American Library, 1962), p. 130.

22. See Siegfried Kracauer, *Theory of Film* (New York: Oxford University Press, 1960), p. 159.

23. See *The Spectre Barber* in *Gothic Tales of Terror*, Vol. 2. Peter Haining, ed., pp. 165–98, and A. W. Schreiber, *The Devil's Ladder*, pp. 248–55.

24. M. G. Lewis, *The Bravo of Venice* (New York: McGrath Publishing Co., 1972), pp. 102–03.

25. Radcliffe, *Manfrone*, Vol. I, pp. 67–73.

26. Rene Lauret, *Le Théâtre Allemand d'aujord'hui*, cited by Lotte H. Eisner, *The Haunted Screen* (California: University of California Press, 1969), p. 122.

27. Radcliffe, *Manfrone*, Vol. I, pp. 71–72.

28. J. S. LeFanu, *Uncle Silas* (New York: Dover Publications 1966), pp. 338–39.

29. Radcliffe, *The Italian or the Confessional of the Black Penitents*, pp. 310–11.

30. Charlene Bunnell, "The Gothic: A Literary Genre's Transition to Film," in *Planks of Reason*, p. 86.

31. James Curtis, *James Whale* (New Jersey: Scarecrow Press, Inc., 1982), p. 88.

PART II

THE ROMANTIC AS MODERN PROMETHEUS

CHAPTER 4

Frankenstein: Are Men Not Gods?

Did I request thee, Maker, from my clay
To mould me Man, did I solicit thee
From darkness to promote me?

—Milton, "Paradise Lost"

In James Whale's *Frankenstein* (1931), the Romantic trappings are present in its quasi-Germanic village of Goldstadt, in the strong expressionistic *mise-en-scène* with its phalliclike tombstones, towers and trees jutting bizarrely out of the landscape, and in huge machines that extend into the night. The concepts mirror the protagonist's soul: the powerful urge to create living matter from dead tissue parallels images suggesting this same paradox, that is, the representation of phalliclike objects that appear on a barren plain. Added to this *mise-en-scène* is the mannered acting of Colin Clive and Boris Karloff and the use of low-angle photography to give power to the characters (Clive for one) and show them against an artificially lit sky. Even the atmospheric elements express corresponding states in the doctor's agitated mind. This artistic expression is a Romantic reaction against the Cartesian duality of the world outside and the world inside. The expressionistic decor of *Frankenstein* (and later *The Bride of Frankenstein*) is part of an anti-Copernican revolution in the plastic arts by which man again stands at the center of the world he represents, but it is the world of Caligari that the director has copied. So while Romanticism in a broad sense was a reaction against eighteenth-century science which left the world as a mechanical system in which man was a stranger, Whale's expressionism creates a world that is not only homocentric but psychocentric, the world of Henry Frankenstein. The creature created by the doctor finds himself a product of the mechanical system in which he, as neither man nor animal, is a stranger. Dr. Frankenstein, as interpreted by Colin Clive, is a neurotic who has projected his fantasies into the act of creation and elaborates them into a form that disguises not only their purely personal origin (egotism) but also their origin in forbidden and repressed desires. The creator has universalized his mental life in a superman who mirrors the psychotic state of the creator. While Whale's egocentric scientist is a rebel against the conventional scientific world, he is also a prophet. Elizabeth (Mae Clarke) says that there is "mystery in his eyes"; Victor Moritz (John Boles) reports of his aloofness: "he walks alone in the woods." Dr. Waldman (Edward Van Sloan) remarks, "he is erratic," and has "an insane ambition to create life." It is Henry's idea "to look beyond the clouds" and glimpse "what eternity is." What ultimately causes the failure in Dr. Frankenstein's plan is not the accidental substitution of brains in the monster, but the fact that Henry, while being a Romantic rebel, is also a rationalist. He creates life, a thing reserved only to God, and in so doing, attempts to make reasonable the mystery of creation. He says to Waldman: "I have discovered the great ray that brought life into the world," and still expurgated from the original print when he brings the monster to life: "Now I know what it feels like to be God." Henry represents the incarnate god of reason that the Romantics denounced and whom the eighteenth century had enthroned under the name of science and the Enlightenment.[1] But in becoming the Promethean figure of modern science, he ironically becomes impotent. Whereas the Count in Browning's *Dracula* has brought life-in-death to those with whom he came in contact, Dr. Frankenstein is interested in bringing a death-in-life to his creation. Once he has aided in the process of creation, however, he is physically and mentally incapacitated and cannot for a time go through the marriage ceremony. His creation, representing the repressed desires that have caused its creator so much strain, has been freed from the doctor's inner self. In a highly evocative situation tinged with the black humor for which Whale is noted, the monster breaks into the bridal chamber in an act that suggests the replacement of the bridegroom by the monster: the creature assumes the role now of procreator. Lust is manifested as something emanating from the monster's uncontrollable "id." The creature becomes Henry's alter ego; while Henry is ironically powerless to protect Elizabeth from his creation, the creature, as a projection of the scientist's baser instincts, attempts to enjoy the favors of Henry's bride-to-be. After the monster has left the room, Henry and Victor break in to find Elizabeth on her bed as if ravished by the creature.

It is not by chance that the monster and creator become interchangeable so that "Frankenstein" is used to designate the creature rather than the doctor, once more asserting the idea of a *doppelganger*. Victor (Henry in the film) in the novel speaks of the monster as "my own vampire, my own spirit let loose from the grave."[2] The critic Harold Bloom, however, says that "The monster . . . is more lovable than his creator and more hateful, more to be pitied and more to be feared. . . . Frankenstein is the mind and emotions turned in upon themselves, and his creature is the mind and emotions turned imaginatively outward, seeking a greater humanization through a confrontation of other selves." These "solipsistic and generous halves of the one self" are what is important in Bloom's conception of the Shelley novel.[3] In general, this is what the Whale films (*Frankenstein* and *The Bride of Frankenstein*) tend to portray, although they are more visually important than "the . . . vivid versions . . . of the Romantic mythology of the self" that Bloom sees in the novel. In Peggy Webbling's play, upon which the film was adapted, the monster assumes the name of his creator and even appears clothed like him. In fact, Webbling extends this doubling to include almost everyone in her play.[4]

The villain-hero of the motion picture, an even more sympathetic character than the vampire of Browning's film, is ostensibly Henry's alter ego, the monster. In the 1930s horror films the monsters are seen as unwilling victims, "all peace destroyed by the horrible and psychological alterations thrust upon them," which makes them attractive to a teenage audience because they "painfully embod[y] the adolescent's nightmare of being hated and haunted by the society which [he] so desperately [wishes] to join."[5] The adult viewers might see the monster as a metaphor for the Great Depression of the 1930s "in which manipulations of the stock-market had recoiled on the manipulators; in which human creatures seemed to be abandoned by those who . . . might have been thought responsible for their welfare; in which men were prevented from . . . feeling themselves full and equal members of society, and were thereby filled with destructive rages."[6] But the more compassionate the villain-hero is presented, the greater the possibility is for ambivalent feelings toward him. It is evident that the monster is envisioned, at least by Mary Shelley and to a degree by James Whale, as the tormented Romantic. The monster suffers from *angst*: he is too human to be associated with the animal world, but too abnormal to be associated with humanity, combining moral culpability with superhuman power and grandeur. In fact the monster becomes a forerunner of the modern existential hero. In *Frankenstein* the existential theme of *Geworfenheit*, the state of being thrown into a world where one does not belong, is advanced, so that by the conclusion the monster's destruction in the burning mill is a pitiable sight.[7] The audience is torn between empathy for it and compassion for the errant creator, because the creature is so much a part of the creator, and because it is so much a part, it is impossible for the creator-romantic lead to destroy it. The villagers, a more objective source of law and order, must perform the service. Concomitantly, Shelley's Victor Frankenstein is as tormented as his creature. When Victor's brother is murdered by the monster, Justine, an innocent servant of Victor's aunt, is found guilty, prompting Victor to cry out: "The tortures of the accused did not equal mine; . . . but the fangs of remorse tore my bosom." And after Justine's death, Victor is seized by "remorse and the sense of guilt, which hurried me away to a hell of intense tortures," so that Victor's "state of mind preyed upon [his] health." He, like Romantic heroes, "shunned the face of man; all sound of joy or complacency was torture to me; solitude was my only consolation." But even when Victor is in the company of his best friend, Clerval, he ruminates: "I am a blasted tree; the bolt has entered my soul . . . a miserable spectacle of wreched humanity." And when Clerval is also slain by the monster, Victor is "absorbed by a gloomy and black melancholy." When he thinks of the approach of his marriage to Elizabeth and the monster's threats on the life of his bride-to-be, he again reflects that "memory brought madness with it, and when I thought of what has passed, a real insanity possessed me . . . sometimes I was furious and burnt with rage, sometimes low and despondent." After the death of Elizabeth he is placed in confinement: "For they had called me mad . . . and a solitary cell had been my habitation."[8]

In the film these Byronic traits are psychologically more pronounced in the creator, while in the monster they are physically more predominant. Together, Henry Frankenstein and his creature complement one another, and accordingly both are forced to suffer an enormous guilt. Frankenstein, the more culpable of the two, must suffer in assuming the role of God and relinquishing his duty after he gives life to his creation. His inordinate pride mirrors the Romantic rebellion against God with its archetype in Lucifer. His creation also must suffer a nameless guilt of alienation, which in turn results in a rebellion against others, driving him restlessly toward an inevitable doom. The moralistic stance of the film version is uncomplicated: man has no right to interfere with the things of God and in Byron's words he must, in the end, proclaim: "knowledge is not happiness, and science / But an exchange of ignorance for that / Which is another kind of ignorance."[9]

Henry Frankenstein, through his experiments, ends by withdrawing into himself, a posture taken by the Romantic. But for the film to satisfy the Hollywood convention, that is, to end happily, Henry must return to the social world. If Mina, in *Dracula*, Madeline in *White Zombie* and Helen in *The Mummy* have to awaken from the trance induced by the villain-heroes to a new life free from the danger of present evil, Henry must undergo a similar metamorphosis in order to live a normal life as the father of a family. His return to health is indicative of his return to normalcy.

In *Dracula*, *The Mummy* and *Frankenstein* images of the death-and-rebirth theme are also found as a part of the gothic literary convention. These films play on the conventions associated with beauty and the beast, but the redemptive quality of love necessary to transfer the beast into a human being is seldom present.[10] Dracula and Ardath Bey are monsters in human form, while the creature of Whale's film is a human in the form of a monster, and even the creator must be transformed into a human being capable of responding to others, rather than remaining at an unhealthy narcissistic stage of development. Only in this way does Romantic man return to ordered society; otherwise he is destroyed like Byron's Manfred or Matthew Gregory Lewis's Ambrosio in *The Monk*.

Whale, in making use of a preface, imitates the framing devices that gothic literature employed in much of its fiction. This artifice usually introduces the main story or a story within the major story. Part of its *raison d'être* is to establish verisimilitude, to authenticate the supernatural machinery that the author puts into operation, or to set a philosophical tone in order that the reader might transcend the "shock" effects for metaphysical reasoning. Mary Shelley's method is like that of a series of Chinese boxes. Each introduction into the tale of the "modern Prometheus" leads the reader into a vortex which anchors the novel of unleashed passion in a rational *mise-en-scène*. The "Author's Introduction" (October, 1831) sets the historical situation which led to the writing of the novel, while the "Preface" (September, 1816) acts as a touchstone to introduce the ideology behind the work:

> the event . . . is exempt from the disadvantages of a mere tale of spectres . . . and however impossible as a physical fact, affords a point of view . . . for the delineating of human passion and more comprehensive and commanding than any which the ordinary relations of existing events can yield.

The above preface gives rise to the fictional letters of Robert Walton to his sister in England providing credence to his meeting Victor Frankenstein by recounting the doctor's tale for his sister to "afford [her] the greatest pleasure."[11] Other nineteenth-century authors carry this convention over from eighteenth-century novelists who "took great pains to disguise their fictions as fact so that they would not be accused of spreading lies."[12] In LeFanu's vampire novella, *Carmilla*, the author attests to the validity of the woman who has written it and to Dr. Hesselius, a prototype of Stoker's Van Helsing, who has treated the case. LeFanu strives for the same plausibility with his framing device as does Mary Shelley:

> As I publish the case . . . simply to interest the "laity," I shall forestall the intelligent lady, who relates it, in nothing; . . . and have determined, therefore, to abstain from presenting any précis of the learned Doctor's reasoning, or extract from his statement on a subject which he describes as "involving, not improbably, some of the profoundest arcana of our dual existence, and its intermediates."[13]

Ambrose Bierce's story *The Damned Thing* creates this same authenticity through the strategem of an inquest as the coroner asks a writer to relate the mysterious death of a young man. In Bierce's *Some Haunted Houses* a Lutheran minister, Mr. Henry Galbraith, recounts the night spent at a deceased pirate's house and relates the strange story which follows. The author adds: "Fortunately for the interests of truth there was present at this conversation Mr. Robert Mosely Maren, a lawyer and litterateur of Columbus, the same who wrote the delightful 'Mellowcraft Papers.' "[14] In LeFanu's *A Chapter in the History of a Tyrone Family*, which deals with revenants and insanity, the author, even before the "Introduction," has under the title "Being a Tenth Extract from the Legacy of the Late Francis Purcell, P. P. of Drumcoolagh." In his *The Murdered Cousin*, later expanded into *Uncle Silas*, there appears in the preface: "This story of the Irish peerage is written, as nearly as possible, in the very words in which it was related by its 'heroine,' " the late Countess D—, and is therefore told in the first person."[15] Gothic literature is suffused with such techniques of which these are but a few. To create a similar realistic atmosphere, Whale exploits the theater's proscenium, opening the film as though it were a staged play and thus legitimizing the genre through an older established vehicle. The film employs a prologue much the same as Mary Shelley uses her "introduction" to the novel[16] to "frighten my readers as I myself had been frightened."[17] In the film's preface Edward Van Sloan adds a note of authenticity to the story by appearing before the film audience as a reputable witness declaring that the film about to be presented is one of the most unusual stories ever revealed. He continues in this same authoritative tone to caution the viewers that the tale may thrill them and may even shock and unnerve them.

Horrifying the audience, however, was no simple matter judging from the film's credits which illustrate the torturous progress of the script's revision: "Screenplay by Garrett Fort and Francis Edwards Faragoh (John Russell and Robert Florey were to go uncredited). Based on the composition by John L. Balderston. Adapted from the play by Peggy Webbling. From the novel *Frankenstein; or, The Modern Prometheus* by Mary Wollstonecraft Shelley."[18] Balderston revised the Peggy Webbling play, *Frankenstein: An Adventure in the Macabre* (1927), without much assistance from the playwright, but his revision was never produced and Universal purchased the rights of both dramatizations for $20,000 plus one percent of the world gross.[19] It seems, however, that the Webbling play has disappeared from both print and stage and that Samuel French distributes an "even more drawing-room version," than her original.[20] Webbling's play in light of World War I and preceding the depression "may be viewed in terms of an age frightened by a spectre of its own creation. It thus presages the most popular modern theme associated with the novel: society's ability to destroy itself." Webbling and Balderston dismiss Mary Shelley's Rousseauistic concept of the noble savage and cast their creature as a brute whose only concern is a desire for pleasure and acceptance.[21] This characterization was carried over into the film script so that Karloff's mute performance was more easily able to mime these basic desires than those of Shelley's cerebrally complex monster. Balderston's play *Frankenstein* (1930) is set in 1880. Using Webbling as its basis, it retains her change in names where Victor Frankenstein is called "Henry" and his friend Henry Clerval is called "Victor." Waldman in the play is both a priest and doctor: in the film Edward Van Sloan's character, although secularized, still voices moral opposition to Henry's experiments and, therefore, retains a hint of the priestly character he had in the play. John Boles, who plays Victor Moritz in the film, is a colorless actor compared to the vibrant performances of the supporting cast; however, the play seems to bolster this casting of Boles in its description of Victor as a "normal young man, [with] charm but not particularly intelligent." He is the perfect foil to Henry, who is introduced in the play as "young, thin, nervous, good looking but now at the point of hysteria." Whale's choice for the role is consummately represented by Colin Clive. Some parts of the film dialogue have been taken almost directly from the play. In both the play and film, Henry, before creating life, conducts a "class" in which his former professor becomes his student. Hè asks of Waldman if he knows what the highest color in the spectrum is. The older man replies "violet." The young doctor then shows his master what he has learned: "Beyond that . . . is . . . an ultra-violet . . . its rays will be used for health. Beyond that is still another ray, hotter than ultra-violet—life-giving—even life-creating! In the beginning of the world—of all things." Waldman then quotes from the opening of St. John's gospel, reminding Henry that the first cause of creation is divine: "In the beginning was the word and the word was God." Henry suggests to the priest that God might be a "ray . . . beyond the visible spectrum." Waldman's scientific mind becomes excited by the speculation of finding "a new electrical force," and Henry, unable to contain himself, boasts of the power of his invention: "In this machine—all the rays of the spectrum—the ultra-violet, beyond that—and the great ray beyond that— which in the beginning brought Life into the world as the hot mass cooled—But you would not understand." The play differs from the film in a major point: Henry is presented as a scientist-alchemist, a derivative of gothic fiction. He not only uses a machine with a galvanic battery but also has discovered an elixir of life. The play's creation scene ends with the monster's arm moving as in the film, but it has no deformed assistant, like Fritz, to taunt the monster. Henry in the play uses a whip and hot iron to keep the monster in check as Fritz does with a whip and fire in the Whale picture. In the play Henry is immediately repentant in creating the monster and tells Waldman, "You warned me, and in my mad presumption I would not listen. I usurped the prerogative of God, I tried to make myself His equal," but at the same time calls his creation "Frankenstein," thus disclosing his bond with the creature to the point that his fiancée, Amelia, says, "Henry! He looks like you!" Instead of little Maria being drowned accidentally by the monster, it is Henry's sister, Katrina, who drowns, but the film keeps the same premise as the play: the creature's devastation at the girl's death by her inability to float. In the play and the film the monster attacks Henry's wife-to-be as she waits for the wedding ceremony to begin, but does not kill her as he does in the novel. As was the original intention in the film, the monster kills Henry, who destroys the mate he was to create for the creature, and is himself struck by lightning. This gives Amelia a chance to marry the unimaginative Victor, a conclusion that was being led up to in the film by showing, at the opening, Victor's love for Elizabeth, Henry's fiancée.[22]

In analyzing the film I would like to concentrate on three sections: (1) the opening graveyard sequence, (2) the creation of the monster and (3) the hunting down and "destruction" of the creature. All three are typical of the spirit of Romanticism that dominates the film.

This sense of melancholy and fated destiny in the novel is conveyed in Whale's version through set design and camera technique. In the graveyard sequence the fluidity of the camera work by Arthur Edeson is distinguished. The circular panning movement by the camera of the mourners as they stand by the grave site is contrasted in the following shot to the vertical movement of Henry Frankenstein and his deformed assistant, Fritz, as they rise momentarily from the bottom of the frame and watch the rites being conducted. The decor of the graveyard has been constructed (together with the Dutch angles) to give the impression of objects sinking into decay; the thrust of the religious figures and objects is to the right, creating a pictorial dynamism that suggests a balefulness of the expressionistic landscape of the mind. Bare tree branches and other objects (crosses, death figures, liturgical paraphernalia, iron fences, hammers and bell poles in succeeding shots) break up the frame vertically and are juxtaposed to the horizontal dimensions of the screen, by which they are framed together with the panning and tracking of the camera. Once the mourners have left the cemetery and the grave digger has filled in the site, Henry and Fritz are free to proceed to exhume another body for experimentation. There is a perverse sexuality as Henry caresses the coffin containing part of the body that he will use to procreate with the electrical elements.

After Henry sends Fritz to steal a brain from Dr. Waldman's class, the next shot is of Elizabeth, Henry's fiancée, reading a letter she received from him to her close friend, Victor Moritz. The letter reveals certain characteristics of the Romantic hero: (1) It is similar to confessional literature of the Romantic-gothic strain full of imperative emotional outpourings: "You must have faith . . . my work must come first, even before you." (2) An antipathy toward the world in which he lives: "Prying eyes can't peer into my secret . . . only my assistant is here to help me." (3) A love of the wild and picturesque: "At night the winds howl in the mountains. There is no one here . . . I am living in an abandoned old watch tower." What follows is even more consciously part of the conventions dealing with the Romantic protagonist. Elizabeth's choice of words in speaking about Henry to Victor reflects the torment of the protagonist by the number of times particular words appear: (1) "He doubted his own sanity," (2) "There was a strange look in his eyes, some mystery," (3) "He just glared at me" and (4) "His manner was very strange." The use of the eyes to convey madness or strange supernatural powers has been seen in *Dracula*, *The Mummy* and *White Zombie* and been observed in gothic fiction. Here too, in *Frankenstein*, Elizabeth's last words, "There was a strange look in his eyes, some mystery," parallel Victor's last words, "His manner was very strange." They represent the "normal" world, but Henry is a man apart: his solitary walks in the woods proclaim this. If social intercourse is restricted by Henry to a few, sexual intercourse becomes prohibitive. There is a perversity of Henry's announcing an experiment on his engagement day, for the only consummation of the engagement proper is in marriage. Henry's consummation is not that of nuptial bliss, but the consummation of a creature that is his other self made from dead men's limbs.

This eccentricity is further characterized by the visit of Victor and Elizabeth to Henry's former professor, Dr. Waldman. Once again in Waldman's conversation with the couple, the center of interest is placed on Henry, the creator, who challenges science and reacts against the world of self-discipline that the university requires. The conflict is between youth (Henry) and age (Professor Waldman), between naiveté (Victor) and the visions of a seer (Henry), between the love of the scientist for his work, which here is egotistical and self-destructive (his "mad dream"), and the love he has for a woman, which is sacrificial and self-effacing. The film's increasingly prominent eroticism veers toward necrophilia. Henry turns from the love of the vibrant woman to the morbid interest in the carrion he wishes to infuse with life.

The opening shots of the creation sequence with its lightning, thunder, wind and rain crosscut between the interior of Frankenstein's tower laboratory where he is working and Fritz on the roof. The tower is situated on a mountain with other peaks surrounding it while the foreground is covered with trees. The scene is reminiscent of gothic novels which use nature not only to establish a "Romantic" setting but to convey a relation between the character's disordered state of mind and nature's destructive forces.

The interior of the lab taken from various angles is in a great depth of field. The camera almost mathematically alternates between high and low shots, conveying an immense spatial interval by positioning Henry down in the lab and Fritz up on the roof. Other shots disorient the viewer's perspective by having the camera placed at an angle that appears other than it is until a character is introduced into the frame: when Henry runs close to the bottom of the frame in a seemingly flat-angle shot to hold the rope that Fritz is using to descend from the roof, the camera begins to tilt down slowly with Fritz to disclose Henry by the rope and reveal that the whole shot was taken from a low angle.

Shots preparatory to the animation of the monster briefly introduce the viewer to the table on which the monster is lying and to the testing of various electrical instruments. Other shots show Elizabeth, Waldman and Victor below at the door and serve several purposes: (1) as an interlude before the final test and, therefore, as a means of protracting the tension;

(2) as a method of dynamizing the space between those in the tower and those below, and contrasting the movement of the camera in the lab to the static shots of those attempting to gain entrance; (3) as a way of having a play within a play; once Elizabeth, Victor, and Waldman are admitted into the lab, they become the filmgoer's surrogates and the kinesthetic conductors of emotional responses indicating how the audience is to respond to the action; and finally (4) as a means to stress Henry's individualism and self-expression pitted against Waldman's adherence to tradition and conformity to the scientific rules for procedure. For Henry, the creation of the monster is an expression of power, of revolt from convention, of the restoration of fallen man to that of perfectible man so much so that Henry is able to proclaim himself a god. Along with this is the irrationality attributed, as far back as Plato, to the poetic fury of the artist, the eccentricity and abnormality that are constantly being stressed about Henry by Victor, by Dr. Waldman and even by Henry's father, Baron Frankenstein. It is the clash between "Apollonian" and "Dionysian" influences that thread their way through gothic literature, the former used by Nietzsche in his essay "The Birth of Tragedy" to signify the presence of form and control over the basically irrational or "Dionysian" nature of the universe. The dichotomy between Henry's methods of procedure and those of his former mentor are amply illustrated by comparing Waldman's anatomy class with Henry's frenzied preparations for his experiment. The empirical approach of Waldman's method is presented in a lecture at Goldstaldt Medical College on the brain, which stresses classical qualities of predictability, cause and effect and adherence to technique. Waldman's style is balanced with an antithesis associated with classicism: "Here we have one of the most perfect specimens of the human brain that has ever come to my attention;" ". . . and here the abnormal brain of the typical criminal." Add to this "Observe . . . the scarcity of convolutions on the frontal lobe . . ." with ". . . as compared to that of the normal brain. . . ." Then there is a return to the main emphasis of the lecture with ". . . and the distinct degeneration of the middle frontal lobe . . .," plus the use of repetition by way of cyclic structure: ". . . whose life was one of brutality, of violence and murder." Henry's "lecture" to Dr. Waldman is less deliberate in its formal elements. The student, for a moment, becomes the master. Henry begins by telling his former professor the great knowledge he has learned from him about the violet and ultra-violet ray but then goes on to prove the older man wrong. His speech is more passionate than Waldman's academic lecture on the brain, and it is filled with subordinate phrases and this clause: "which you said was the highest color in the spectrum." After saying this, he departs from Waldman's controlled report.

Henry, for instance, varies the length of the sentence structure: (1) "You were wrong," (2) "Here in this machine I have gone beyond that." By announcing this he creates an ellipsis in the structure, and concludes with a lyrical description of this scientific investigation: (3) "I have discovered the great ray that first brought life into the world!"

With the actual "creation sequence," the pace of the film is more frenzied and yet a perfect equilibrium is set up with reverse angles and steady repetition of shots showing Henry and Fritz, the visitors and the laboratory machinery. As the "creation sequence" continues, the table with the monster on it becomes increasingly important. Between the time the table begins to rise to the time it descends, there is constant rapid editing. Although the shots of the electronic equipment are statically composed, the activity they generate together with the montage is intense compared to the fixity of the human figures looking toward the skylight where the monster's body rests. Up until this time the repetition of the shots in rhythmic cadence has contributed to the tension, but the first close-up, and it is extremely important as such, after the descent of the table to ground level and the unveiling of the monster's body, is of the creature's hand and arm moving. This is again repeated two shots later while another couplet of shots takes up the maniacal chant of Henry, "It's alive!" until it builds into a crescendo.

With the experiment's success, Henry expresses his utopian definition of a scientist to Waldman and further distances himself from his mentor. In his quasi-poetic speech about the necessity of learning what lies beyond the grasp of science, he exhibits the *hubris* of the Promethean: "Have you never wanted to look beyond the clouds and the stars or to know what causes the trees to bud and what changes the darkness into light?" Frankenstein ends with "Well if I could discover . . . what eternity is, for example, I wouldn't care if they did think I was crazy." And for the remainder of the film Henry does experience a descent into madness through his creature's rampage about the countryside, which is only remedied by the "death" of the monster and the young scientist's rebirth from the fiery windmill.

The monster's first appearance is quite impressively staged by Whale in four shots. The first is a long shot of the lab door as it opens and the monster walks in backward so his face is hidden from the camera. The second is a medium shot with the monster's back to camera. The camera dollies back as he walks backward through the door slowly turning around in a counterclockwise direction; the heaviness of his boots can be heard. In the third shot, a medium close-up, the monster's face looks full front at the audience. The sequence ends with a close-up of the monster's face looking full front. Such successive stages of montage are created to elicit a response of terror in the audience by first hiding the creature's face from the camera (however illogical it seems to have the monster enter backwards) and then presenting consecutive stages in cutting from a medium shot to a medium close-up shot to a close-up. Whale's editing objective has nothing to do with the reaction of an individual character in the film, but solely to impress the audience with the creature's awesomeness. In this sequence Whale has the camera concentrate on the monster's hands, as he had done in the creation sequence, to give the creature a means of expressing human emotion. Whale has the monster raise his hands to the light coming in from the lab's skylight. When the light is withdrawn, the camera tilts down to the monster's hands in close-up, opened (palms up) evoking a feeling of confusion. When he is injected with a hypodermic (after killing his tormentor, Fritz) the camera shows his hands moving in a pathetic manner as though he cannot comprehend what has happened to him. Again, the monster's hands are emphasized when he strangles Waldman in self-defense as the doctor is about to dissect him. Later on, his hands play an important part when he receives flowers from Maria, and when he looks down at his empty hands after he has thrown the last flower in the lake.

The expressionistic devices that have been noted in the opening graveyard scene are accentuated in the laboratory. The tower windows usually seem to be placed at odd angles in the background of the frame, thus foreshortening the dimensions of the room so that the background looks narrower and smaller in height than the foreground (especially the scene in the monster's cell). Good use is made of the monster's shadow, which seems to double his actual size. The creature's gestures and halting gait are reminiscent of Lang's workers in *Metropolis*, and a rather ungainly Caesar in *Caligari*. Low-angle photography and cross beams that cut diagonally through the frame, as well as the geometric design cast by the light reflected on the stone staircase in the tower, tend to splinter the overall balance of the shot and create their own tensions (in the lab, in the monster's cell). At times light and shadow seem to be painted onto the sets.

The attack on Elizabeth in her bedroom by the monster is sexually suggestive, a type of Oedipal invention where the son usurps the father's place and rapes his "mother." If one remembers the toast the Baron initiates on the wedding day, "a son to the house of Frankenstein," it is ironic and quite in keeping with Whale's black humor to remind the viewer that the monster is indeed "a son of Frankenstein."

The final search for the monster by night with the conventional torch light processions weaving amid the countryside might owe something to

The White Hell of Pitz Palu by Fanck and Pabst made two years before. In the tracking down of the monster and setting fire to the windmill (borrowed from Ingram's *The Magician*, 1926), the conflagration physically and symbolically illuminates the darkness, casting chaos aside, making way for the restoration of order and purifying the town from the villain-hero's domination.

Only when the monster has died in the flames of the burning windmill can the Baron once more proclaim, and this time with more certainty: "Here's to a son to the house of Frankenstein!" Not only has Henry vanquished his rival "son," he has destroyed his alter ego. He is now free to proceed in a normal relationship with Elizabeth, while the monster, given birth in a stone tower, dies in a wooden one. Yet the monster was resurrected for Whale's sequel in 1935 in a more elaborate and more grotesque film than its predecessor.

The next film, *Island of Lost Souls*, is a picture of the "new" Eden gone awry and of a man who, like Henry Frankenstein, also claims to be a god, but whose paradise must, in the end, be destroyed by the purging fire of justice before the romantic leads rest secure in one another's arms.

NOTES

1. Wylie Sypher, however, sees a similarity between the science and Romanticism of the nineteenth century. Both proceed from an anthropomorphic view of the world. The Romantic creates a world as his will or idea while with scientific laws there was a compulsive logic of cause and effect extending man's mind into nature by a theory of force or energy, a reflex of man's own will. Wylie Sypher, *Loss of Self in Modern Literature and Art* (New York: Vintage Books, 1962), p. 84.

2. Mary Shelley, *Frankenstein or the Modern Prometheus* (New York: New American Library, 1965), p. 74.

3. Harold Bloom, "Afterword" to *Frankenstein*, p. 215.

4. Steven Earl Forry, *Hideous Progenies: Dramatizations of Frankenstein from Mary Shelley to the Present* (Philadelphia: University Pennsylvania Press, 1990), p. 96.

5. Walter Evans, "Monster Movies: A Sexual Theory," in *Sexuality in the Movies*, ed. by Thomas R. Atkins (New York: Da Capo Press, 1975), p. 148. Also see Walter Evans, "Monster Movies and Rites of Initiation," in *Journal of Popular Film* Vol. 4 no. 2 (1975), pp. 124–42.

6. S. S. Prawer, *Caligari's Children: The Film as Tale of Terror* (New York: Da Capo Press, 1980), pp. 22–23.

7. Sympathy is further enhanced through two shots that are "seen through the revolving mill wheel, [where] maker and Monster appear as doubles." See

list of illustrations in Martin Tropp, *Mary Shelley's Monster* (Boston: Houghton Mifflin Company, 1977).

8. Shelley, *Frankenstein*, pp. 86, 153, 173, 181, 189.

9. Lord Byron, *Manfred*, Acts. II, sc. iv, 11. 61–63, in *Types of Philosophic Drama*, ed. by Robert Metcalf Smith, Ph.D. (New York: Prentice-Hall, 1928), p. 320. Destiny speaks here to Manfred.

10. In *Frankenstein* and *The Bride* temporary transformations do occur with dire consequences: Maria befriends the monster in *Frankenstein* and drowns; the hermit befriends him in *The Bride* and his cottage burns to the ground.

11. Shelley, pp. xiii, 29.

12. Les Daniels, *Living in Fear: A History of Horror in the Mass Media* (New York: Charles Scribner's Sons, 1975), p. 2.

13. LeFanu, *Carmilla*, in *Best Ghost Stories of J. S. LeFanu* (New York: Dover Publications, 1964), p. 247.

14. Ambrose Bierce, *Some Haunted Houses*, in *Ghost and Horror Stories of Ambrose Bierce*, ed. by E. F. Bleiler (New York: Dover Publications, 1964), p. 66.

15. LeFanu, *A Chapter in the History of a Tyrone Family* and *The Murdered Cousin*, in *Ghost Stories and Mysteries*, edited by E. F. Bleiler (New York: Dover Publications, 1975), pp. 189, 216. See the following in their use of framing devices to create verisimilitude:

Lewis's *The Monk* contains stories within stories; one such being the "History of Don Raymond, Marquis De Las Cisternas."

Maturin's *Melmoth the Wanderer* has a series of interpolated tales with a lengthy framing story dealing with John Melmoth who uncovers a dreaded secret about one of his ancestors which is placed in the perspective of English history.

The framing device may also be seen to give credence to the fantastic in Wilkie Collins's *The Dream Woman*, Frederick Marryat's *The Werewolf*, and F. Marion Crawford's *The Upper Berth*.

Ann Radcliffe's *Gaston De Blondeville* employs a framing device of more than 76 pages. Mrs. J. H. Ridell in *The Haunted House at Latchford* uses a title to create the needed believability: "Mr. H. Stafford Trevor, Barrister-At-Law Introduced by Himself."

J. Meade Falkner's *The Lost Stradivarius* fills the introduction of possession by the dead with a plethora of historical associations.

16. I will use the 1831 text for all quotations taken from the book instead of the 1818 text. The reasons for this are (1) Percy Shelley's contribution to the 1818 text of *Frankenstein* was not substantial, (2) James Rieger is a proponent of the 1818 text, but Rieger's account of Shelley's changes contains several errors and (3) Rieger's questioning of the authority of the 1831 edition has "more to do with justifying his reissue of the 1818 text than with any elasticity in the facts of authorship." See David Ketterer, *Frankenstein's Creation: The Book, the Monster, and Human Reality* (Canada: University of Victoria, 1979), pp. 107–10.

17. Shelley, *Frankenstein*, p. xi.

18. Michael Brunas, John Brunas, and Tom Weaver, *Universal Horrors: The Studio's Classic Films, 1931–1946* (North Carolina: McFarland & Company, Inc., 1990), p. 20.

19. Forry, pp. 91–92.

20. George Levine and U. C. Knoepflmacher, editors, *The Endurance of Frankenstein: Essays on Mary Shelley's Novel* (Los Angeles: University of California Press, 1979), p. 286. The revised Webbling play was deposited with the Library of Congress on September 7, 1928.

21. Forry, pp. 93, 99.

22. All quotations from the Balderston play are found in Forry, pp. 252–86.

CHAPTER 5

Island of Lost Souls: The Eden of the Grand Guignol

To defy Power, which seems omnipotent:
. . . to hope till Hope creates
From its own wreck the thing it contemplates.
                                —Shelley, "Prometheus Unbound"

Island of Lost Souls (1933), directed by Erle C. Kenton, and adapted from H. G. Wells's *The Island of Doctor Moreau*, presents an exotic locale, and its villain-hero, Moreau (Charles Laughton), is himself a Romantic idealist, attempting to change beasts into men. *Hubris* causes Moreau's downfall, for he, like Henry Frankenstein, dares to usurp God's authority.

Both *Frankenstein* and *The Island of Doctor Moreau* are pessimistic works with a dichotomy at the heart of their narratives: an optimistic outward journey with new, bright ideas of humanitarianism and the chastened return whereby man falls far short at playing God.[1] Mary Shelley's novel is less so, perhaps, because of the pre-Darwinian age in which it was written. Darwin dealt one of the final blows to Romantic man's image of himself as the center of the universe by postulating that man was only part of a series of lower forms of life in the evolutionary process. Wells's pessimism expresses all the doubts about the benefits of science for which mankind was not sufficiently prepared to appreciate, and as one of Thomas Huxley's biology students, he must certainly have remembered when writing *The Island of Doctor Moreau* (1896) a series of lectures entitled *Evolution and Ethics* (1893), where Huxley described the evolutionary process as "full of wonder, full of beauty, full of pain," for "suffering is the badge of all the tribe of sentient things, attaining to its highest level in man."[2]

In the Wells and Kenton works, man as scientist, meets Darwin head-on exercising his godlike power to transform lower forms of life into his own image and likeness thereby accelerating the evolutionary process. But man is doomed to failure. Both Shelley and Wells (by extension Whale and Kenton) argue against these utopian ideals which seem attainable through science. Even the Captain of the *Covena*, Davies, both in the novel and film is as bestial as anything Moreau has produced on his island, and the thirties movie-going audiences may have seen in Moreau's capricious experimentation on the beast-folk a parallel to those who willingly blamed "a system which appeared to thrive on an arbitrary suspension of the individual's inalienable right to the pursuit of happiness."[3]

Regardless of the socio-economic implications in the film, the photography of Karl Struss, responsible the year before for *Dr. Jekyll and Mr. Hyde* (1932), is excellent. The film opens with a shot of a ship enshrouded in mist and cuts to the prow with the name *Covena* as it emerges out of the fog, which disappears as quickly as it surfaced. The following shot of the doctor who observes a man adrift is in soft focus so that his white clothes, which seem incandescent, act as a bridge between the heavily fogged scenes and the clearer shots to follow. This atmosphere establishes the quasi-dreamlike ambiance of Kenton's film while off-screen sounds contribute to the mystery surrounding the ship. Edward Parker (Richard Arlen), having been saved from a shipwreck, tells Dr. Montgomery on the *Covena* to send a wireless to his fiancée, Ruth Thomas (Leila Hyams), at the port of Apia, saying that he is safe. Edward inquires if Montgomery is a doctor, and the latter responds cryptically that he was at one time. Much more mysteriously sinister is the Montgomery of Wells's novel that Edward Prendick meets:

This man . . . *had come out of immensity merely to save* my life. Tomorrow *he would drop over the side and vanish again* out of my existence . . . But in the first place was the *singularity* of an educated man living on this *unknown little island*, and . . . the *extraordinary nature of his luggage*. . . . [I]n his personal attendant there was a *bizarre quality* that had impressed me profoundly. These circumstances threw a *haze of mystery around the man*. They *laid hold of my imagination* and *hampered my tongue*. Towards midnight we stood side by side . . . and I began my gratitude. . . . "Thank no one . . . I injected and fed you *much as I might have collected a specimen. I was bored*, and *I wanted something to do*. If I'd been *jaded* that day, or *hadn't liked your face*, well . . . *it's a curious question where you would have been now*.[4]

The first seven lines describe a character in the gothic mold, the secret that surrounds him and his effect on Prendick. In the film Struss employs soft focus to dramatize the "haze of mystery around" Montgomery; in the last five lines this physical description becomes internalized through a self-reflexive psychological delineation: the intelligent man of the world who through mere whim decides to save another's life, but whose feelings are removed from normal human emotions.

As the doctor and Edward walk about the deck, the audience hears and afterwards sees that the ship is a floating menagerie of wild animals, further confusing the viewer as to the nature of the vessel and its cargo. The dialogue between the ship's brutal captain and Dr. Montgomery in the presence of Edward casts mystery over the entire enterprise: the cargo, announces Captain Davies to Edward, contains animals from Mombasa going to an undisclosed nameless island not on the map, one with a stinking reputation over the South Seas. As for Dr. Moreau, the captain describes him as a grave robber. The stock device of mysterious islands presided over by strange doctors is an intriguing part of the scientific romance genre, and like many stock devices it is economical in the associations it conjures up. Before the mysterious Moreau is met, there is another instance aboard the boat which gives the viewer time to ponder who Moreau is. A deformed servant of Dr. Montgomery carries a bucket of food to the howling dogs. When the servant is struck down by the captain, Edward goes over to pick him up and a ghastly discovery is made. The camera zooms in on the man's ear, covered with hair and pointed like a dog's. When he regains consciousness, the servant rushes to the captain (face to the camera in an extreme close-up) baring his long canine teeth. Under different circumstances, Wells's literary counterpart makes this discovery of M'ling, the dog-man: "I could hardly repress a shuddering recoil as he came . . . and placed the tray before me on the table. The astonishment paralyzed me. Under his stringy black locks I saw his ear! It jumped upon me suddenly, close to my face. The man had pointed ears, covered with a fine fur!"[5] Wells uses words like "repress a shuddering recoil" juxtaposed to "bending amiably," then reverts to the reaction shot, as it were, "astonishment paralyzed me." The word "ear," which ends the sentence, is followed by an exclamation point creating a dialectic of the simple sentence with an ordinary observation followed by the jarring punctuation mark that brings the statement to an abrupt halt. The ensuing sentence needs no such punctuation, but the vocabulary acts in a similar manner to a zoom shot: "It jumped upon me suddenly, close to my face." The paragraph ends in a topic sentence with a discovery of "the pointed ears . . . covered with fur" and another exclamation point. Earlier on in the novel

Prendick first detects this strange creature and Wells prepares the reader for the sight through the first-person narration, presenting the beast-man in a similar way to Whale's monster by deliberately showing him in successive stages.

> He was standing on the ladder with his back to us. . . . He was, I could see, a misshapen man, short, broad, and clumsy, with a crooked back, a hairy neck, and a head sunk between his shoulders. . . . , and had peculiarly thick coarse black hair . . . forthwith he ducked back, coming into contact with the hand I put out to fend him off from myself. He turned with animal swiftness. . . . The black face thus flashed upon me startled me profoundly. It was a singularly deformed one. The facial part projected forming something dimly suggestive of a muzzle, and the huge half-open mouth showed as big white teeth as I had ever seen in a human mouth. His eyes were bloodshot at the edges, with scarcely a rim of white round the hazel pupils.

Linguistically, this excerpt serves the same purpose as Whale's sequence: the gradual revelation of the monster's face to create a greater impact on the viewer. In Wells's novel, the beast-man is first seen "with his back to us," the narrator giving a description of him. The sentence, "He turned with animal swiftness," summarizes succinctly what the "man" is by the way he moves. But even before this, his progress toward the narrator is prepared for by another "shot": "and forthwith he ducked back, coming into contact with the hand I put out. . . . " Next comes the description of his physiognomy as he stands face-to-face with the narrator: first the general description with words like "the black face," "singularly deformed," and then a more particular description with "half opened mouth," "big with white teeth," "eyes . . . bloodshot." Yet, however detailed these descriptions are, one advantage the movie has over the novel is that the film shot presents an immediate intellectual and emotional complex rendering the temporal prolixity of Wells unnecessary.[6]

The soft focus shots of the *Covena* sequence give way to clarity when Moreau's boat is docked alongside the freighter to receive its cargo. Moreau, the villain-hero, is shrouded in mystery in the film version. The viewer is prepared in advance for this by Edward's inquiries concerning Moreau and his island to a sailor who gives an evasive answer that adds to the secrecy: "I don't know, and if I did know maybe I'd want to forget." Even when Edward is unceremoniously forced off the boat and on to Moreau's, we only observe the doctor in long shot from a high angle so that his face cannot be seen, and when pictured again in a second shot, his back is to the camera, prolonging the suspense. Only when Moreau sits at the wheel of the vessel does the audience see this face clearly.

The approach to the island is through mist, and silhouettes of beast-men are seen on the walls of a cave that leads to Moreau's jungle paradise. Before they enter the cavern the doctor prefaces his remarks to Edward with cryptic words that suggest the strangeness of the island. He also admonishes Edward to be cautious while on the island and to remain silent after he leaves. Moreau secretly formulates his plan to have Edward mate with one of his most perfect specimens, a panther-woman, whom he has given the semblance of beauty, but when this fails and Ruth Thomas reaches the island, Moreau plans to have her raped by one of his beast-men. The sexual perversity in the film seems rather tame by today's standards, but the film seethes with eroticism and sadism.

As in many sequences throughout the film, emphasis is placed on off-screen sound or dialogue which Kenton employs contrapuntally. For example, in the scene where Moreau has invited Parker to dinner along with Montgomery, the urbanity of the table talk is contrasted to the sound of the cups rattling in a servant's hand as frightening cries are heard coming from the House of Pain where Moreau surgically transforms beasts into the likeness of humans. The enigmatic dialogue of Moreau that attends this is threatening without the least tone of sternness. Accompanying the sounds of screaming, Moreau cautions Parker by saying that he relies on his discretion. Parker replies with no more than a nod, while Moreau, drinking a brandy, warns the young man that he hopes it will be so.

But there are other signs which speak more significantly than words of the unknown terror that resides in that off-screen space. As Moreau and Montgomery leave the room there is an extensive tracking shot through the gardens; iron bars are seen in the background to all accessible entrances into the house. Moreau walks up to the iron gate surrounding the house and opens it. He eagerly inquires of his partner if he thinks Letta will be attracted to Parker or if she has the ability to be a woman with the appropriate emotional impulses. The image of incarceration is found throughout the film, and it is ironical but totally within context that while giving the panther-woman the freedom to be sexually attracted to the "man from the sea" (as Edward is called), the shadows of bars that enclose the compound are constantly seen. As Moreau walks like a caged animal up and down Letta's cell, the camera pans back and forth in short movements; shadows of the bars are reflected on the wall from a window. The doctor tells his creation that he wants to leave her alone with the man who has come from the sea to talk about the world that Parker has left. But he forewarns Letta to say nothing about himself, the Law and the House of Pain. Moreau holds Letta's hand and leads her down a pathway in the garden like a father with a young child, but not with such an innocent purpose. A panther is heard as Moreau and Letta pause by its cage, and the sound is carried over to Edward, seated in his room, linking Letta with her "mate." The growling animal and the barred windows in Edward's room emphasize that he is just as much a prisoner as Letta and suggests not only the constitutional make-up of the woman herself but of a sexuality that lies close to and is embedded in her animal nature. Kenton charges the atmosphere with sexual electricity. It is only now that the director allows the viewer to observe her exotic beauty, long frizzled hair and skimpy two-piece sarong; she is the embodiment of primitive sensuality. Ape-men suddenly block the path of Moreau and Letta but at the doctor's command they disappear, yet their presence is a reminder of man's animal drives aroused at the sight of a beautiful woman, and so assists in Wells's bitter allegory of man's complete trust in science to advance him to a godlike level through the creative process.

As in much of Kenton's film, revelation comes a bit at a time in unraveling the mystery surrounding the island and the doctor: the noise on deck of the *Covena*, finally revealing the menagerie; the screams from the House of Pain followed by the vivisection performed by Moreau, a beautiful native woman who turns out to be a panther. This device for unveiling slowly is also exploited in the novel:

> I fell into a tranquil state midway between dozing and waking. From this I was aroused . . . by a rustling amidst the greenery on the other side of the stream. . . . Suddenly upon the bank of the stream appeared something—at first I could not distinguish what it was. It bowed its head to the water and began to drink. Then I saw it was a man, going on all-fours like a beast![7]

When Letta (she has no counterpart in the novel) becomes sexually attracted to Edward, nestling up to him on a sofa, a quick pan shows Moreau watching her progress through the ever-present barred windows. Letta asks Edward if he comes from the sea. He tells her of his being afloat for three days, while Letta expresses her desire for him to remain on the island. Suddenly horrible screams are heard from the House of Pain. Edward starts to run out and Letta runs after him. In the garden the camera tracks them as Edward rushes ahead, followed by Letta. She tries to soothe him by saying it isn't anything, but Edward will not be put off and vehemently replies that somebody is being tortured. He runs to the doorway of the House of Pain. Moreau and Montgomery are seen over the operating table on which a beast-man is screaming. While Moreau yells to Edward to get out, Montgomery shuts the door after Edward leaves to inform Letta that they are vivisecting humans, fearing that he may be the next victim. The scene just described combines sex, voyeurism and sadism. The diagonal panning movement to Moreau suggests the bamboo barlike coverings over the windows in their diagonal placement. The scene points to Moreau's scientific-sexual voyeurism and is intercut with the attempted seduction of Edward. The notion of the man from the sea is also sexual since the sea is a symbol of fertility, and Moreau's design is to have Edward fertilize his female panther-woman. Edward brings the seed of life which ironically Moreau, who has cultivated overgrown orchids, lilies (fertility symbols) and huge asparagus (gigantic phalli), cannot hope to accomplish. Therefore, the man who comes from the sea becomes a reservoir of the possibilities of existence which precede every form and support every creation. Edward has been rescued from the sea, and this immersion in water signifies regression to the preformal, reincorporation into the undifferentiated mode of preexistence. His immersion repeats the cosmogenic act of formal manifestation. And although the "island of Dr. Moreau" does not disappear through immersion, which is an equivalent to a dissolution of forms, it is purified through fire.[8] Counterpoised to the eroticism of the situation are the screams of the vivisected creatures and the reinforcement of the images of incarceration by the barred windows. The sudden freedom and depth of space created by the tracking movement as Edward rushes to the House of Pain with Letta is contrasted to the operating room shot with its low lighting fixtures and beams that form right angles that cut portions of the frame. Both Letta and Edward run to the main gate which is barred: they leave the enclosure through the side door.

Their fleeing through the jungle is the second of three sequences that punctuate the film: (1) with Moreau and Edward; (2) with Edward and Letta; and (3) with Ruth, Letta, Montgomery and Captain Donahue as they attempt to make their escape. The village of the beast-men into which Letta and Edward have made their way, only to be rescued by Moreau, is headed by the Sayer of the Law (Bela Lugosi). As the beast-men are about to attack Letta and Edward, Moreau makes them recite the Law, after he has run the gong. Moreau is seen on a plateau; Edward, Letta and the Sayer are in the midground below. The other creatures are behind them with a glowing camp fire toward the background of the frame. Moreau rings a gong and all come running to the camp site. Cracking a whip, he compels them to reply to a catechesis about the Law. The Sayer retorts, "Not to run on all fours. . . . Are we not men?" There is a shot showing misshapen creatures bowing up and down chanting these final four words. At the conclusion of the lengthy recital the Sayer intones that Moreau's is the House of Pain. The creatures once more repeat this. Edward looks horrified at the proceedings, while Moreau walks down the hill and at a gesture from him all disperse but Edward and Letta.

With the exception of the framing shots in which everyone is included, several things become apparent. First, Moreau, as the sequence progresses is seen less often but his presence is audibly manifested offscreen through the cracking of the whip. Then too, while a shot might center on one character (the Sayer, for example), it is the offscreen space occupied by Moreau that attracts interest because of the Sayer's arm pointing to the doctor. In reality Moreau "appears" in every one of the shots, even if it is only his off-screen presence. Also, in proportion to the decrease in the number of times Moreau appears, there is a rise in the number of times Letta and Edward appear. Increasingly longer are the intervals among the composite shots of Letta, Edward and the Sayer which suggests a breakup in the security of the group by isolating them amid the dangers from the beast-folk. To increase this spatial isolation, Edward appears alone twice and the Sayer alone once. Once Moreau has the creatures under control, their appearance on screen decreases and the focus of interest shifts (1) to the reactions of Letta and Edward, since they occupy the majority of shots in the sequence (five in all); (2) to interaction among the three principals, Letta, Edward and the Sayer, since the Sayer acts as an intermediary between Moreau and the man and woman, and then between Moreau and the creatures: and (3) most importantly to the creatures and their creator. Edward and the Sayer perform subsidiary roles that parallel those of Moreau for not only are they framed in separate shots as is Moreau, they act as buffers to the various hierarchies of physical, moral and spiritual development within the group. On the lowest level are the beast-folk, after them comes the wisest of their kind, the Sayer, then Letta, an almost perfect human, followed by Edward. At the apex of this scale is Moreau, the creator of the Law. The contrapuntal effect is also not lost. The words of the Sayer, "are we not men?," are juxtaposed to their animal-like figures as the creatures also repeat the phrase.

After the incident at the beast-man's village, Moreau shows Edward how he has progressed from creating new forms of plant life, to working upon animals and finally into transforming animals into men by giving them articulate speech. In the novel as in the film, Moreau expresses his aloofness as creator and his lack of concern about playing God in his mad drive to create human life. As horror films invert religious iconography, so too does the novel. Moreau becomes the antitheses of the loving creator, and his sin is in breaking the "great chain of being" that links all of creation into a oneness:

The thing before you is no longer an animal, a fellow-creature, but a problem . . . I wanted . . . to find out the extreme limit of plasticity in a living shape . . . I have never troubled about the ethics of the matter. The study of Nature makes man at least as remorseless as nature. I have gone on, not heeding anything but the question I was pursuing.[9]

As Edward and Moreau in the film look out from the laboratory to the misshapen creatures that were unsuccessful experiments and do the mindless work of supplying power for the electrical generators, one is reminded of Legendre and his zombies who run the mill. Moreau tells Edward that as he improves on each experiment he feels like God creating a new life form. In the novel it is Edward who comes to the realization that "Moreau, after animalising these men, had infected their dwarfed brains with a kind of deification of himself."[10]

The shots at the electrical generators present a distorted view of the new Eden. Kenton makes sure that Moreau's earthly paradise is framed by countless bars that turn it into a fortress prison, which is clearly a counterpart to the gothic castle or "old dark house." The shots of the two men become progressively closer so that by the conclusion Moreau and Edward do not occupy the same screen space, so disparate are their views on life. Moreau's lecture on the creation of plant and new forms of animal life is a parody of chapters one and two of Genesis in the Old Testament. The final line of dialogue by Moreau might well have been taken out of the censored section of *Frankenstein*, when Henry knows "what it feels like to be God." In the novel, Wells has Edward excoriate a higher god, "a blind fate" which even Moreau is subjected to as mad genius.

I lost faith in the sanity of the world when I saw it suffering the painful disorder of this island. A blind fate, a vast pitiless mechanism, seemed to cut and shape the fabric of existence, and I, Moreau by his passion for research, Montgomery by his passion for drink, the Beast People, with their instincts and mental restrictions, were torn and crushed, ruthlessly, inevitably, amid the infinite complexity of its incessant wheels.[11]

But in the film the only god is Moreau; there is little room for Wells's philosophy. Moreau is the "blind fate" even to the mating of male and female and is ready to try the ultimate experiment, confiding to his assistant his hopes for sexual union between his panther-woman and Edward. After he watches them part in the moonlight where he has been observing the two, Moreau says to Montgomery: "She was tender like a woman. How that little scene spurs the scientific imagination of old! Are you wondering how much of the murderous animal origin is still alive? How nearly a perfect woman she is? It's possible I may find out with the aid of Mr. Parker." The biblical prophecy is fulfilled in romantic fiction: "So God created man in his own image . . . male and female, . . . and God . . . said to them, 'Be fruitful and multiply, and fill the earth' " (Genesis, 3: 27–28). The Moreau who play-acts God, however, is not only the Devil in disguise with the traditional icono-graphic close-shaven goatee and moustache, he is also the mythical serpent of Eden with his seductive reasoning, completing a picture of one who is more demonic than divine. The near seduction of Edward, the animal-like movements of Letta and the reflected images in the pool all add to the ambiance. It is only later in the scene at the pool that Edward discovers what she is through her clawlike fingers that caress his body. This discovery, together with the animal cages in the background of the shot, suggests, more than anything else, the genesis of the exotic but strange childlike woman which Edward sees before him. It also confirms her animalistic qualities, and makes Edward realize she is a creature like the other inhabitants of the island. Moreau momentarily admits defeat to Montgomery when he sees the bestial qualities creep back into his creation. But immediately afterwards he grabs Letta by the back of her hair and says triumphantly with a laugh that he will expunge the animal nature from her and make her completely human. He ends by saying that Parker is attracted to her and time, along with the monotony of life on the island, will lead Parker to mate with her. This scene has been interspersed with shots of Letta stretching provocatively on a couch. These shots together with the dialogue of Moreau imply not only a sadistic but voyeuristic impulse to watch her make love to Edward.

When Ruth Thomas and Captain Donahue appear on the island, paral-leling the opening trek of Edward and Moreau to his fortress-like house, Moreau substitutes the seduction of Edward by Letta for the rape of Ruth by one of the beast-men. Though it is the very antithesis of the scene of Edward and Letta by the pool, it is highly charged with sexual overtones. The attempted rape scene by the ape-man combines voyeurism and undertones of sadism. The opening shots in Moreau's trophy room, irrespective of dialogue which is banal and unimportant, give an inkling of the immediate peril that the captain, Edward and Ruth are placed in as they prepare to retire to their separate rooms for the night. Quadrangular-shaped bars are prominently situated in the foreground of the frame, again suggesting imprisonment and accentuating the chiaroscuro effect with shadows cast by the crisscrossing lattices of the windows upon the room and its occupants.

A pan shot of the trophy room that Donahue, Edward and Ruth are in reveals stuffed animals and various specimens preserved in jars which carefully insinuate and equate Moreau's experimentation with Edward and

Ruth who are being used for the same purpose. Even Ruth's bedroom with massive bars on the windows as well as the portal within her door suggests her animal-like entrapment, although the bars are also there to prevent the "animals" outside from entering it.

Once Edward sees Ruth safely to her room there are a series of short parallel shots increasing the tension between the attacking ape-man whom Moreau has sent to rape Ruth and the semiclad woman preparing to go to bed. The voyeurism on the part of the ape-man is complemented by shots of Ruth's disrobing (358 frames) behind the bars of her window, followed by a closer shot of the ape-man, revealing his face. At the end of this shot Ruth has kept the candles lit, while the next shot has Moreau blowing them out, one by one, in another room, signaling the darkness of evil overpowering the brightness of virtue. Ruth is the fair-haired virgin, while her counterpart, Letta, is the dark-haired temptress, possessing all the animal instincts Ruth is careful to conceal.[12] Yet both Ruth and her lover remain passive spectators, affected by but not effecting a change in the conditions. It is left to the half-human panther-woman and a discredited alcoholic medical doctor to save the two.

The tempo of the shots increases by alternating between the ape-man and the sleeping virgin, but this is a beast who ironically has already been transformed, from the beauty of his own nature to semihuman deformity. To add to this Ruth is photographed through gauze (the mosquito netting) giving the scene a gossamer effect as compared to the ape-man shot behind the bars that cover Ruth's window. In one shot all four elements come into play: (1) the seductive silhouette of the woman in the foreground; (2) the netting behind her; (3) the iron bars in the background; (4) the ape-man. The entire shot progresses from a foreground of soft femininity and diaphanous draperies to a background of iron bars and muscular savagery.

When Edward hears Ruth's screams and runs to her room, he must shoot his pistol through the barred portal of her locked door at the ape-man attempting to get in from the window. However, Edward is not successful with his pistol (a Freudian phallic symbol), but does frighten the ape-man away. In the conclusion of this sequence a pivotal action occurs. Montgomery breaks up his association with Moreau, telling him that Uran tried to break in and attack Ruth. He then realizes what Moreau meant by not needing Parker any more. Moreau tells him to mind his own business, which infuriates Montgomery into saying, "You're insane even to think of it and I'm through with you here and now." "Are you going back to England? To prison?" Moreau inquires sarcastically. With finality, Montgomery answers that he would rather go to prison. The darkness in which

Moreau is placed during his confrontation with Montgomery complements Moreau's dissimulation while the shadow of the barred windows on the walls suggests that Moreau's house and island are no less a prison than the one which awaits Montgomery.

The two movements that end the film are polar: the escape to the boat through the jungle and the retreat by Moreau back to his house. When the creatures attack Moreau they advance to the camera as Moreau, with whip in hand, retreats from the camera. This movement contains three main caesuralike pauses to retard the action which is taking place: (1) Moreau's ringing the gong as he had done in the beginning to save Edward and Letta, and his snapping the whip and asking them "What is the Law?"; (2) his recalling to them the House of Pain, followed by another general onrush of the creatures; and (3) the Sayer of the Law suggesting to the others that Moreau be placed in the House of Pain to be vivisected like themselves. At one point the escapees leave through a door at frame right, while Moreau enters a door toward frame left, so that the viewer is forced to focus on two simultaneous but dissimilar actions: freedom and life on one hand for the escapees and torture and death on the other for Moreau.

During the fighting that ensues between Letta and the ape-man not a sound is perceived, but off screen are the noises of the creatures as they subjugate Moreau to the House of Pain. The off-screen sound is quite effective here for it generates tension within a viewer who is attempting to grasp the significance of two spaces that claim equal importance: the powerful on-screen activity and that within the off-screen space.

Only when Letta screams do the others realize she has stayed behind to kill the attacking ape-man. Her last words to Edward are part of the aquatic imagery with its theme of rebirth that runs through sequences of the film. As Edward holds her in his arms, she asks, "You go back to the sea?" while off screen are heard the sounds of the angry beast-men at Moreau's house. When Edward wishes to take Letta's body to the sea, Montgomery answers, "It's better that we leave her here. The fire will soon destroy all of Moreau's work." If water represents rejuvenation and rebirth, fire becomes the symbol of purification.[13] The island of Dr. Moreau may indeed be purified and returned to that true paradise, before the Fall, where evil did not exist.

In the novel, Moreau's death occurs "off-page" but Montgomery and Prendick are led by one of the beast-men to his body in the jungle: "He lay face downwards . . . one hand was almost severed at the wrist, and his silvery hair was dabbled in blood. His head had been battered in."[14] In the film it is done with simplicity and brevity; only Moreau's screaming is heard as he is sadistically tortured. His final vivisection takes place off screen, his last shrieks heard in the empty courtyard before the House of Pain.

The final shot has the three sitting in a small boat: Montgomery is lighting a pipe, his back is to the camera; Ruth and Edward are sitting beside one another facing the camera. In the background the mountainside is ablaze. Ruth and Edward turn to look around and Montgomery says softly, but with a commanding tone, "Don't look back." As he starts to row, background music is heard over the fade to black. The injunction of Montgomery to the two lovers parallels God's destruction of the cities of Sodom and Gomorrah: "Flee for your life; do not look back or stop anywhere . . . lest you be consumed. . . . And lo, the smoke of the land went up like the smoke of a furnace" (Genesis 19: 17, 28).

The novel's conclusion filled with Wells's pessimism for a perfectible mankind leaves Edward, seared with the horror of Moreau's island, becoming a creature apart, like the beast-folk, an outcast, a self-imposed exile living among the multitude of London.

> I look about me at my fellow men. And I go in fear. . . . I feel as though the animal was surging up through them; that presently the degradation of the Islanders will be played over again on a larger scale. . . . I shrink from them . . . and long to be away from them and alone. . . . And even it seemed that I, too, was not a reasonable creature, but only an animal tormented.[15]

In the next film to be discussed, James Whale's richly cinematic *The Bride of Frankenstein* (1935), man again plays god. And like Moreau's beast-men, Frankenstein's creation turns against its master. This act has its archetype in Lucifer's battle with God in Milton's *Paradise Lost* and occurs with alarming regularity in the horror film genre, which might be seen as poetic justice, a suturing technique to conform to the 1930 Production Code.

NOTES

1. V. S. Pritchett, *The Living Novel* (London: Chatto and Windus, 1954), Chap. on "Scientific Romantics," pp. 116–24.
2. Lovat Dickson, *H. G. Wells: His Turbulent Life and Times* (New York: Atheneum, 1969), pp. 66–68.
3. Phil Hardy, Tom Milne and Paul Willemen, eds., *The Encyclopedia of Horror Movies* (New York: Harper and Row, 1986), p. 52.
4. H. G. Wells, *The Island of Dr. Moreau*, in *Seven Science Fiction Novels of H. G. Wells* (New York: Dover Publications, 1934), p. 89.
5. Wells, p. 100.

6. A. R. Fulton, *Motion Pictures: The Development of an Art from Silent Films to the Age of Television* (Norman: University of Oklahoma Press, 1960), Chap. 10, "From Novel to Film." Also see Ezra Pound, cited in Joseph Frank, "Spatial Form in Modern Literature," in *The Sewanee Review*, LIII, Nos., 2, 3 and 4 (1945).

7. Wells, p. 105.

8. Mircea Eliade, *The Sacred and the Profane*, trans. by Willard R. Trask (New York: Harcourt, Brace and World, Inc., 1959), p. 130.

9. Wells, pp. 133–34.

10. Wells, p. 121.

11. Wells, p. 152.

12. This repression causes the cultured man to use surrogates to express his animality. See Sigmund Freud, *On Dreams*, trans. by James Strachey (New York: W. W. Norton and Company, Inc., 1952), chap. 3. Leslie Fiedler in his work, *Love and Death in the American Novel*, has this as his thesis in the chapter on "James Fenimore Cooper and the Historical Romance" (chap. 7).

13. Fire purges evil in *Frankenstein* and *The Bride of Frankenstein*, as well as in such widely diverse pieces of fiction as Poe's *Fall of the House of Usher*, Mrs. J. H. Ridell's *Old Mrs. Jones*, Maugham's *The Magician*, Stoker's *Lair of the White Worm* and H. Rider Haggard's *She*.

14. Wells, p. 159.

15. Wells, pp. 181–82.

CHAPTER 6

The Bride of Frankenstein: A Friend for the Enemy of God

The fallen angel becomes a malignant devil. Yet even that enemy of God and man had friends and associates in his desolation; I am alone.

—Mary Shelley, *Frankenstein*

The Bride of Frankenstein opens with a framing device that takes place in 1816 at the time Byron was with the Shelleys in Geneva, but Whale deliberately avoids specificity here as well as in the main story that Mary Shelley unfolds. Although the sequel to the 1931 *Frankenstein* film is itself removed from the immediate present (1935), employing expressionistic sets and lighting (the Baron's castle, Pretorius's house) and decorative devices such as candles, horse-drawn carriages and period costuming (Pretorius's clothes and the peasants' outfits), Elizabeth and Henry wear the modern dress of the 1930s. According to Forrest Ackerman, however, the characters' dress "appears to be early 1920s," and Whale even changed references of cars and trains to carriages, going so far as to describe the telephone used between Pretorius and Fritz as an "electrical machine" and deleting a scene in the Goldstadt Morgue where the date 1869 is seen on a sign.[1] The anachronisms that still exist only make the film more interesting and bizarre.

The framing story contains expressionistic contrivances of shadows outlined by lightning during a stormy night, the eccentric posturing of Gavin Gordon's Lord Byron and the Shelleys' angular-framed mansion with its tall gables. Byron, looking out the window at the storm, expresses the Romantic interest in the display of nature by his anthropo-morphizing it: "The crudest, savage exhibition of nature at her worst without. . . . I should like to think that an irate Jehovah was pointing those arrows of lightning directly at . . . the unbowed head of . . . England's greatest sinner." Two conventions characteristic of Romantic literature are present: the use of a prologue to create its own moral parameters for the main story by employing stock figures who represent various virtues and vices, and the Romantic's rebellion against God by making himself an equal, this chaotic situation mirrored in the tumult of nature. In *The Bride of Frankenstein*, Whale has Mary make the classic statement of the moral purpose of her book/film as Van Sloan had done in *Frankenstein*: "to write a moral lesson [about] the punishment that befell a mortal man who dared to emulate God." Mary's ethical posture also serves as a foil to Byron's decadent aestheticism: "I take great relish in savoring each separate horror." Even though Mary is speaking about the film that has preceded *The Bride*, she is also implying a similar moral aim for the 1935 film. She will write a sequel (*The Bride of Frankenstein*) because her publishers did not see her moral purpose earlier. The idea of having the narrator of the story, Mary Shelley, part of the fictional tale she is recounting binds the narrator with the story she narrates. If Victor Frankenstein in the Shelley novel claimed himself to be a part of the thing he created, it is natural for the actress, Elsa Lanchester, to assume the part of the "bride" and Mary Shelley. The narrator, therefore, be-comes a persona in her own fiction, an important part of the action, so that the moral fable becomes doubly effective. Shelley/Lanchester both become the creator of the story as well as the creature created in the story. Miss Lanchester said: "James' feeling was that very pretty, sweet peo-ple . . . had very . . . evil thoughts. . . . So James wanted the same actress for both parts to show that the Bride of Frankenstein did, after all, come out of sweet Mary Shelley's soul."2

Romantic literature contains many examples of this moralizing, but only a few need to be commented upon. Clara Reeve in *The Old English Baron* makes clear-cut divisions between good and evil and fills her preface with moral and religious sentiments: "The business of romance is, first, to excite the attention; and, secondly, to direct it to some useful . . . end [for too often] . . . mankind are naturally pleased with what gratifies their vanity; and vanity . . . may be rendered subservient to good and useful purposes."3 This is not far removed from Horace's theory in his *Art of Poetry* where he explains how a work of art can heighten interest in such qualities as prudence, good sense and good taste by suggesting their social desirabil-ity.4 In English literary criticism, Sir Philip Sidney is the earliest critic of note to enlarge upon the ancients. In his *An Apology for Poetry* (1595), Sidney declares that the end of art "is to lead and draw us to as high a perfection as our degenerate souls, made worse by their clayey lodgings, can be capable of."[5] In the nineteenth century *Wieland, or the Transformation* aims to illustrate "some important branches of the moral constitution of man." Its author is the "moral painter" who exhibits his novel in "its most instructive and memorable forms."[6]

In Charles Robert Maturin's preface to *Melmoth the Wanderer*, the author-priest writes:

> The hint of this Romance . . . was taken from a passage in one of my Sermons. . . . At this moment is there one of us present, however we may have departed from the Lord, disobeyed his will, and disregarded his word . . . who would . . . accept all that man could bestow, or earth afford, to resign the hope of his salvation? . . . [T]here is not one . . . on earth, were the enemy of mankind to traverse it with the offer![7]

And since *Melmoth* is concerned with the "enemy of mankind" and the various people he attempts to seduce, the entire novel becomes an "exemplum" of the medieval type to illustrate what becomes of men who traffic with evil. Leigh Hunt in writing an instructive story for *The Indicator* in 1819 says in *A Tale for a Chimney Corner*:

> A ghost story . . . to be a perfect one, to add to the other utility of excitement a moral utility, . . . should imply some great sentiment,—something that comes out of the next world to remind us of our duties in this; or something that helps to carry on the idea of our humanity into afterlife even when we least think we shall take it with us.[8]

In *Uncle Silas* by LeFanu, the heroine's brief epilogue points to the moral force intended in the story:

> This world is a parable—the habitation of symbols—the phantoms of spiritual things immortal shown in material shape. May the blessed second-sight be mine—to recognize under these beautiful forms of earth the Angels who wear them; for I am sure we may walk with them . . . and hear them speak![9]

Marie Corelli introduces her novel *The Sorrows of Satan* with the words of the narrator, Geoffrey Tempest:

> I know that many men . . . are in the tangles of sin, but too weak of will to break the net in which they have become voluntarily imprisoned. . . . Will

they realize as I have been forced to do . . . the . . . active Mind, which behind all matter, works unceasingly, . . . a very eternal and positive God? If so, then dark problems will become clear to them, and what seems injustice in the world will prove pure equity![10]

These few examples have been selected from a richly abundant stock in gothic literature. And so, Elsa Lanchester's Mary Shelley, in *The Bride of Frankenstein*, is voicing in the prologue what has been a standard custom in the genre. She concludes by saying that she wishes to complete the tale: "It's a perfect night for mystery and horror; the air itself is filled with monsters." Byron continues with the imagery by replying to Mary: "I'm all ears. While heaven blasts the night without, open up your pits of hell!" The scene is set. The night becomes a correlative for the story, and the cosmic and mythical polarities of heaven and hell are employed in speaking metaphorically of the unraveling and exploration of evil.

The adaptation, which includes several other incidents described in the novel that were not in the 1931 film, contains the monster's meeting with the blind man and the creation of the mate. The feat was accomplished by William Hurlbut and the playwright John L. Balderston, who wrote the stage version of *Dracula* and the script for Freund's *The Mummy* and *Mad Love*, which are more somber productions of gothic themes than the flamboyant *Bride*. Most of the minor characters in *The Bride* provide the humor: Minnie (Una O'Conor), the pompous Burgomaster (E. E. Clive), and Karl (Dwight Frye), but also to some extent Dr. Pretorius (Ernest Thesiger who carries the prissiness of Whale's *Old Dark House* to *The Bride*). Other scenes are also invested with the irreverent humor that only Whale could provide: the monster and the hermit (O. P. Heggie), the monster with Pretorius in the crypt, and the "bride's" discovery of her "lover." There is even a standing joke in the use of the words, "It's alive!" When Minnie rushes into the castle to warn the inhabitants of the monster's presence, she tells Albert, the butler (Lucien Prival), that "It's alive!" When Henry, thought dead and placed on the hall table in the castle, moves his arm as the monsters do on the operating table in *Frankenstein* and in *The Bride*, Minnie screams out, "He's alive!" Henry repeats this over again when he creates a mate for the monster. In adding these instances together, it may not be so far from the mark to say that "while the macabre gothic touches make for humour, they also weaken the horror" so that the film succeeds more "on a level of parody than on the level of pure horror achieved by *Frankenstein*."[11]

Henry's first speech to his wife, Elizabeth, typifies the Promethean figure who gives to mankind "the secret God is so jealous of, the formula for life." He revels in the idea when he tells Elizabeth of his power to create a man and even an entire race, boasting that in time he might have found the secret of eternal life. Elizabeth attempts to dissuade her husband by stressing the morality involved: "It's the devil that prompts you. It's death, . . . that's in it all and at the end of it all." Then, almost prophetically, she continues: "A strange apparition has seemed to appear in the room; it comes, a figure like death. . . . It seems to be reaching out for you, as if it would take you away from me." This "figure like death" is, first of all, a foreshadowing of the coming of the monster. In the Shelley novel Victor tells of Elizabeth's presentiment of impending danger: "But on the day [their wedding] that was to fulfill my wishes and my destiny, she was melancholy, and a presentiment of evil pervaded her." She announces to Victor: "Something whispers to me not to depend too much on the prospect that is opened before us." As the monster approaches, the elements mirror this change:

The wind . . . now rose with great violence in the west . . . ; the clouds swept across [the moon] swifter than the flight of the vulture and dimmed her rays, while the lake [was] . . . rendered still busier by the restless waves that were beginning to rise. Suddenly a heavy storm of rain descended.[12]

Although Mary Shelley wrote the novel in 1816, a fiction work dealing with the same subject matter preceded her novel. A sixpenny book of tales published by William McKenny about 1798 reveals a story by an anonymous author entitled *The Black Spider*. The hero is a German named Rodolpho de Burkart who experiments with a galvanic battery and is a pupil of a famous professor of alchemy.

The new buried corpse of a young female which had been stolen from a neighbouring cemetery was . . . deposited in the apartment of Rodolpho . . . [who] . . . entertained the belief that the mere muscular motion first caused by the application of galvanism, might by its continued action . . . cause the heart to beat, the lungs to inflate, the blood to flow; and then thought the reanimation must ensue . . . [H]e gradually applied the powers of this battery to the corpse before him—it caused at first a sort of tremor of the whole body,—then muscular action commenced . . . —he thought he heard a sigh—he stood aghast and motionless till he was sure he heard a moan, and then the corpse before him half uplifted its head, and raised its arm—it started half upright—opened its eyes—gazed wildly—and sunk again.[13]

Three years after Shelley's *Frankenstein* Leigh Hunt wrote in *A Tale for a Chimney Corner* (1819) about the moral questions posed by reanimation through galvanism: "Reanimation is perhaps the most ghastly of all ghastly things. . . . When the account appeared . . . in the newspapers of the galvanized dead body, whose features as well as limbs underwent such contortions, that it seemed as if it were about to rise up, one almost expected to hear . . . news of the other world."[14]

In the Whale film when Elizabeth makes known her fears to Henry there is an immediate cut to the castle hall entrance and the sounds of heavy knocking. Pretorius is introduced; he is a second prefigurement of the "figure like death," and Elizabeth's speech has prepared for his appearance on screen. Again Whale's paradox: the "figure like death" (Pretorius is dressed all in black) is interested in bringing life to the dead but unlike the image of "death," he is a droll character, a foil to Henry. The imagery of death is carried on in the conversation. Minnie, while answering Pretorius's repeated knocks at the castle door, says to herself, "Don't knock the castle over; we're not all dead, yet." When Pretorius meets her, he ironically says to Minnie that he is "on a secret matter of *grave* importance." This brief encounter carries on the images that Henry and Elizabeth have used in their conversation about the secrets of life, but the Pretorius-Minnie conversation at once places them on a less-serious and more-ironic level.

Pretorius is also a man in rebellion against God, but he assumes a more whimsical attitude. After displaying one of his miniature creatures which he calls "the very devil," a sophisticated, urban creature in evening dress, he tells Henry: "There's a certain resemblance to me. . . . Sometimes I have wondered whether life wouldn't be much more amusing if we were all devils, with no nonsense about angels and being good." Later, half admitting his madness to Henry, Pretorius says: "I . . . grew my creatures . . . as nature does, from seed. . . . Leave the charnel house and follow the lead of nature, or of God if you like your bible stories, 'Male and female created He them.' 'Be fruitful and multiply.' Create a race, a man-made race upon the face of the earth." Scoffing at the biblical myth of creation in Genesis, the scientist still wishes to emulate God through the act of creation. The ludicrousness of Whale's mismatched creators who role-play as God is evident; they become a parody of Promethean proportions upon whom, through the eccentricity of Whale, the nobility of purpose has been inverted. Henry creates a huge grotesque monster; Pretorius creates small, finely delineated beings. Henry is presented as an overwrought individual, highly sensitive; Pretorius is calm and even quixotic. Henry becomes a victim of circumstances; Pretorius becomes his victimizer. Where Henry loses control of the monster, Pretorius gains control. Pretorius has created from "seed"; Henry has created from "dead tissues."

Henry's monster is most human and pathetic in scenes where he is surrounded by nature, and both are highly stylized creations of Universal's art department. While Boris Karloff must mime his pathos, Shelley's monster is gifted with vocal articulation, addressing Victor with the words:

> Have I not suffered enough, that you seek to increase my misery? Life . . . is dear to me. . . . I ought to be thy Adam, but I am rather the fallen angel, whom thou drivest from joy for no misdeed. Everywhere I see bliss, from which I alone am irrevocably excluded.[15]

To aid the visual pathos in the film, the monster is not identified with Adam but with the "second Adam," Jesus. He is raised on a beam of wood as though on a cross and thrust into a cart to be taken to prison. This is not only part of Whale's inversion of images but also a part of his sardonic humor. And if his "crucifixion" at the hands of the townspeople seems to point to the Bible, so too the monster's bursting the bonds in prison and overcoming the two guards point to a "resurrection." As *Dracula* has its inverted and perverted Christ-images. so does *The Bride of Frankenstein*.

The scene between the hermit and the monster is, no doubt, meant to bring out the latter's humanity as Mary Shelley was able to do through the monster's lengthy discourses. He spies on an old man living in the cottage with his daughter and son, Agatha and Felix: "the old man . . . taking up an instrument . . . played a sweet mournful air . . . and I withdrew from the window, unable to bear these emotions."[16] Discovered by the brother and sister, the monster is beaten out of the house by Felix. In the film he is discovered by two hunters and is driven out while the house is accidentally set on fire. The lonely hermit in the movie (O. P. Heggie), dressed in a long coarse robe resembling one of Christ's disciples, plays Schubert's *Ave Maria* on his violin (the "sweet mournful air" of the novel). The piety does not wear well now, but interspersed with this is the humor: the monster and hermit smoking and drinking together, and the creature's keeping time to the old man's music. The scene is also placed here to illustrate the power of spiritual love (*agape*) and human kindness over the monster. In one shot, as the hermit thanks God for sending him a friend, the crucifix on the wall in back of the old man becomes strangely illuminated. In a slow fade-out the only object left in the upper part of the frame is the glowing crucifix.

In *The Bride*, therefore, grotesque scenes such as this act syntagmatically to combine images into a unit which depends for its value on the opposition to what precedes and what follows it, and one realizes that Whale is not simply playing it straight. It is like reading Defoe's *Moll*

Flanders and Richardson's *Pamela*, where humor and sobriety are on such a thin line of balance for the modern reader that he is constantly being challenged as to the authors' intentions. The admixture of such incongruous elements in *The Bride*, which makes the 1931 film seem sedate by comparison, leaves this pleasantly discordant effect.

The film also suffuses the humor with undertones of necrophilia which have been subdued in the opening three reels. The monster being pursued seeks refuge in a graveyard where, in the earlier film, Henry had rifled tombs to supply organs for his creation. Upon entering a vault the monster uncovers the body of a girl in her coffin and attempts to make love to it by calling it "friend" and stroking its face. At this moment Pretorius arrives with Karl and Ludwig, two murderers, to steal a corpse. Paying the men, the doctor admits to himself that he likes the crypt and will stay around. On the coffin Pretorius sets up a modest supper and during its course the monster appears. Pretorius asks the creature if he knows what he is and who Frankenstein is. The reply is indicative of the monster's desires and perfectly parallels that of his creator: "Yes . . . made me from dead. I love dead, hate living." The monster picks up the skull from the coffin and holding it gently in both hands says: "Woman . . . friend . . . wife?" This macabre touch ends on a droll note of the two murderers who would rather give themselves up than be "resurrectionists." As Karl adroitly remarks, "This is no work for murderers!"

The final and most pronounced form of necrophilia is the creation sequence, which commences with an establishing shot of the tower laboratory. A large number of shots are then filmed with Dutch angles. This visualizes, in expressionistic terms, the tension and conflicts leading to the creation of a mate for the monster. Throughout the sequence the beating of a kettledrum is heard which simulates the beating heart of the young woman who has just been murdered by Karl for the experiment.

The creation sequence in *The Bride of Frankenstein* is more elaborate than the one in the 1931 film. The entire sequence explores the space of the lab either by the tilting, dollying or panning of the camera, but this does not fully explain the sequence's rapid pace and, furthermore, many of the shots employing a static camera rely only on movement within the frame as *Frankenstein* did. Moreover, there are many shots in which movement within the frame is minimal or does not exist at all. What tends to give the semblance of movement in the sequence is due to the percussive editing by Ted Kent and to the wordless passages orchestrated by motifs that signal the presence of certain characters or actions: the music that accompanies the creation first begins with the incessant beat of the kettledrum and concludes 160 shots later with the full orchestra playing the theme music that introduces the bride.

To distort space Dutch angles are frequently employed so that alternating shots complement each other by positioning one shot at the opposite angle of the next. This rocking effect produces a disequilibrium within the frame itself. Within such a space not only is the character given a dynamic thrust so that his body or a portion of it severs the frame in half by the diagonal position of his figure, but the Dutch angle posits a moral and ethical problem in the creation of a mate and suggests the difficulty of such an undertaking succeeding. The lack of equilibrium mirrors the minds of these "mad" scientists; how can such research be pursued when diagonals break up the narrative space and splinter the harmony of the horizontal plane resulting in an unrealistic and unsubstantial film space?

The first two shots of Pretorius and Henry moving about a machine registering the heartbeat of Fritz's female victim start out normally, but the next ten of the scientists are filmed on an angle. There is a pause in this unsettling atmosphere as Henry and Pretorius prepare the body for its ascent to the top of the tower. The second plane of conflict is now introduced in an establishing shot of the tower battlements. These planes meet when the platform is raised to the top of the tower with its large phalliclike lightning conductor emblematic of Henry Frankenstein's creative power.

Intermittently there are 12 isolated shots of the machinery (even Pretorius and Henry placed in the frame form a symbiotic relationship with the scientific instruments) varying in length from 12 frames to 67 frames. Although the shots of the machinery are static, they are part of the film's rhythm. As they are repeated, they become increasingly percussive including shots of Henry and Pretorius, the kites in the sky, and the lightning streaking across the frame.

As the suspense increases with the preparation for the imminent elevation of the platform bearing the monster, the Dutch angles reappear. When the platform begins its ascent, emphasis is directed to low- and high-angled shots of the rising table within the lab, but when Dutch angling is apparent, the space becomes even more disjointed with shots of Henry's body counterpoised to the Dutch angle so that while the lab appears tilted to the right, his figure is bent to the left, looking upward. Sometimes the position of the body alone suggests a Dutch angle where there is none, as when Henry is crouched by a control panel while the platform begins its descent. Since the majority of shots in the creation sequence are short, those of the operating table with the body on it rising to the roof assume importance because of their duration, the upward tilting of the camera as it follows the movement of the table through space, the momentary stasis of the camera when the platform is level with it, and the already-mentioned alternation of high and low angles in its ascent. This places the focal point of the drama both on the emotional level in the piece's sustained length and narrative level since it is the climactic point of the sequence.

The animation of the body recalls the 1931 film. The characters are blocked so that they remain on either side of the frame with the bride in the center. There are no distorting angles, and the shots are in perfect balance. In successive shots the bride is seen in a medium-long shot, a medium shot, a medium-close shot, and close up, thereby imitating the first glimpse of the monster in the 1931 film. This rapid editing correlates to the movements of the monster's head, which are abruptly swift in their inquiring gaze.

After Pretorius announces, "The Bride of Frankenstein," the monster approaches, attempts to win his mate and is rejected. There then appears a skillfully edited piece in which the monster's hand rests on a lever which can blow the entire tower to pieces. Elizabeth comes to the laboratory door and Henry reluctantly opens it. The monster tells Henry to leave while forcing Pretorius to remain. "You stay, we belong dead," he says. Then follows this montage of shots:

1. The monster's hand reaching for the lever,
2. The bride looking down as if dejected,
3. The monster's face lifted upward, snarling,
4. The monster's hand reaching for the lever,
5. The bride hissing at the monster,
6. The monster's face shedding a tear,
7. The bride hissing,
8. The hand of the monster pulling down the lever,
9. The laboratory exploding,
10. An exterior shot of tower exploding,
11. Henry and Elizabeth running out of the tower door while mortar and rock fall from above,
12. An exterior shot of the tower exploding,
13. Inside the tower: Pretorius's back to a wall; the place falling in,
14. An exterior shot of the tower exploding,
15. Inside the tower; the tower in flames and smoke,
16. An exterior shot of the tower bursting apart; a huge hole appears in the wall,
17. An exterior shot of the tower toppling down,
18. As in shot 16; the tower bursting apart,

19. The remainder of the tower crumbling to pieces,

20. Elizabeth and Henry running up a hill; they embrace and look off screen toward the camera,

21. Elizabeth and Henry in an embrace while still looking on. Henry, stroking Elizabeth's head, repeats words of endearment.

To begin with, the conflict is enhanced in these 21 shots by distending time so that tension is spatially augmented by prolongation of the tower's explosion led up to with the shots of the hand (1, 4 and 8), and is interspersed with reaction shots of the bride (2, 5, 7) and those of the monster (3, 6). After shot 8 there are a series of shots which alternate between those inside (13, 15) and those outside (11, 20, 21) and various shots of the tower beginning with shot 10. The effects of the blast are also prolonged through shots 12, 14, 16 to 19 so that the successive stages in the tower's demolition appear to overlap one another in an effort to increase the temporality of the explosion.

In the end, the bride, the monster and Pretorius must be destroyed, because the film is a morality play where evil is punishable by death. Henry alone is left to be a living lesson to all—even though in four short years the monster will be resurrected by Universal in *Son of Frankenstein*, and the Baron's son will repeat his father's mistakes.

In the novel it is necessary that the monster die after his creator, Victor, is dead. This coincides with other *doppelganger* tales which *Frankenstein* stresses. The monster speaks to Robert Walton, the narrator: "I shall die. . . . He is dead who called me into being; and when I shall be no more, the very remembrance of us both will speedily vanish."[17] But the remembrance has not vanished and while it might be thought that Roger Corman's adaptation of Brian Aldiss's *Frankenstein Unbound*, which updated Mary Shelley's story, was the final nail in the coffin for gothic horror fans, MCA Television thinks differently and is planning to use big-name directors and actors to produce remakes of the classic Universal monster films on cable network.[18] What new horrors can be found in the old formulas remains to be seen.

The next category that this book takes up deals with Romantic man as a symbol of Destiny, the scientist as villain-hero manipulating forces which he creates himself in order to direct the lives of others.

NOTES

1. Forrest J. Ackerman, "Forward" to the script of *The Bride of Frankenstein* ed. by Philip J. Riley, Vol. 2 of Universal Filmscript Series of Classic Horror Films (Atlantic City: MagicImage Filmbooks, 1989), p. 17.

2. Gregory W. Mank, "Production Background" for script for *The Bride of Frankenstein* (Atlantic City: MagicImage Filmbooks, 1989), p. 30.

3. Clara Reeve, *The Old English Baron*, in *Seven Masterpieces of Gothic Horror*, edited by Robert Donald Spector (New York: Bantam Books, 1971), p. 105.

4. Horace, *The Art of Poetry*, in *Criticism: The Major Texts*, ed. by Walter Jackson Bate (New York: Harcourt, Brace and Company, 1952), p. 49.

5. Philip Sidney, *An Apology for Poetry*, in *Criticism: The Major Texts*, p. 87.

6. Brown, *Wieland, or the Transformation* (New York: Harcourt, Brace and World, Inc., 1926), pp. 3–4.

7. Maturin, *Melmoth the Wanderer* (Lincoln: University of Nebraska Press, 1972), p. 3.

8. Leigh Hunt, *A Tale for a Chimney Corner*, in *Gothic Tales of Terror*, Vol. I (Baltimore: Penguin Books, Inc., 1972), p. 352.

9. LeFanu, *Uncle Silas* (New York: Dover Publications, 1966), p. 436.

10. Marie Corelli, *The Sorrows of Satan* (Illinois: Palmer Publications, Spring 1965), pp. 3–4. Equally moralistic is her first major novel that deals with the supernatural, *A Romance of Two Worlds*, published in 1886. (New York: Rudolf Steiner Publications, 1973).

11. Alan G. Frank, *Horror Movies* (London: Octopus Books Ltd., 1975), p. 20. Also see Janice R. Welsch and Syndy M. Conger in "The Comic and the Grotesque in James Whale's Frankenstein Films" in *Planks of Reason*, edited by Barry Keith Grant (Metuchen, N.J.: Scarecrow Press, Inc., 1984), p. 293.

12. Shelley, *Frankenstein, or the Modern Prometheus* (New York: New American Library, 1965), pp. 182–84.

13. *The Black Spider*, in *Gothic Tales of Terror*, Vol. I, p. 180.

14. Hunt, *A Tale for a Chimney Corner*, in *Gothic Tales of Terror*, Vol. I, p. 353. Whether or not Mary Shelley read *The Black Spider* is a matter of conjecture, but Leigh Hunt no doubt read *Frankenstein*, although Shelley's preface to the novel where she speaks of galvanism was not written until October 15, 1831.

15. Shelley, pp. 95–96.

16. Shelley, p. 103.

17. Shelley, pp. 210–11.

18. Thomas Tyrer, "Tales From the Tube: Why TV is Afraid of Scary Series" in *Electronic Media* (October 28, 1991), p. 32.

PART III

THE ROMANTIC AS A SYMBOL OF DESTINY

CHAPTER 7

The Invisible Man: "A Reign of Terror"

I do not feel as if I were a man,
But like a fiend appointed to chastise
The offenses of some unremembered world.
                                        —Shelley, *The Cenci*

It is young Frankenstein's destiny in the Shelley novel to become ac-
quainted with theories of galvanism. Destiny, he says, "was too potent,
and her immutable laws had decreed my utter and terrible destruction."[1]
Destiny at first is something abstract for him: later, when he has created
life, the creature becomes a symbol of that destiny, and in its hands lies
Victor's fate. This concept of "destiny" permeates Romantic literature.

Coleridge's Ancient Mariner is fated for his crime against creation to
teach all who pass, love and reverence for the things created by God. He
is God's human instrument of communication, and says: "I have strange
powers of speech; / That moment that his face I see, / I know the man that
must hear me: / To him my tale I teach" (ll. 587–90). The poem with its
overt parablelike structure is not unlike Sue's *The Wandering Jew*, or so
many other Romantic figures. He has the characteristics of a Byronic hero:
a tormented and solitary life as an agent of an almighty power, bright
penetrating eyes and the ability to influence the lives of those with whom
he comes in contact.

In the next two films to be discussed, humans attempt to act as agents
of destiny and in this way play-act at a godly pastime. Dr. Griffin, in James
Whale's *The Invisible Man*, hopes to conquer the world through invisibil-

ity, while in Browning's *The Devil Doll* an escapee from Devil's Island plans, with the aid of miniature creatures, to murder those who unjustly sent him there.

Primarily, the villain-heroes are destiny figures because of their desire to exercise control over the lives of others. Unlike the necrophile's desire, theirs is not one of unholy love; unlike the Promethean figure theirs is not the desire to create. These destiny figures are associated with the lust to domineer, which is predicated upon their motivation for revenge. They are not impartial judges of men's fates because this would detach them from the narrative and would not allow the viewer to identify with them. Their superiority, which places them in control, arises from their power over nature that surpasses those of other humans. This does not prevent the destiny figure from succumbing to his own fate because he is human and because there is an external moral code to uphold in film narrative enforced by the industry and an internal moral code of closure demanded by the audience where evil is punished and good rewarded. Unlike today's horror films, films of this decade belong to an aesthetic whereby the opposition of good and evil unifies the narrative. The motivating force in these stories that prompts the villain-hero to become "overseer" of men's fates gives the Romantic hero his *raison d'être*. Since his actions are motivated by vindictiveness, this proclivity gives the villain-hero his aura of evil, his devotion to destruction. It is this convention taken from gothic literature that is to be analyzed next, but before this takes place it is interesting to speak about the fiction dealing with destiny as a symbol of man's fate. *Frankenstein* was used as a first example, and indeed it serves as a treasury of many conventions that find their way into gothic literature. At the beginning of the story, every step Victor takes is fraught with significance: "Chance—or rather the evil influence, the Angel of Destruction, which asserted omnipotent sways over me from the moment I turned by reluctant steps from my father's door—led me first to M. Krempe, professor of natural philosophy." He sees in Professor's Waldman's words the unfolding of a design manifested by fate and in it his own downfall: "Such were the professor's words—rather let me say such the words of the fate—announced to destroy me." Becoming a disciple of Waldman, Victor feels, has "decided my future destiny."[2] Destiny appears in many guises in Romantic literature, which is sometimes more concrete although hardly less symbolic. In Sheridan LeFanu's *Sir Domonick Sarsfield*, destiny is the Devil as tempter; in Mary Shelley's *The Mortal Immortal*, it is a young man who, like the Wandering Jew, Melmoth and Dracula, remains as a warning for those who desire perpetual youth: "Thus I have lived on for many a year—alone, and weary of myself—desirous of death, yet never dying . . . the ardent love that gnaws at my heart, never to be returned—never to find an equal on which to expand itself."[3] In *The Judge's House* by Bram Stoker, the evil spirit of a magistrate sits in judgment on all who dare to enter his house, and in Bulwer-Lytton's *The Haunted and the Hunters* it is the image of death-in-life and life-in-death in the form of a mysterious stranger who has "mastered great secrets by the power of Will" and can "retard the process of years."[4] In *Gaston De Blondeville*, fate in the form of a ghostly knight in armor comes so that the guilty might be punished and the innocent set free. In Maturin's novel, *Melmoth*, the ambassador of the enemy of mankind seeks to tempt people and thus subvert their eternal happiness. Eugene Sue's *Wandering Jew*, a man cursed with eternal life, is the symbol of chastisement to man; he confesses to himself, as God's instrument of punishment, his horror at the thought of bringing cholera to Paris: "A solitary wanderer, I left in my track more mourning, despair, disaster, and death, than the innumerable armies of a hundred devastating conquerors could have produced. I then entered this city, and it was decimated."[5] For Fernand Wagner, in Reynolds's *Wagner the Wehr-Wolf*, it is Faust who exemplifies Wagner's destiny by offering him eternal youth not simply by selling his soul to Satan but by becoming a werewolf when the full moon rises.

Characters in gothic fiction usually ascribe unnamed fates for their actions, and in Anne of Swansea's (1764–1838) *The Unknown! or the Knight of the Blood-Red Plume*, Werwrold, a knight, takes leave of his love, Erilda, with these words: "irresistible fate leads me hence. . . . You behold in me a houseless wanderer, against who the vengeance of Heaven is imprecated, doomed, for a term, to be a solitary inhabitant of earth."[6] Antonia, the heroine of Lewis's *The Monk*, is warned by a gypsy of her destiny: "Lovey maid, with tears I leave you, / Let not my prediction grieve you: / Rather, with submission bending, / Calmly wait distress impending, / And expect eternal bliss / In a better world than this."[7] Geoffrey Tempest encounters destiny in the form of the urbane Prince Lucio Rimanez, Lucifer in his earthly disguise in *The Sorrows of Satan*. The artist, Scott, in Robert W. Chambers' *The Yellow Sign* meets his destiny in the form of a strange young man who, giving the impression of a "'plump white grave-worm,"[8] has died and is ever present to the painter as a reminder of his own death. Count Rosalvo, turned bravo in Lewis's *The Bravo of Venice*, laments his misfortune in grandiloquent terms: "Fate has condemned me to be either the wildest of adventurers . . . or one, at the relation of whose crimes the world must shudder! To astonish is my destiny. Is it not the hand of fate, which has led me hither?"[9] Wieland, who murders his wife and children in Charles Brockden Brown's novel, believes that he is commanded to do so by a higher law: "I brought thee hither to fulfill a divine command. I am appointed thy destroyer, and destroy thee I must. . . . I was commissioned to kill thee . . . [cease] to contend with thy destiny . . . my wife!"10

The films, as opposed to the gothic literature above, are rooted in pseudoscience and rely on the preternatural instead of the supernatural, embodying a single personage who becomes arbiter of the destinies of various individuals. The first of these strange men is Jack Griffin, "the invisible man."

The Invisible Man (1933) by James Whale is hardly an atmospheric film when compared to his *Frankenstein* films or *The Old Dark House* (1932), but its opening is evocative of the gothic film genre: the snowy night, the howling wind, the strange man's costume. The novel brings this out, and it is well to introduce some of the passages from Wells's 1897 work.

Griffin exhibits the characteristics of the gothic villain-hero. As a scientist he is as solitary a figure as Henry Frankenstein:

> The stranger did not go to church. . . . Communication with the world beyond the village he had none. . . . He rarely went abroad by daylight, but at twilight he would go out muffled up enormously, . . . and he chose the loneliest paths and those most overshadowed by trees and banks.11

Like the Romantic hero, this modern-day gothic protagonist suffers in mind and body, not from an unknown sickness or moral lassitude, but from physical peculiarities that separate him from the rest of mankind, a victim of his own scientific experiments. He is somewhat akin to Stevenson's Dr. Jekyll in this account: "I had not expected the suffering. A night of racking anguish, sickness and fainting. I set my teeth, though my skin was presently afire; all my body afire; . . . there were times when I sobbed and groaned."

Griffin, although his scientific purpose is realized in achieving complete invisibility, moves from sanity to madness, a disorder of the Romantic imagination. He begins to formulate plans with his former colleague, Dr. Kemp, that sound nightmarish: "an Invisible Man . . . must now establish a Reign of Terror . . . take some town like your Burdock and terrify and dominate it . . . issue his orders. . . . And all who disobey his orders he must kill." The dream becomes reality when Griffin commits his first murder. His plan to dominate the world begins with the brutal description, by Wells, of Griffin's wrath on Mr. Wicksteed: "He . . . broke his arm, felled him, and smashed his head to jelly." He then seeks revenge on Kemp for having conspired with the police, becoming arbiter of men's destinies just as he had predicted to his colleague: "Death starts for . . . [Kemp] to-day. He may lock himself away . . . get guards about him, put on armor if he likes; Death, the unseen Death, is coming."12

The mad desire to rule others is brought about by Griffin's invisibility. Wells attempts to explain the scientific principle behind the discovery in a chapter entitled, "Certain First Principles" where he investigates the laws of the refractive index of a substance. Whale has rightfully omitted this; Claude Rains, swathed in bandages, in the sitting room of The Lion's Head Inn with his chemicals about him is a nineteenth-century version of an alchemist. Yet he is presented more sympathetically than Wells had written him. Whale's "invisible man" desperately tries to return to normal, but is thwarted; he attempts to seek friendship and the love of the woman he once knew, but madness takes over. The drug that produces the gift of invisibility also produces the curse of insanity.13

There are several key sections to be covered in *The Invisible Man* either through analysis of the shots:

1. The opening scene through the snow and the arrival of the invisible man at The Lion's Head Inn;
2. The scene between Flora and Dr. Kemp in Dr. Cranley's home;
3. The attempted arrest of the invisible man at the inn;
4. Flora's first meeting with Griffin
5. The capture of Griffin,

or through analysis of the dialogue:

1. The discussion by Dr. Cranley on the effect of monocane,
2. Kemp's first encounter with the invisible man.

The opening scene with the invisible man trudging through the snow is memorable, for it sets the *mis-en-scène* and uses careful cutting, camera angles and camera movement to emphasize the drama. The Romantic hero is shown coming out of the dark snowy night to disturb the peaceful lives of the people of Iping; it is to be the first test of his power to control. To begin with, Whale has allowed the credits to become part of the *mise-en-scène*. As the credits appear the sound of the snow storm mimicked by the music can be heard and seen over them until there is a complete fade-out and fade-in to the opening scene. The titles are stark white over a black background and form an easy transition between credits and narrative. The white credits on black are also a good transitional device for the scene that opens the film: the white of the snow against the black of the night.

The opening shots are meant to create a sense of mystery. A figure in long shot comes toward the camera as he trudges up a hill on a country road. The man is seen in profile; his face looks masked. He stops at a signpost (his back to the camera) and wipes the snow from it. It reads "To Iping, 1/2 mi." The stranger leaves the sign at the crossroads and takes the route which goes off into the background. These shots, skillfully observing the stranger from various camera positions, like the opening chapter of Wells's novel, introduce him to the viewer and yet never allow the viewer to see distinctly his bandaged face. The audience also comes to learn the direction the man is headed. Slowly Whale unveils his setting through a wipe by having the stranger literally move his hand across the snow-covered sign to clear the name, not only for himself, but for the viewer, who is made aware of exactly how far the man has yet to travel. Up until now most of the movement has been within the frame, giving a certain rigidity to the setting that parallels the frigid scene where everything is still but the sound of the wind and the falling snow. The insert The Lion's Head is a transitional device and like the road sign quickly announces the scene of the action.

Once inside The Lion's Head, with its contrasting warmth, noise and good-humored fellowship, the camera is quite mobile. Whale sets his scene and explores, in a most interesting manner, the limited space of The Lion's Head, causing the pub to appear larger than it really is. The camera work is careful and methodical, filled with so much cinematic diversity that the constant dollying in to and out of groups of people, and the panning and tracking back and forth about the pub never become tedious. This is due in no small part to the photographer, Arthur Edeson, Whale's cameraman on *Frankenstein* and *The Old Dark House*. The director arranges actors geometrically so that they indicate where the center of focus is to be found. For example, the men who are playing darts are grouped in a triangle about the table while in another shot a similar triangular configuration is formed with a barmaid, Milly, at the apex. Although the camera constantly refers the viewer to the men at the dart game (this happens three times in the sequence), one is always amazed at the unexpectedness of returning to the players since, in reverting to the same spot, the viewer is presented with a new perspective of the game and men each time.

As in *Frankenstein* and *The Bride of Frankenstein*, the first appearance of the stranger is composed of several shots: first in long shot, then in a low-angle medium shot, and finally in low-angle close-up. The jarring cuts, so different from the smooth movement of the camera that had previously explored the space of the tavern, imitate the startled reaction of the people in the pub to the intrusion of the stranger. There is something more. The tavern scene is part of a filmic convention. It represents one of the places where the natural and preternatural worlds meet. Up until the time when the invisible man enters the inn, the camera moves quite freely. Once he arrives, not only does the humor and good fellowship cease, but the camera becomes less fluid, and the shots become more percussive. Yet the drollery that characterizes Whale's horror films strikes a purposefully discordant note which straddles the margin between slapstick and black humor, between the normal and abnormal situations that he sets up.

The next scene between Flora (Gloria Stewart), Griffin's fiancée, and Kemp (William Harrigan), her father's (Henry Travers) assistant who is also in love with her, is not only good from a cinematic point (although it too, like the one between Flora and Griffin, first appears static), but it also reiterates themes used in this film and horror films of the decade. Cinematically there is in both blocking and cutting an attempt to show the love of Flora for Jack Griffin (Claude Rains, the invisible man of the title) by repeatedly having Kemp and Flora so positioned that they are separated from each other by a table with a bouquet of flowers, and even when they are together in the frame their body language (she, her head on the chair; he standing looking out of frame) indicates their lack of mutual understanding. Constantly Flora attempts to evade the advances of Kemp; she by moving out of the frame and he by moving into it.

The characteristics of the villain-hero come through in Flora's talk with Kemp about Griffin: "so strange . . . so excited and strung up." This description is similar to the dialogue between Elizabeth and Victor about Henry in the film *Frankenstein.* Kemp concurs with Flora's sentiments, for Griffin has had utter contempt for his partner. Yet Flora also sees Griffin through the eyes of love: "He was always so keen to tell me about his experiments." This antithesis of reactions is now built up by presenting the two contrasting characters: Kemp, "the straightforward," practical scientist with an underlying dullness in his adherence to the rules, and Griffin, who "worked in secret" while barring the door and drawing the blinds before he opened the cabinet in his laboratory. As a romantic villain Griffin has "meddled in things men should leave alone." He says this of himself before he dies, yet those who "meddle in things" in horror films are basically men ahead of their times. Usually what they suffer is greatly disproportionate to what they have done to merit such suffering, at least initially, and is usually brought about by their research. Kemp tries to tempt Flora to leave Griffith by saying that Griffith cares only about his experiments. This prefigures Griffin's growing insanity as seen in his talk with Kemp and later on with Flora.

The attempted arrest scene of Griffin by the constable at The Lion's Head is quite effective in its use of editing. Whale cuts back and forth so that initially neither Griffin nor the constable appear within the same space. This preserves the distinctness between the two as they fight with words. The well-defined space, however, is broken down with a voice-over on the image. Griffin is seated by a desk with a book before him; he faces the camera and says: "I give you a last chance to leave me alone." In the next shot the constable with the townspeople behind him replies defiantly: "You've committed assault. . . . And you can—" There is a shot of Griffin still seated with the sound-over of the constable's voice finishing his line, "—come along to the station with me." From this point Griffin is shown in low-angle shots that stress his superior position, and his dialogue continues to be superimposed over the shots of the constable and townsmen, his presence dominating the scene even when he is not visible in the shot. Significance is placed now on Griffin's escape from the townspeople, and Whale does this by concentrating on the invisible man's mysterious apparel. He emphasizes the artificial nose worn by Griffin not only by a close-up, but by the enjambment of Griffin's dialogue into the shot; each object of clothing he discards to allude the police is presented in two shots, one following the other: the taking off of the nose in two shots, the removing of the glasses and throwing them away in two more shots.

Toward the end of the scene and for one shot only Griffin and the other men occupy the same space for the first time, but even here he is separated from them by the space in the midground where a table with chemical apparatus is placed. For the most part eye trajectories and voice-over have smoothly bridged the definite spatial parameters that divide the two groups.

If Griffin's madness is hinted at in his escape from the police at Iping, it is reinforced by Dr. Cranley's description to Kemp of monocane's terrible effects. Made from a flower that grows only in India, it has sent a dog, on whom it was tried, mad. Invisibility has its roots in the drug that produces insanity, a complaint suffered by many villain-heroes and at one time thought a divine gift; it separated mortals from those who had direct communication with the gods and performs a similar function in the horror film by segregating the "mad" characters from the "common herd," the Cranleys and the Kemps of this world. Whale simply makes use of pseudoscience ("monocane") to explain the cause of madness which for some of the villains constitutes their "genius." Henry Frankenstein, Dr. Gogol in *Mad Love*, and Henry Jekyll are emotionally scarred because of their superior intelligence. Griffin's megalomanaic speech to Kemp only emphasizes, in a more direct way, this disorder when he says to Kemp: "everyone deserves the fate that's coming to them: panic, death, things worse than death." When asked why he has become invisible, Griffin gives no altruistic motive as others do in films of this genre, but at the same time there is no moral culpability in his act: he says that for him it was just a scientific experiment that no one in the world has ever done. But this scientific curiosity changes when the monocane enters his system.

In a marvelous diatribe disclosing the effects of monocane on his system to the terrified Kemp, one that Wells did not include in his novel, Griffin discourses on the power that is his to rule and subjugate people and his plans to murder a few individuals just to show what he can do as an invisible man. The only thing approaching this in the novel are Griffin's remarks where he warns Kemp by letter of his imminent death. The tone of Rains's rich voice is sardonic. His insanity was suggested in Dr. Cranley's speech on monocane; it is reinforced in Griffin's plans shared with Kemp, and it is confirmed and embellished upon in Griffin's dialogue with Flora. In fact, he uses some of the same words while varying the meaning of others:

1. Griffin [to Kemp]: "the power to rule, to make the world grovel at my feet"

    Griffin [to Flora]: "Power . . . to rule, to make the world grovel at my feet!"

2. Griffin [to Kemp]: "The drugs I took seemed to light up my brain."

    Flora [to Griffin]: "It alters you, changes you, makes you feel differently."

3. Griffin [to Kemp]: "Just these fingers around a signalman's throat, that's all."

4. Griffin [to Flora]: "Power to make multitudes run screaming in terror at the touch of my little invisible finger."

Another quality associated with the Romantic villain-hero is the strange or exotic. It has already been pointed out that monocane is a drug derived from a plant grown in India. The rareness of the plant coupled with the rareness of the disease and the complete eccentricity of the character is not unlike Wilfred Glendon's use of an exotic Tibetan plant in *Werewolf of London* (1935).

In the scene between Griffin and Flora seated by a window in his bedroom physical movement has been reduced to a minimum. It is a companion piece to that between Kemp and Flora. In the opening of this scene Flora and Griffin are seated close together in a medium-long shot, but by the end of the scene the camera has the two blocked so that they are distinctly separated to convey that momentary rupture between them by the positions they have taken: he, with this back to her, facing the window and she in profile, seated to the right of the frame, looking at him. Quite precisely Whale widens the gap between them the times he presents a two shot. During this scene Griffin's madness becomes apparent. He begins with loving concern for the woman he cherishes, telling Flora that there is a way back to becoming visible and that he will come to her. Then he modulates his words so there is a hint of his growing madness: "I shall offer my secret to the world with all its terrible power," and finishes with monumental megalomania: "The nations of the world will bid for it, thousands, millions. The nation that wins my secret can sweep the world with invisible armies!" Flora attempts to calm him, speaking of the resourcefulness of her father to help Griffin return to normal and of the lovers' eventual reunion. Flora's talk of their reunion is undercut by having them segregated in their own spaces while Griffin descends into madness: "Your father? Clever? . . . He's got the brain of a tapeworm, . . . beside mine. Don't you see what it means? Power . . . to rule, to make the world grovel at my feet!" Flora in desperation pleads with Jack and stresses the effects of the drugs, even hinting that they can produce insanity. The employment of the Dutch angles now increases the stress as Griffin speaks of insane plans for conquest. These angles are preceded by an expressionistic body language, whereby Griffin's figure is arched to create a diagonal in the frame. Added to this is the low angle that displays Griffin's insane strength, and the words he utters are appropriate to the form within the frame: "Power, I said! Power to walk into the gold vaults of the nations [low Dutch angle of Griffin] . . . into the secrets of Kings, even the Holy of Holies. Power to make multitudes run screaming in terror—" When he speaks about the power of invisible hands, he thrusts his before the camera so that they appear larger than life: "—at the touch of my little invisible finger. Even the moon's frightened of me! . . . The whole world's frightened to death!" Everything contributes to the effectiveness of characterization: the camera angle, the editing, the blocking, the focal length and the dialogue. As Griffin's plans for domination assume greater importance, Flora's ideas of domestic happiness fade.

At the conclusion of this scene, when Flora leaves Griffin's bedroom, it appears that they are reconciled. He promises her that he will return and even kisses her hand. Yet, after what has taken place, all their remonstrances cannot efface the fact that their union will never occur and that Griffin, despite his plans of conquest, remains a pathetic figure losing his struggle to regain the normal life he had with Flora by not reckoning the depth of his madness.

The final almost wordless section which details Griffin's capture takes place on a farm. The police surround the barn and literally "smoke him out." As Griffin's footprints are observed in the snow, the police inspector begins to raise his gun. In long shot the steps of the invisible man through the snow approach the camera, which tilts down when the prints reach the bottom of the frame so that the shot almost becomes a direct overhead angle. The sounds of a gun are heard, the footprints stop and an impression of a body is made in the snow. The inspector, along with the others, kneels over the indentation. The sequence ends with a dissolve to the hospital waiting room.

As Griffin is dying in a hospital bed and before he becomes visible, he says, repeating the words Kemp used to speak about him, that he interfered in things that should be left alone by man. It is a standard reply from the repentant villain-heroes of these films. Some film antagonists experience remorse over their crimes, and unlike their literary counterparts, do not die fighting. In the conclusion of Wells's novel, Griffin takes on a group of men until he is crushed to death by them: "His hands were clenched, his eyes wide open, and his expression was one of anger and dismay."[14] It is a far cry from his cinematic twin, but the film script had to contend with a code. Even madmen like Whale's Griffin are made to realize in their final moments that what they have done was wrong. Whale has done an extraordinary job on a rather ordinary novel. The heroine is left to mourn her loss alone with no immediate prospect for a happy union because no romantic lead exists.

The strength of the invisible man lays in his insubstantiality; but by the same token he found it necessary to rely on others to help him accomplish his plans. With the next film, Tod Browning's *The Devil Doll*, the power to direct the lives of others is taken to an even more outlandish degree when an escaped convict, played by Lionel Barrymore, enslaves and miniaturizes people to carry out his designs against those who have sent him to die on Devil's Island.

NOTES

1. Shelley, *Frankenstein, or the Modern Prometheus* (New York: New American Library, 1965), p. 41.

2. Shelley, pp. 45, 47.

3. Shelley, *The Mortal Immortal*, in *Classic Ghost Stories* (New York: Dover Publications, 1975), p. 130.

4. Bulwer-Lytton, *The Haunted and the Haunters*, in *Classic Ghost Stories*, p. 327.

5. Eugene Sue, *The Wandering Jew* (New York: Modern Library, 1940), pp. 233–34.

6. Anne of Swansea, *The Unknown! or The Knight of the Blood-Red Plume*, in *Gothic Tales of Terror*, Vol. I, edited by Peter Haining (Baltimore: Penguin Books, 1973), pp. 247 and 244.

7. Lewis, *The Monk* (New York: Grove Press, 1959), pp. 62–63.

8. Robert W. Chambers, *The King in Yellow and Other Stories* (New York: Dover Publications, 1970), p. 2.

9. Lewis, *The Bravo of Venice* (New York: McGrath Publishing Co., 1972), pp. 13–15.

10. Brown, *Wieland, or the Transformation* (New York: Harcourt, Brace and Ward, Inc., 1926), pp. 193–94.

11. H. G. Wells, *The Invisible Man* in *Seven Science Fiction Novels of H. G. Wells* (New York: Dover Publications, 1934), p. 199.

12. Wells, pp. 264, 285, 291 and 293.

13. The film's multigenre characteristics make *The Invisible Man* "overall a horror film, but because science is emphasized as a cause it overlaps into the science-fiction genre, and the invisible scenes fall readily into a comic-fantasy category." Paul Jensen, *The Invisible Man*, a Retrospective," in *Photon*, no. 23, p. 22.

14. Wells, p. 141.

CHAPTER 8

The Devil Doll: "Three Lives Must Pay"

They have made effigies comparable with my image, . . . to my death they have led me—O God of Fire destroy them!
—Abraham Merritt, *Burn Witch Burn!*

Although not as atmospheric as *Mark of the Vampire* or the opening sequences of *Dracula*, *The Devil Doll* (1936) is Tod Browning's best sound horror picture and bears a striking resemblance to his earlier work, *The Unholy Three* (1925). In the silent film, Lon Chaney, in a woman's disguise, owns a doll shop and employs a midget dressed as a baby to steal jewels of wealthy clients; Lionel Barrymore in *The Devil Doll* disguises himself as a woman and uses living dolls for a similar crime. Both films take place during Christmas and in both a police detective comes within inches of discovering the stolen gems hidden in the children's toys.

The screen script for *The Devil Doll*, credited to Tod Browning, Garrett Fort, Guy Edore and Erich von Stroheim, is based on Abraham Merritt's novel *Burn Witch Burn!* A comparison between the film and the novel reveals some interesting differences. The film contains a series of conventional characters: a crippled wife-scientist with a hunched back (Rafaela Ottiano), an imbecilic servant girl, Lachna (Grace Ford) and a mad scientist (Henry B. Walthall) who wishes to transform the world into miniature people to ward off global hunger. The scientist-husband is an ersatz godlike being who creates a perfect diminutive "Eve" on his operating table, and his wife and partner, Malita (with a white shock of hair and large protruding eyes) resembles the monster's mate in *The Bride of Frankenstein*. But the real villain-hero of the story is Paul Lavond (Lionel Barrymore), who justifies his all-powerful control of the three bankers who sent him to Devil's Island by saying that he must clear his family name and enable his daughter to marry the man she loves. He is the symbol of destiny whose sole purpose in life is to administer justice.

The two romantic leads, Lorraine (Maureen O'Sullivan), daughter of Lavond, and Toto (Frank Lawton), the taxicab driver whom she loves, are like those in other horror films, passive to the action of the plot. They are even further removed from the story because the heroine is related to the villain and, therefore, not the persecuted maiden of the conventional film genre. The love affair between Lorraine and Toto is sentimental and toward the close of the film this mawkishness persists when Lavond, unrecognized by his daughter, kisses her on the forehead and says that he was sent to her by her father before he died in the swamp at Devil's Island. He goes off into the night, sacrificing his love for her happiness even though she comes to cherish his memory when his name is cleared. The film ends on an ambiguous note. Lavond tells Toto that where he is going he will not need the money he has acquired, suggesting he will do away with himself. By having destroyed Rodin, paralyzed Coulvet, and sent Matin to prison, Paul Lavond has fulfilled his mission of punishing those who sought to crush him.

The novel is quite different. It is pedestrian, without much color, attempting to report, in a hard-hitting documentary style, the facts as seen through its first-person narrator, Dr. Lowell, who writes a preface to the story he is about to unfold. The device, common in such horror stories, is meant to give credence to the work and enable the reader to suspend disbelief in what is to follow. Merritt's novel takes place in New York City during the prohibition, and the majority of the characters are Mafia types with a Mr. Ricori at the head. Madame Mandilip is indeed a witch who kills people indiscriminately with her dolls. Once the victim is murdered a soul transference takes place and the doll becomes animated with the spirit of the individual who (before being murdered) has modeled the doll for Mandilip. Dr. Lowell, as a man of science, does not believe in the supernatural and is typically incredulous until the very end. In his forward he writes about this conflict, which is so characteristic in horror films and which contains that mysticism and love for the exotic past that are part of Romantic literature. In the forward he questions whether the forces and energies that the modern world labels myth and superstition are of an older wisdom:

born before history, . . . burning in Egypt before ever the Pyramids were raised; . . . known to the sons of Ad whom Allah . . . turned to stone for their sorceries ten thousand years before Abraham trod the streets of Ur of the Chaldees; . . . and still burning, still alive, still strong.[1]

The screenplay gives to Paul Lavond the necessary motivation for the attacks on the three bankers. In the novel Mandilip is presented as a symbol of destiny that truly makes her the incarnation of evil without justification; she elicits no sympathy like Paul Lavond. Dr. Braile, in the novel, speaks of the unknown perpetrator of the murders that occur as a malign god who sports with people's destinies:

> It's a bit like being God and unloosing the pestilence upon the just and the unjust alike. . . . No one who believes that things on earth are run by an all-wise, all-powerful God thinks of Him as a homicidal maniac. . . . If you believe things are in the hands of what is vaguely termed Fate—would you call Fate a homicidal maniac?

From the diary of nurse Harriet Walters, a victim of Mandilip, we get a description of the "witch," who, with a young girl (a slave to the old woman's will) named Laschna, runs a doll shop. Mandilip is described as about six feet in height, brown skin, with a powerful physique and very large breasts. She has gray hair and a long face, noticeable for a mustache. It is her dark vibrant eyes, however, that hold Miss Walters. The other two prominent features about Mandilip are her beautiful hands and deep, rich, contralto voice.[2]

Madame Mandilip is able to mesmerize her victims, obtaining complete control over them and implanting certain suggestions in them. When nurse Walters is in Mandilip's shop, she experiences, under hypnosis, a strange sensation emanating from the mirror in the room of the doll maker. In dealing with the mirror as a metaphor, philosophers from Plato to the eighteenth century conceived the mind as a reflector of the external world, throwing forth a radiance in art,[3] while for the Romantics, mirrors were envisaged as areas in which the real world and the world that is a reflection of reality merge into one that becomes more unreal and nightmarish.[4] Merritt employs these notions for a purely surrealistic effect as the nurse enters the inner room of the doll shop.

> I had the peculiar experience with the mirror . . . as though I were looking not at its image or my own image but into another similar room with a similar me peering out. And then . . . the reflection of the room became misty. . . .

I could see only myself . . . getting smaller and smaller until I was no bigger than a large doll.[5]

This becomes a foreshadowing of when the nurse's spirit is transposed into that of the doll Mandilip has made. Merritt uses other dreams like this to foreshadow events, such as Dr. Lowell's dream which ends in the death of his closest friend, Dr. Braile.

As in many horror films, the dichotomy exists between scientific fact and the supernatural. Part of the working out of the plot convention of both the novel and the film is that the superstition becomes fact, and the man of science learns to hold these positions without contradiction. *Burn Witch Burn!* is no exception. Lowell tells Braile that he cannot believe Mandilip has possessed nurse Walters' soul: "I have never seen a soul. . . . .Show me a soul, Braile, and I'll believe in—Madame Mandilip." Lowell becomes as much of a disbeliever as Jeffrey Garth in *Dracula's Daughter*: "Nothing can be supernatural. If anything exists, it must obey material laws. We may not know those laws—but they exist nevertheless."[6] By the concluding chapter, however, Lowell becomes convinced of the supernatural when he hears Mandilip's voice issue from Ricori's mouth, after the doctor has attempted to explain away Mandilip's demise and her "death-dolls."

Garrett Fort scripted *Dracula's Daughter* a year after *The Devil Doll*. *Dracula's Daughter* contains several similarities to *Burn Witch Burn!* Perhaps it is not a coincidence. Dr. Lowell is very much like Jeffrey Garth and uses psychiatry and hypnotism in his work. Madame Mandilip is like a vampire and Laschna is her victim; she is one of her slaves just as Lili is a slave to Countess Zeleska in *Dracula's Daughter*. Mandilip, like the Countess, also asks women to pose for her in the nude. When Lowell brings Laschna out of a trance he put her in to learn information about Mandilip, the girl immediately dies, as does Lili in *Dracula's Daughter* when Dr. Garth attempts a comparable strategy. Lowell uses the same type of Luys mirror to hypnotize Laschna as Garth does to hypnotize Lili.

Although the book has little sexual suggestiveness, the control of men's minds has sexual undertones, for Mandilip is an enchantress. The gangsters, together with Lowell, come to her shop and, hypnotized by her, drop their weapons upon seeing her transformation: "Before us stood a woman of breath-taking beauty—tall and slender and exquisite. Naked, her hair, black and silken fine, half-clothed her to her knees." At this point, the recalcitrant nurse Walters doll that is in her hand wreaks her vengeance against Mandilip. The doll thrusts the daggerlike pin through Mandilip's throat, twisting it savagely. The witch throws the doll toward the fireplace and it touches the coals. The dolls at her feet disappear and a flame arises from them wrapping itself around the doll maker. At this point the narrator, noting the change in Mandilip, says: "I saw the beauty melt away. In its place was the horse-like face, the immense body of Madame Mandilip . . . [S]he stood, then toppled to the floor. And . . . the spell that held us broke."[7]

The incredibly fantastic plot of the Merritt novel, with several comic episodes that also characterize the films of the 1930s but are absent from *The Devil Doll*, moves at a brisk pace which saves *Burn Witch Burn!* from becoming tedious. Browning does away with the witch and substitutes a man posing as a woman, who creates, through scientific means, living dolls which do his bidding. This allows Barrymore as Mandilip to play two parts similar to the Chaney vehicle spoken about earlier.

Four sequences will be taken from the film to illustrate the power of the villain-hero to control others: (1) The creation of the miniature girl, spelled "Lachna" in the film; (2) The paralyzing of the bankers Rodin (Arthur Hohl) and (3) Coulvet (Robert Greig); and (4) the confession of the third, Matin (Pedro de Cordoba).

To begin with, old Marcel, as a scientist, has high-minded principles, although, like most scientists in the horror films of the period, he is mad. And his wife, Malita, likewise takes eccentricity to the point of caricature, heightening the macabreness of the situation. Marcel's noble ideals contrast sharply with Paul Lavond's desire for revenge. One need only consider the bread lines of the depression and the quasi-totalitarian government of the Roosevelt years to see the Swiftian "modest proposal" that Marcel makes when he announces his intention:

Think of it, Lavond, every living creature, reduced to one-sixth its size, one-sixth its physical need, food for six times all of us. . . . I've found a way to reduce all atoms of the body simultaneously to any desired degree and still maintain life . . . only, in reducing the frame all records are wiped off. No memory left. No will of its own. A creature capable of responding only to the force of another will.

The dialogue gives the viewer an idea of the pseudoscientific jargon that began to come increasingly into play in the films of the thirties (especially in *The Invisible Ray* and *The Invisible Man*). Yet to call these pictures "science fiction" is to anticipate the coming of the genre in the early fifties. The characters of the fifties became a little more coldly scientific without the Romantic aura that those of the thirties inherited from an earlier literary fiction.[8] Paul Lavond in *The Devil Doll* retains this Romantic aura, and it is this aspect that must be considered.

Lavond tells Malita his reasons for escaping from Devil's Island, which are far from the humanitarianism that prompted Marcel's flight with him:

> [W]hen a man saves an ambition in a dirty dungeon for 17 years, it becomes almost an insane obsession. Well, with Marcel it was science, with me it was hate, hate and vengeance [he laughs]. . . . I was once a very successful banker. Three men, my partners, lied and tricked me into prison. Well, three lives are going to pay for it.

There really is no distinction between Marcel's self-styled madness and Lavond's insane obsession. In fact, the quixotic ideals of the former become the instruments of the latter's pragmatism. Marcel's work is not science; it is akin to Pretorius's necromancy. Science here becomes a means to control men's lives and for Lavond a power that he wields. It is the same purpose for which Dr. Griffin uses science in *The Invisible Man*, inaugurating a reign of terror.

Lavond one night listens at the head of the stairs to Malita and Marcel talking in the laboratory. The viewer now sees through Paul Lavond's eyes as he walks downstairs into the laboratory where Marcel and Malita are leaning over the lab table transforming Lachna, their servant, into a miniature creature. Browning's editing style in this creation sequence is more predictable, more conservative than Whale's in building up an air of mystery. Besides employing a subjective camera, Browning utilizes longer takes with asynchronous dialogue enjambed into other shots for smoother elision and has the center of interest, Lachna, in an off-screen space on the lab table. When the miniaturized woman is introduced she receives considerable film time (163 frames). Malita eagerly remarks: "You've corrected her brain, Marcel, she's no longer the stupid half-wit."

Marcel ironically tells his friend, "Lavond, tonight, out of this mist [vapors from the experiment], you will see the birth of a new mankind, in full control of its destiny." But a little later in the same scene, Malita tells Lavond that the lilliputian shall respond to his will. In truth the creature has no will of its own, only the will of those who govern it. It is through Marcel's will, or that of his wife or Lavond, that Lachna responds at all. After Marcel's statement about the new creation, a rapid acceleration of shots that contain no dialogue takes place once again as the experiment progresses to its conclusion so that the main thrust is on the visual images. Several Dutch angles are utilized to set the visual image on edge, including the laboratory equipment which is exploited for its pictorial effect to fragment the screen space. Marcel dies during the experiment and Lavond assists Malita in completing it, so most of the attention is centered on her with increasingly tighter shots of her physiognomy framed by the glass retorts in the laboratory. Browning is not as elaborate in his camera movement or set ups as is Whale. In fact, most of the shots have little camera movement within the lab. The movement is basically within the frame. This situation gives a percussive cadence to the *mise-en-scène* that is quite crisp, efficiently executed and economically presented.

Since much of the actual experimentation on Lachna is conducted off screen, and because of the minimal amount of camera movement, eye trajectories are often used to establish the presence of the actors and their locations within the laboratory. There are few surprises in this film-making approach, but the form is without flaws and a good balance is obtained overall between verbal and visual content.

The remaining sequences deal with the bankers who, prior to the film's opening, had sent Lavond, through their testimonies, to prison. It might be an arguable point that for a movie made during the depression, the real villains in *The Devil Doll* are the greedy bankers, miscreants of American populist film. Hoover had adamantly blamed them for undermining his economic reforms,[9] and unquestionably in the moving-going public's eyes at that time the bankers in the film are justifiably punished for depriving Lavond of freedom and economic security, while his manipulation of them makes the villain-hero a sympathetic figure with whom the audience can empathize.

Paul Lavond, made up as Madame Mandilip, a doll manufacturer, goes to Rodin's office. Before the disguised Lavond leaves, Browning invests her conversation, and subsequent talk to Rodin, with dramatic irony immediately comprehended by the audience. She says, "once you're in my shop, I'll wager you'll do anything I ask." When she lures the greedy Rodin into her establishment she urges him to go into partnership with her after showing what marvels her "toys" can perform. The necessary suspense is created by a series of ironic visual and verbal insinuations that give the commonplace in Browning films such menacing overtones. As Rodin enters Madame Mandilip's shop she says, "To think that I really have you here." Rodin does not seem to understand, and Mandilip continues, "I mean, that you're going to be my partner and help me." The banker, however, does not want his name to be associated with the financial enterprise and Mandilip reassures him with a laugh, "Oh, I wouldn't dream of using your name. You'll just be my *silent* partner." As she cautions Rodin about the steep stairs down to the workshop, her voice is carried over to the shot of Malita preparing the device for his miniaturization.

"Now this is the room where we keep all our little secrets," says Madame Mandilip, as she conducts him through the workshop door. She asks Malita, "Is everything ready for Monsieur Rodin?" and gives a sly wink while her back is to the banker. She points to Lachna, the "apache" doll, and entreats Malita to bring the miniature stiletto, saying to Rodin: "All our accessories are carried out down to the most minute detail." There is a cut on this final word to a shot of Malita picking up the stiletto with Mandilip's voice-over: "For example, on our ponies [there is a close-up of Malita dipping the stiletto into a little vial of dark liquid] the harness is exact." Then another shot of Mandilip sitting down (with a slightly low angle to give a menacing effect), and saying, "and on our little dolls the collars are all different, but mind you, suitable to the breed." From the left of the frame Malita's hand juts out with the miniature stiletto as Mandilip continues "—and our apache dolls we supply with a dainty little stiletto." All this time Rodin is situated off screen, and only when she hands him the knife is there a shot of the two seated face-to-face. He says, "This is an authentic little replica itself." She takes the miniature knife back from him with much courtesy and then jabs it into his leg, letting slip the falsetto with the words, "It hurts." Rodin starts to get up from his chair but is paralyzed. This is part of the Browning trademark, the fantastic disguised as the mundane. A grown man is paralyzed and sits helpless from the effects of a knife less than one-half inch long. With a shot of the paralyzed victim, Lavond is heard to say in his own voice: "Don't be too alarmed, Rodin, you're not dying." Then a cut to Lavond is made. He is now the transformed man who has gone through death and resurrection:

> Look at me [shot of Rodin] . . . and see what seventeen years in the grave has done to me [shot of Lavond who has removed his wig while talking]. No, Rodin, without my hatred I never could have lived to exhume myself. What swine you three are [a two shot]. You're going to help me to recover what I can. . . . That's why you're not going to die.

Barrymore's make-up is part of Browning's sinister transvestitism that conceals evil and hatred under a mask of benevolence and vulnerability. A number of qualities have contributed to the tautness of this scene: the dialogue's irony, the juxtaposition of the "old lady's" sweet voice with the seemingly inoffensive but drug-tipped stiletto, the sinister hand of Malita coming into the frame with the diminutive knife, and the off-screen presence of the victim, as Madame Mandilip talks innocently away. Only when the disguised Barrymore hands the stiletto to Rodin is the banker seen again, and this is almost a total rear shot so that Mandilip predominates. The voice-over is used afresh as Rodin, paralyzed, can hear but not respond to the words of hatred uttered by his former partner. When Rodin's face is seen in full, it is contorted with shock and pain. This is the shortest of the three attacks perpetrated by Lavond, and after a dissolve occurs to the interior of the shop, it is already presumed that Rodin has been miniaturized.

Lavond, once again disguised as Madame Mandilip, enters the Coulvet home. When she asks to look at Madame Coulvet's necklace, one is reminded of Chaney's female impersonation in *The Unholy Three*. Going to wealthy people's houses with a midget disguised as a baby, he discovers the jewels that the woman of the house is wearing and where they are kept. Lavond also does this, not only to steal the jewels, but to plant the doll in the house in order to work his revenge. Mandilip leaves Coulvet's house with the ironic remark, "Thank you a thousand times, Monsieur. You'll never know how happy it makes me to leave one of my dolls in your beautiful home."

The sequence which follows is completely wordless and leads to the paralyzing of Coulvet. Browning sets the scene for what is to come: the vanity table where Mme. Coulvet places her valuables before retiring, the twin beds in relation to the jewelry case, the doll resting in the sleeping Coulvet child's arms in the nursery and Mandilip under the balcony of the master bedroom. Browning manipulates the action so that all proceedings coalesce. For one thing, there is a repetition of shots of Mandilip outside the house giving silent instructions to the doll wriggling from the sleeping child's grasp. Then there are repeated shots of Coulvet asleep. To increase suspense, for the viewer knows the sleeping man will be attacked, the temporal and spatial continuum is extended. First there is the doll's climb to the vanity table, the removal of the jewels, and their disposal by dropping them from the balcony into Mandilip's basket, a process repeated a second time. The rest of the sequence deals with the doll's approach to Coulvet's bed in long shot so that the viewer is constantly aware of the spatial distance involved in the attainment of the doll's and its master's end. The doll advances to the foreground of the frame, slowly but steadily to emphasize the shortening distance between it and the victim. These shots appear longer in duration so as to augment the suspense until Coulvet is paralyzed. The attack itself occurs below frame as Lachna plunges the dagger into the banker. Madame Coulvet's discovery of her immobilized husband, her attempts to question him and her screams when she discovers his condition are voiced-over the shots of the doll descending the balcony to Mandilip who watches from below.

The incredible attack epitomizes the Browning directorial trademark; it combines an *outré* situation with the most matter-of-fact direction. Although use is made of matte shots and oversized furniture that the extremely large MGM set was able to accommodate, the detailed reality of the upper-class milieu renders the horror of the situation even more grotesquely credible. The actors in Whale's expressionistic sets and consciously lit interiors do not inhabit the day-to-day reality of a Browning film, for even when there is an apparent studio set, like the scenes that take place on the Eiffel Tower in *The Devil Doll*, Browning inserts stock footage of cars below to create a sense of realism.

The scene that prefaces the attack on Matin takes place at a restaurant where the agitated banker is talking to his doctor: "Do you think I can close my eyes, after seeing poor Emile. Doctor, what could have frightened him so? What could he have seen?" The doctor, shaking his head, answers: "He'll never be able to tell us. He'll be hopelessly paralyzed for the rest of his life . . . a brilliant mind imprisoned in a useless body." Matin mutters to himself one meaningful word: "imprisoned." At this point a waiter enters from the right with the check, and from the left of the frame with her back to the camera comes Mme. Mandilip selling mistletoe. She bends down before the seated Matin as if to offer him some and is told by the banker to go away. Picking up a piece of paper on the table Matin sees a note that contains biblical references headed by a title, READ YOUR BIBLE. Matin, after questioning the waiter, hands the paper to the doctor, while outside Mandilip looks through the restaurant window, smiles, bows her head and proceeds on. There is a dissolve to a profile of Matin at his desk with a Bible going through the references and writing them down. The piece of translated cryptogram reads: "This . . . night . . . tenth hour . . . thou shalt likewise . . . enter . . . the shadow of death . . . Confess . . . and be saved." The camera zooms in on the words "Confess and be saved," but before calling the police, Matin burns the section, "Confess and be saved," which he has cut from the rest of the translated piece.

Here is the typical economy of Browning's style. Again the audience is set up for the unexpected to occur to Matin who, like Coulvert before him, admits of insomnia. The irony comes after the episode is played out and Matin has translated the biblical passages. "Confess and be saved" become the paramount words which the camera emphasizes with the zoom. If Matin is to be saved from Lavond's vengeance he must confess. But if he confesses, he will be imprisoned just as Coulvet's mind is "imprisoned in a useless body," just as Rodin is "imprisoned" as a living doll that obeys Lavond's commands. This one word recalls Lavond's years on Devil's Island, and on the word "imprisoned" Browning has a waiter move into the frame from one corner and Mme. Mandilip move in from another to converge on Matin. Matin's image is obliterated by Mandilip's, and this symbolically suggests that the doll maker has the banker already in his power.

The final sequence, Charles Matin's confession, is preceded by the appearance of the commonplace. Browning moves slowly. The opening shots, acting as a framing device, take place outside the Matin mansion where Mandilip walks with a basket. A clock, which will become increasingly important as a sign of Matin's approaching death, strikes the quarter hour. This is accompanied by a fade to the Christmas tree inside the mansion and a dissolve to Mandilips's doll hanging on the tree as an ornament. The first-floor interior set is constantly juxtaposed to the study on the second floor, as the doll, Rodin, in his apache costume attempts to make its way upstairs.

The shots lead the viewer first through the exploration of the immediate first-floor entrance area and gradually bring the climax of the action to the second floor when the doll enters Matin's sitting room. The film's sequence concludes, as it began, outside, with Paul Lavond's name vindicated. The suspense is a matter of exploring the mansion's grand stairway, emphasizing its vastness and the doll's obstacles in ascending it to carry out Lavond's commands.

The final shots need a bit of explanation from the point where the doll has successfully eluded the police and gotten into Matin's room, to the conclusion where Matin in fright yells, "Monsieur Lavond, wherever you are, in heaven's name listen and have mercy. I confess. You're innocent. We were the guilty ones." As short as the remaining shots are, they, taken as a whole, are woven into a sustained piece of horror by actually imparting a sense of protracted time. The entire remaining piece works on three separate time values: (1) the time the action unfolds in the film, which is established as 15 minutes; (2) the time it takes for the projection of the sequence, which is approximately six or seven minutes; and (3) the subjective time lapse experienced by the viewer, which appears longer than the plot time. There is less camera movement in this final section, yet the fragmentation of the characters' actions is increased and begins to occur almost immediately in the devil doll's descent from the Christmas tree on the ground floor: (1) an establishing shot to locate the doll; (2) three shots of his descent from the tree; (3) one shot of his gaining access to the stairs; (4) three shots of his encounter with a policeman; and (5) six shots of the doll up the staircase interspersed with shots of the police on the first floor and Matin, the inspector and his men on the second floor.

The editing of the final portion of the sequence illustrates Browning's handling of the crosscutting between the upper torso of Matin and his legs where the doll will strike, to the doll itself, to the clock and to Mandilip outside. To portray anxiety on the victim's face, Browning usually has longer shots showing the upper portion of Matin's torso, his nervous fingers playing with his handkerchief. While not innovative, the employment of these familiar codes to illustrate inner feelings is part of Browning's method that he acquired in silent films. Juxtaposed to the pictorial presentation of Matin's anxiety the off-screen sound of a clock is heard announcing his impending death. These two banal images, one visual the other audial, are united into one trope to heighten the psychological stress.

To show the proximity of the danger Matin is in, the shots of the doll approaching Matin's legs become progressively longer in screen time, while shots of the clock become gradually shorter, although its off-screen presence can, at times, be heard. Just as the doll approaches Matin's legs there is a cut-away to the clock reading 10 P.M. Shots of Mandilip are made increasingly longer to register, in the first instance, her grim determination to mete out punishment and, in the second instance, to present her satisfaction at Matin's confession, as his voice is heard over her image. This is similar to the conclusion of Coulvet's punishment with the voice of his wife heard over a shot of Mandilip's gratified countenance.

With the exception of the attempted attack by the doll on Lavond, instigated by the mad Malita, the film ends on a happy note with the joining of the lovers in a sentimental tryst on the Eiffel Tower, which becomes a sign of pure love, the ethereal, unselfish kind which is not mixed with the sordidness of the world below. Above exists the self-sacrificing love of the young couple; below exists the base selfishness of the bankers. In the same spirit of self-sacrifice Lavond departs never making his identity known to his only child, the punishment he must endure for his crimes.

This was the next-to-last film Browning made, and its good moments outweigh its sentimentality. It is certainly more macabre than *Mark of the Vampire* and has a greater sustained horror with none of the "staginess" and slow pacing of *Dracula*. *The Devil Doll* will remain Browning's last great horror film.

The final segment in this book deals with the "tormented hero," the most tragic of all the villains.

NOTES

1. Abraham Merritt, *Burn Witch Burn!* (New York: Liveright Publishing Corporation, 1952), p. 6. A more faithful adaptation of this novel is the 1961

Mexican film entitled, *The Curse of the Doll People*. Unfortunately it is a "B" film and cannot compare with Browning's version. Two other films with similar themes are Bert L. Gordon's *The Fantastic Puppet People* (1958) and Roy Ward Baker's *Asylum* (1972). In literature see Fitz James O'Brien, *Wondersmith*, in *Terror by Gaslight: More Victorian Tales of Terror*, ed. by Hugh Lamb (New York: Taplinger Publishing Company, 1976), pp. 114–45.

2. Merritt, pp. 40, 94.

3. M. H. Abrams, *The Mirror and the Lamp* (New York: W. W. Norton and Company, Inc., 1958), p. 59.

4. Eisner, *The Haunted Screen* (California: University of California Press at Berkeley, 1969), p. 125.

5. Merritt, p. 96.

6. Merritt, pp. 97, 109, 128–29.

7. Merritt, pp. 191, 209, 211–12.

8. The "human monster" created in the thirties had been transformed in the fifties into something completely abnormal, "not of this world" yet so much a part of it because man had been responsible for these aberrations of science. See Susan Sontag, "The Imagination of Disaster," in *Against Interpretation* (New York: Dell Publishing Co, Inc., 1966).

9. Peter Roffman and Jim Purdy, *The Hollywood Social Problem Film* (Bloomington: Indiana University Press, 1981), pp. 47–48.

PART IV

THE ROMANTIC AS TORMENTED HERO

CHAPTER 9

Dr. Jekyll and Mr. Hyde: The Beast in the Man

... there is no future pang
Can deal that justice on the self-condemn'd
He deals on his own soul.

—Lord Byron, "Manfred"

Robert Louis Stevenson's *The Strange Case of Dr. Jekyll and Mr. Hyde*, published in 1886, is a modern gothic novel. There are no castles, assassins, monks, skeletons, ghosts, secret passages or exotic locations. But there is Jekyll's house with its two entrances, his compulsion when under the influence of Hyde to perform acts of lust-murder, and the torment of a man who, attempting to free himself of his animal nature, finds only imprisonment in the body of a "troglodyte."

Like many Romantics, Stevenson says his inspiration for the morality tale came from a dream. Again like the Romantics, Stevenson wrote, as if writing in a trance, a straight terror story which, due to the influence of his wife, became more allegorical in nature.[1] In Romantic literature according to Arnold Hauser.

> The dream becomes the paradigm of the whole-world picture, in which reality and unreality, logic and fantasy . . . form an indissoluble and inexplicable unity. The surrealist finds his best inspiration in . . . the "mystery of the subconscious" [which] translates objects into strange, horrible . . . forms.[2]

Stevenson's dream allegory depicted the "war in the members," the conflict between the external world and the inner man, and a departure from the Romantic ideal where man and nature become one.

The novel, like the film version, also contains other allegorical techniques, among which are the entrances to Jekyll's house: one "ancient [and] handsome," the other, from which Hyde departs in the rear, "show[ing] no window, nothing but a door on the lower story and a blind forehead of discolored wall in the upper; [bearing] . . . the marks of prolonged and sordid negligence." If this Janus-like feature of Jekyll's house mirrors his own soul so does his change of signature under the influence of Hyde. Hyde's deformity is made even more evident in the handsome wardrobe of Jekyll which becomes ill fitting with Hyde's physiognomy. His name alone suggests the hidden and secret part of Jekyll's nature and contributes to the allegory.

In the novel the animalistic side of Hyde is brought out early in the murder of Sir Danvers Carew, which is reserved in the film for the finale: "Mr. Hyde broke out of all bounds and clubbed him to the earth . . . with ape-like fury, he was trampling his victim under foot and hailing down a storm of blows, under which the bones were audibly shattered." This savagery might be contrasted to the butler's description of the tormented Jekyll. "Once I heard it weeping!. . . . Weeping like a woman or a lost soul." And again by way of contrast: "Utterson was amazed to find . . . a copy of a pious work, for which Jekyll had . . . expressed a great esteem, annotated, in his own hand, with startling blasphemies." This despair together with his hatred for all organized religion is part of the Romantic villain-hero's make-up. Yet Jekyll both in the novel and the film is not without fault. He is too proud, too self-confident and even hypocritical, "already committed to a profound duplicity of life." But even as Jekyll, his suffering is increased by the recognition of the duality in human nature: "I was no more myself when I laid aside restraint and plunged in shame, than when I laboured . . . at . . . the relief of sorrow and suffering." When Jekyll is transformed into Hyde, Stevenson underlines the dichotomies in Hyde's nature in a subtle way: "I felt younger, lighter, happier in body; within I was conscious of a heady recklessness, a current of disordered sensual images running like a mill race in my fancy . . . and the thought . . . braced and delighted me like wine." But even when Hyde murders, his emotional split is evident: "I mauled the unresisting body, tasting delight from every blow; and . . . I was suddenly struck through the heart by a cold thrill of terror . . . I saw my life to be forfeit; and fled from the scene . . . at once glorying and trembling." Successive transformations bring increasing tortures: "I sought with tears and prayers to smother down the crowd of hideous images and sounds with which my memory swarmed against me."[3] The protagonist of Stevenson's novel qualifies as a Romantic hero: damned, tortured, proud and even defiant, with an underlying melancholy remaining. Fredric March managed to convey these qualities both as Henry Jekyll and Edward Hyde and win an Academy Award for best actor.

What transforms the film version (1932) into gothic terms is the skill of its director, Roubel Mamoulian, whose careful supervision orchestrates the film's visual poetry. For Mamoulian, film aspires to the condition of music and selecting the right poetic image for the camera was as important as selecting the dramatically pertinent sounds for the film's track. In this selection process Mamoulian moved away from realism whenever dramatic purposes called for it.[4]

Yet Mamoulian was not always praised for his innovative work in film. Dwight Macdonald, former critic of "The New Yorker" magazine, has called him "glib, imitative, chic, with a fake elegance, a pseudo-wit and a suggestion of oriental greasiness," and his productions have been dismissed as pretentious. A year after the film premiered, Macdonald wrote that "a Mamoulian production can be depended on to overstress the note."[5] Certainly for today some of March's acting looks like overripe theatrics, but Mamoulian ingeniously manipulates the filmic medium to poetically wed image to sound. He has said "symbolic imagery, presumably unrelated, or a seemingly irrelevant sound can be a tremendous weapon for a dramatic intensification of a scene."[6] In so doing he moves away from the realism of the image to express by means of coded signifiers the psychological make-up of the characters in the film. In no other horror film of the thirties has the use of filmic codes associated with the subjective camera and various forms of montage (including wipes, editing for symbolic effect, dissolves, superimpositions and sound montage) been employed more effectively. In most films such coding ordinarily connotes passage of time, but Mamoulian extends these codes to increase the viewer's knowledge of the characters that simple visual or verbal details alone could not provide. In fact, what attracted Mamoulian to films was not dialogue but imagery, "the magic of the camera, the rich, exciting possibilities in editing."[7] In *Dr. Jekyll and Mr. Hyde*, a wipe, for example, not only bridges narrative syntagmas, but becomes one with the signified, commenting on both synchronic and diachronic levels of action. The tension this produces in the viewer is in direct proportion to his ability to see all forms of signification as dialectical: the image together with the coding device (visual as well as audio) creates a new meaning within the *mise-en-scène*. For this reason alone it is necessary to treat the discussion of *Jekyll and Hyde* differently from the rest of the films in this book, for Mamoulian complements Stevenson's "cinematic imagination already at work before the cinema had become a reality."[8]

By employing the subjective camera and montage, Mamoulian defines the very nature of the fantasy: a parable of good and evil that is atavistically connected with man's imperfect human nature. This chapter will cover the technical devices insofar as they define the Romantic hero/lead beginning with the employment of the subjective camera[9] in the opening sequence of Jekyll's preparation and arrival at the lecture hall, the realistic use of synchronous and asynchronous sound and the first transformation of Jekyll into Hyde. The next area covered includes the exploitation of montage in the form of wipes used to make ironic comments on the characters through spatial differentiation, the joyous organ-playing sequence with its symbolic editing, the dissolves and superimpositions to highlight the differences between Ivy and Muriel, and the utilization of sound when Jekyll frees Muriel from their engagement.

The opening sequence with the subjective camera in the restored version is much longer than what was in circulation before 1988 in America. William K. Everson states that when *Jekyll and Hyde* did become available in the early seventies it contained the cuts ordered by the Production Code for its reissue in the thirties.[10] The subjective camera sequence is a lengthy three minutes twenty-six seconds of film time; the first half takes place in Jekyll's ornate mansion, the second half occurs on route to the lecture hall at St. Simon's Medical University and in the lecture hall where the camera gradually frees itself from the first-person point of view. The scene opens with the subjective camera from Jekyll's viewpoint as it tilts down moving from organ pipes to a music sheet. Bach is being played. A shadow of a man's head is seen on the music sheet and the camera continues its tilt downward to a pair of hands playing the organ. These are the hands that later on will be used to signify the change that Jekyll undergoes in becoming Hyde. Out of the eight shots that make up this first half of the subjective camera sequence, three are devoted to Jekyll's hands. The camera moves with his hands as he changes the stops on the organ and it tilts up again to the sheet. Throughout Mamoulian employs an audio-visual enjambment to make images flow smoothly by connecting various asynchronous combinations of sound and image. For example, as Jekyll's butler, Poole (Edgar Norton), reminds the doctor of his university lecture, the camera swiftly pans from Jekyll's hands playing the organ on the voiced-over words, "It's a quarter to three, sir, —" to the butler on the completion of his sentence "—and your address at the university is at three." As Jekyll in voice-over replies, "So it is, Poole—" there is a cut to

Jekyll's hands playing the organ and a continuation of his sentence, "—So it is . . . You know, Poole, you're—" then a cut to Poole as Jekyll finishes his thought, "—a nuisance." Poole answers "Yes, sir," and the doctor resumes, "—but I don't know what—" with another cut from Poole to the music sheet on the organ and Jekyll's reply, "—I would do without you." We hear in another voice-over the obsequious servant reply, "Thank you, sir," while the doctor proceeds with, "Your sense of duty is as impregnable as Gibraltar, even—" At this point there is another shot of Poole as Jekyll in voice-over finishes with, "—Bach can't move it."

The viewer is at once drawn into the character of the doctor without having seen him. But what the audience does see in the subjective shots of the room bespeaks of refinement, elegance and taste: the grand pipe organ, the graceful hands and white cuffs of the doctor's shirt, the objet d'art, the expensive, leather-bound books and the room's large airy space. His voice is cultured, somewhat petulant, and even bombastic, but basically there is a kindness behind Jekyll's remarks and yet a distinct tone, with all the bantering, that he is still the master. At this point in the sequence the camera (Jekyll) follows Poole out of the room. The butler stops in the foyer outside the music room to ask Jekyll, "Will you wear your overcoat or cape, sir?" The camera (Jekyll) in the foreground replies, "Give me my cape." Not only is this the first long take in the sequence moving from the music room into the grand foyer with its marble floor, but the dialogue creates a three-dimensional effect in sound; Poole's voice is somewhat distant in the background while Jekyll's voice booms decisively out in the foreground.

Mamoulian continues to build up the audience's interest in the doctor's identity through the subjective camera, necessitating the use of asynchronous dialogue (Jekyll's voice) which in turn produces tension. First, by allowing the viewer to concentrate on the *mise-en-scène*, he, as participant of the action through the subjective camera, intimately shares the protagonist's experiences. Second, once the sound of Jekyll's voice is heard, the viewer immediately desires to know what his physiognomic proportions are like, and in some way attempt, while the camera moves through space, to add to the viewer's frame of reference a visual analogue that accompanies the cadence and timber of the voice. This becomes a form of subliminal editing because, in the process, the viewer mentally juxtaposes the images before him with the unseen protagonist as the subjective camera takes on a more definitive autonomy by becoming Jekyll. Precisely at this point the camera (Jekyll) continues to follow Poole as he goes to the entrance hall closet beside a mirror. The camera (Jekyll) turns to the mirror and for the first time we see Jekyll's reflected image fixing his cravat; he is a young, handsome man in his thirties, distinguished and proper. Later on in the first transformation sequence we shall see in a parallel situation, with the same type of subjective camera movement, the hideous face of Hyde revealed as he approaches a mirror in his laboratory to examine his other self. In this present sequence Jekyll with cape, hat, gloves, and stick walks away from the mirror and the camera pans in the direction of the front door. Poole opens it and outside a carriage awaits. The camera (Jekyll) moves to the carriage, exchanging pleasantries with the coachman, Jasper, perched in the front seat; Jasper talks directly back to the camera. When the doctor gives Jasper the destination, the camera is focused on the back of the coachman as he drives to St. Simon's. Mamoulian dissolves from the coachman's back into another shot of the coachman's back but in a different location, right before the entrance to the university. The second half of the subjective camera sequence now begins. Various people salute the camera (protagonist) as the coach passes by, and the doctor responds in turn to an officer, several doormen and students. In the first of the nine shots of the lecture hall sequence, the subjective camera explores the space not only through the use of the pan and dolly on the visual level, but also through the trajectory of vision that various characters impose upon the space when looking directly into the camera from the opposite point of view. The camera (protagonist) gazes at them and they back at the object of perception, thus delimiting the boundaries of the narrative space.

Not only the asynchronous dialogue, but the movement of the camera adds to the audience's impressions of the individual in this half of the sequence, since it is an extension of him. It is a precisely balanced movement exhibiting a classical symmetry and augmenting the picture we have of the man's orderly and fastidious temperament. Jekyll, after speaking to the lackey, moves his gaze from the right to the left of the frame to bring into perspective the coachman. This movement is followed by one that pans from left to right to focus in on the students, and then again from the students at the right of the frame to the left where the doorman is stationed. Operating as a nexus in these panning shots, the dollying camera now moves into the auditorium and continues to pan first from right to left and then from left to right to explore the student-faculty audience in a distinctly different manner from the camera movement outside the lecture hall. The investigation of space within the auditorium is altered by the fact that the camera is at a fixed focal point resulting in a panning movement that establishes a disengagement between the camera (protagonist) and the assembly. Since the zoom lens was not in wide use in 1932, Mamoulian continues to examine space through a series of logically systematized shots. As soon as the camera fixes on two students and then on two teachers, it loses its subjectivity so that the viewer no longer sees the action from the first-person point of view. Once the student speaks confidently to a friend alongside him, the camera has relegated its role of first-person observer to that of omniscient narrator; this detachment increases the tension produced by the disengagement of the camera from its subjectivity, resulting in the viewer's expectation of seeing Jekyll from an objective viewpoint. Moreover the shots of the two students and the professors enable a tenuous contact with the focal point formally provided by the subjective camera in indicating, through the character's sight lines, the off-screen space occupied by the protagonist. Mamoulian cuts on the action of the students pointing to the teachers below to those teachers whose gaze is directed off screen to Jekyll and from them to Jekyll on the sound of his first spoken word to the assembled group. In the nine shots that comprise the lecture hall sequence, therefore, Jekyll's presence is continually recalled so that the camera, while remaining detached from its subjective point of view, is, nevertheless, still centered on the doctor. His commanding presence among the group is further accentuated by low angle shots with the camera tilted slightly to the right to give a forward thrust to his figure.

At the conclusion of the lecture Mamoulian does not jarringly cut from a close-up of Jekyll to a long shot of the students and teachers departing from the building. Instead he dissolves the close-up of Jekyll into the larger space of the courtyard, and also bridges the gap by having the discourse of the lecture dissolve into the sound of the masses. Audially and visually he has once again made a transition effective, emphasizing through the slow dissolve the impact of the lecture on the assembled students and teachers.

In terms of the narrative, however, the most important use of the subjective camera, and the most visually exciting one, is Jekyll's transformation into Hyde. It is the most forthright presentation of filmic expressionism, which relies heavily on camera movement and asynchronous sound, depicting the subjective feelings of Jekyll that verge on the grotesque. This cinematic expressionism, the offshoot of the Romantic notion of Fichte's world-positing ego, becomes the extreme manifestation of Romanticism where inner psychic states are projected onto the milieu.

Mamoulian's build-up to the transformation of Jekyll into Hyde is one of increasing tension and is very elaborately choreographed. For such a long sequence, the director has made only 13 cuts (the entire sequence up to and including Hyde's looking into the mirror to see his other self runs approximately four minutes and forty seconds). The first shot with its racks of retorts, distillation apparatus and test tubes with chemicals in reaction, partially explores the laboratory space, but more importantly, it is an elaborate introduction to position Jekyll into the sequence. In many suspense films the axiom is usually to begin quietly and end with a cut on action within the frame. This procedure has been reversed by Mamoulian. The camera, from the opening, is almost always in motion either through panning or dollying, changing the perspective of the objects in the lab, adding a stereoscopic effect to the scene and establishing the tone of the sequence.[11]

The most important image within the sequence is Jekyll's hands for they stand as a form of synecdoche for the entire changeover in his nature. His hands are the first to change each time Jekyll undergoes a transformation: in this sequence; the second time he takes the drug when he learns that Muriel will not return from abroad with her father as expected; under the tree in the park and finally outside the Carew home. In the laboratory section, Mamoulian pans three times to Jekyll's hands in one subjective shot which punctuates the dialogue between him and Poole, separating two levels of action: on one level the servant is concerned for Jekyll's health, and his fiancée, Muriel (Rose Hobart), is concerned about his broken dinner engagement; on the other is Jekyll's mixture of the chemicals which the camera constantly draws to the viewer's attention and which is uppermost in Henry's mind (the shot is taken from a subjective angle). Even the nonsubjective shots emphasize the protagonist's hands. Mamoulian further increases tension by the repetition of Jekyll lifting the solution to his lips and putting it down again. This gesture retards the flow of the main action and allows Jekyll's eye trajectory to become the main signal to explore off-screen space in order to distend the time until Jekyll's metamorphosis.

The transformation scene begins with an extraordinary mirror shot which becomes a symbolic way of representing the *doppelganger*. The shot ends with the mirror and the completely transformed figure of the once-handsome Jekyll. In the opening after Jekyll quaffs the liquid, the camera dollies away from the mirror, goes into soft focus and begins its rapid clockwise movement around the room (initiating Jekyll's hallucination) producing a kinesthetic effect on the audience. At the conclusion of the shot it refocuses and begins to pan and dolly in the opposite direction back toward the mirror. A pastiche of dialogue, heard over the off-screen sounds of Jekyll's heart beating, gaspings and a piercing noise like that of a generator, are phrases that have been heard through the course of the film, but here they become grotesque placed in juxtaposition to one another from the mouths of disembodied individuals. The asynchronous snarling sounds are used as an extension of character when the subjective camera begins its movement back toward the mirror. The appearance of Hyde's mirror image has been carefully led up to and the time stretching of the sequence has been allowed maximum play to present the audience with a final perverted figure of the alter ego. The scene goes a long way to prove Maya Deren's comment "that the best use of cinematic form (camera, editing, etc.) appears in those commercial films which seek to describe an abnormal state of mind and its abnormal perception of reality."[12]

The second major coding device Mamoulian employs is the wipe. It must seem, at first consideration, to be the most objective and functional of all filmic contrivances. Mamoulian uses the wipe not simply for cutting from one scene to another, but by its temporal duration, allows it to inform the viewer the way he should examine the scenes that it conjoins. Five wipes employed in the film are significant. The first wipe takes place in the free ward sequence where Jekyll is comforting a sick, old woman who needs an operation. Dr. Lanyon (Holmes Herbert), Jekyll's close friend, comes into the ward to tell him about the party at the Carew's that night. Jekyll insists that he will perform the operation himself, much to Lanyon's disgust at the thought that the wealthy doctor would give up a dinner to operate on a penniless patient when other doctors are available. The shot is shown in the following manner:

Jekyll by the bedside of an old woman; The patient has her eyes on Jekyll, looking up at him. Lanyon is departing.

JEKYLL

Oh, Lanyon! You make my excuses to the general, and I'll make mine to Muriel, myself.

LANYON

Oh! eh, all right!

A DIAGONAL WIPE FROM SCREEN LEFT MOVES ACROSS THE FRAME AND HALFWAY THROUGH THE FRAME IT STOPS so that Jekyll's fiancée, Muriel Carew, is seen on the left side of the frame, beautifully dressed while in the right half of the frame the old lady in the ward is seen looking up to Jekyll (who is now out of the frame). AS THE DIAGONAL WIPE BEGINS TO OPEN MORE there is established a full shot of Muriel and Hudson, a servant.

HUDSON

Yes, Miss Muriel?

MURIEL

Oh, will there be almond cakes with the coffee, Hudson?

HUDSON

[At this point the WIPE BEGINS TO MOVE AGAIN so that the servant and the remainder of the shot is seen.]

I'm sorry miss, but I don't think so.

MURIEL

Oh, but we must have almond cakes. Send for them immediately!

The effect of the wipe is not only to bridge time and space. In analogizing the two shots Mamoulian opts for the didactic effect. The old lady with her hand resting beseechingly on that of Jekyll (already out of frame) appears now to be supplicating Muriel, and, furthermore, the old woman's gaze is toward the left corner of the frame now occupied by the doctor's fiancée. Not only has the trajectory of the sick woman's gaze bridged the spatial-temporal hiatus, but also the position of her arm directs the viewer's attention to the left-hand corner of the frame. The wipe is also used to counterpoint social and ideological differences: the infirm and impoverished old woman implores Jekyll to be the one to save her life, not with words but with a look and a slight pressure of her hand on his; contraposed to this is the vibrant, wealthy young girl imploring her servant, with a series of importunate words, to order a mere trifle for the dinner party. The diagonal wipe, briefly holding the contiguous shots, forms a type of visual-verbal *zeugma* which places the importance of saving life on the same level as that of a dessert.

The second use of the wipe also makes use of antithesis. Jekyll has sent Poole to Ivy Pearson's house with a 50-pound note because he realizes that he, under the influence of his other self, has brutally mistreated the singer. Ivy (Miriam Hopkins) opens the envelope in the presence of the landlady, Mrs. Hawkins (Tempe Pigott).

A WIPE BEGINS FROM THE RIGHT OF THE FRAME MOVING IN A DIAGONAL SWEEP, CUTTING THE SCENE IN HALF, revealing on the right Jekyll's fiancée, and on the left, Hyde's mistress, Ivy.

MURIEL

You made me suffer so and now you tell me nothing.

[AS THE WIPE CONTINUES Henry is seen seated on a couch next to Muriel.]

JEKYLL

I tell you, no man ever needed another or loved another as I need and love you.

The contrasting images work antithetically; there is a dichotomy between the socially and economically inferior mistress and the socially and economically superior fiancée. Muriel is worshiped by Jekyll like a woman in a romance, far removed from the sadomasochism involved in the treatment of Ivy by Hyde. Moreover, there is a paralleling of the two situations in the dialogue. Muriel tells Jekyll that he "made me suffer so" by which she means mental anguish over his safety. With the image of Ivy, however, still in the frame, one can imagine her saying the same thing to Hyde but in a totally different context. Jekyll tells Muriel that he needs her and her love, but it can easily be argued that these words might well be placed in the mouth of Ivy with her growing infatuation for the doctor. Thus the second wipe is used as another *zeugma*. Here single phrases within one dialogue stand in a similar visual relation to another series of associations but with some alteration in their meaning.

The third wipe is a rather complex one. Jekyll has set out for the Carew house where the General (Halliwell Hobbes) is to announce Jekyll's forthcoming marriage to Muriel. Being early, Jekyll goes through the park and sits on a bench under a tree where a bird is singing. Jekyll, looking up to the bird, quotes from Keats's "Ode to a Nightingale": "Thou wast not born for death, Immortal Bird! / No hungry generations tread thee down." In close-up a bird is seen singing. Looking up again, Jekyll sees a cat on the same limb of the tree as the bird, and getting up from the bench raises his stick in protest. The cat, off-screen, attacks the bird and destroys it. Jekyll sits down distressed and in an ironic tone repeats the first line he uttered from Keats. He looks down at his hands as they begin to change. The violence against the bird brings about the reluctant transformation, without the potion, of Jekyll into Hyde. Once the change occurs he, as Hyde, replies, "But it is death . . . death!"

[1.] Hyde in a great focal depth runs to the background through the park. THERE IS A DIAGONAL WIPE FROM RIGHT TO LEFT OF THE FRAME WHICH STOPS DIRECTLY AT THE POINT OF DIVIDING THE SCREEN IN HALF [but even as the wipe begins there is sound of people's voices at the Carew party in honor of the forthcoming marriage].

[2.] AT THE EXACT SPLITTING OF THE SCREEN IN HALF BY THE WIPE: General and lady in conversation. THE CAMERA CONTINUES IN A CRANE SHOT TO PAN ACROSS AND DOLLY IN WHILE LOWERING THE ANGLE TO COME TO A SHOT of Muriel seated in a chair. To the left of the wipe is Hyde walking quickly in a deep focus shot through the park so that by the time THE CAMERA STOPS at Muriel [and as THE WIPE PROCEEDS SLOWLY

ACROSS the rest of the screen], Hyde is a mere speck of an image remaining in the frame. There is dialogue among the guests as to Jekyll's lateness.

[3.] As Muriel and Mr. Utterson converse THERE IS A DIAGONAL WIPE FROM LEFT TO RIGHT OF THE SCREEN revealing Ivy on the left, Muriel on the right in medium shots. Ivy is drinking champagne.

MURIEL

Do you think anything has happened to Henry?

MR. UTTERSON

On a night like this my dear? Nonsense!

MURIEL

Why is he late then?

THE WIPE STARTS TO COMPLETE ITS MOVEMENT, FIRST PUSHING the old gentleman out of the picture then the figure of Muriel as she sits fanning herself.

MR. UTTERSON

There, there, my dear. It's not his lateness; it's your impatience. He'll be along shortly.

MURIEL

I hope so . . . I hope so.

The diagonal wipe of shot 1, held for a few seconds so that it evenly divides the two opposite corners of the frame, contains several instances of visual and audio counterpoint acting as metaphors and indicating the great gulf that exists between Muriel and her intended husband.

1. The noise of the party suggesting through sound the large number of people is contrasted to the quiet of the park.

2. The extreme depth-of-field shot in the park is contiguous with the limited space within the Carew living room,

3. The high-angle shot in the opening scene in the living room is placed next to the flat-angle shot in the park,

4. The moving camera in the house, which explores the room where the characters remain in fixed positions, is opposed to the relatively static camera position in the park depicting Hyde's movement within the frame,

5. The final medium-close shot of Muriel, when the camera comes to rest, is conterminous with the extreme long shot of Hyde just before the wipe cuts him off from view.

Shot #3, encompassing the diagonal wipe, is full of irony. Both shots are approximately the same medium length and a definite comparison is meant to be drawn between Ivy and Muriel: the former is overjoyed at the prospect of never seeing Hyde again, the latter is in despair at not having seen Jekyll; Ivy is in a flutter of activity, Muriel is in somber repose.

The fifth and final wipe comes after Hyde has killed his mistress but is conterminous with the dinner party fiasco at the Carews. The General and Muriel are saying goodby to Dr. Lanyon, the last of the guests to leave. After Lanyon departs the General gives vent to anger.

GENERAL

I'll kill that scoundrel, Jekyll, if I ever set eyes on him again!

MURIEL

No father, something terrible must have happened. I'm sure he can explain. I believe in him!

GENERAL

I forbid you to see this man again!

MURIEL

I love him, Father . . .

A VERTICAL WIPE BEGINS FROM THE LEFT TO THE RIGHT OF THE SCREEN, REVEALING HYDE IN LONG SHOT AT A TAVERN.

MURIEL

. . . and I'm going to marry him!

GENERAL

[facing left of frame. THE VERTICAL WIPE HELD A MOMENT HERE]
Muriel, you will have nothing more to do with that man!

HYDE

[to the proprietor, facing frame right]
Give me a pencil and paper, quick!

PROPRIETOR

Yes, sir!

THERE IS NOW A COMPLETION OF THE VERTICAL WIPE ACROSS THE SCREEN.

The vertical wipe begins with Muriel's words, "and I'm going to marry him." From the left hand side of the frame Hyde is seen at a tavern. The verbal and visual irony is predicated on the wipe coinciding with the particular phrase, for if Muriel knew what her lover really was like she would never make the utterance. When the vertical wipe is directly in the center of the frame allowing for a split screen, the General is seen facing to the left of the frame (Muriel's image having been eliminated with the wipe). Facing to the right is Hyde, the wipe not being completed so that the viewer cannot see the tavern keeper whom he is addressing. The effect is that the wipe, being held for an instant, enables the General to "address" not only his daughter but Jekyll/Hyde. The fact that the General is in medium shot and speaking while Hyde is in long shot and silent gives the General's words a greater force suggesting who is predominantly stronger at the moment; Jekyll has lost control of his other self.

Besides these wipes, which are a form of editing from shot to shot, other forms of montage in *Dr. Jekyll and Mr. Hyde* appear with equal force to comment on the characters' motivations. Certain symbolic images juxtaposed to the characters are incorporated quite naturally within the *mise-en-scène* through panning and give the shots an even flow (the statue of Eros and Psyche by Ivy's bedside and the two flowers facing close to one another in the pond of the Carew house where nearby Henry is seen kissing Muriel, etc.). There is, however, a montage of symbolic shots that depends on a percussive editing style to enforce the mood of the situation conveyed through the music which unites the disparate shots.

When Jekyll obtains General Carew's permission to marry Muriel in a month's time, he rushes into his house and sits down joyfully to play the organ. While he is playing, a succession of close-ups of objects that are within the large study are projected:

1. Profile of Jekyll seated at the organ, playing,
2. Jekyll's face smiling as he plays the organ [profile],
3. Jekyll's hands on the keyboard,
4. A candelabrum, with eight lighted candles on a wall sconce,
5. A bronze statue of an athlete with one arm raised holding a wreath,
6. A marble head of a young man with a smile on his face,
7. Poole's face directly facing the camera with a large smile,
8. The fireplace, flames rising up,
9. Jekyll in foreground; Poole in midground [organ music stops]. Poole says, "I beg your pardon, sir, but Miss Pearson is waiting for you in the consulting room."

The shots begin with an establishing one and then proceed in detailing the whole: shots #2 and #3 describe the feeling of joy within the man. The others, even shot #7, become symbolic extensions. The tapered lighted candles of shot #4 suggest brightness, warmth and comfort; in shot #5 the victory of the athlete becomes Henry's victory in obtaining the General's consent to a speedy marriage. Shot #6, as in #5, represents another instance of symbolically representing and mirroring the emotional state of the doctor. Shot #7 (a human figure treated as an object which prepares the viewer for shot #9) logically follows on shots #5 and #6 in detailing the figures of men (as well as that of Jekyll himself in shot #2). But shot #8, although allied to shot #4 through a similar cause and effect (a fireplace gives, like candles, both light and warmth) is somewhat ambiguous because of its sinister overtones. As the flames leap up, they suggest the idea of excessive passion and the destruction it can produce. The final shot (#9) of Poole's announcement seems to lend greater weight to the previous shot. Jekyll cannot ease his conscience by paying 50 pounds for what he, as Hyde, has committed against Ivy Pearson.

The next form of montage used by Mamoulian deals with dissolves and superimpositions, which can be illustrated with one pertinent example, and defines, like the wipes and editing, Jekyll's character even more.

As Jekyll and Lanyon leave the room of the Carew home after the dance, there is a dollying in on Muriel and a dissolve with her superimposed briefly over a long shot of Jekyll and Lanyon walking down a flight of stairs in a darkened street. By the time Lanyon begins to talk, after a few steps down the stairs, the image of Muriel dissolves. The transition by itself is not remarkable but for the fact that when Jekyll (continuing on the same walk with his friend from Carew's home) has just come out of Ivy Pearson's flat after rescuing her from a man who has physically molested her, there occurs another superimposition.

The two doctors come down the stairs of Ivy's tenement. A SUPERIMPOSITION of Ivy's naked leg swinging and her seductive voice.

IVY

Come back soon, won't you? Don't say you can't. Come back soon. Come back.

The intensity of the shot is increased by the duration of the superimposition, for whereas the superimposed chaste image of Muriel's figure is seen on the screen briefly, the sexual implications of the second superimposition are quite obvious, and what is more, the brevity of the first and the prolongation of the second suggest more than a way of linking a shift in time and space. They imply a psychological connection of the impression these women have made in the memory of Jekyll. The superimposed image of Muriel ends as soon as the dialogue between Lanyon and Jekyll begins. The image of Ivy's bare leg continues through Lanyon and Jekyll's discussion as they leave Ivy's apartment where she has attempted to seduce Jekyll. It is quite obvious that Lanyon's words to Jekyll, "I thought your conduct quite disgusting. You ought to control those instincts," and the dissolve of the image of Ivy's leg at this last statement are meant to have a cause-effect relationship. James Twitchell connects this split in personality with the Victorian age itself. He equates the dual natures in Jekyll as having a basis in societal sexuality, making a case for a literal interpretation of the double standard used by Victorian men who were able to sustain long engagements to chaste women like Muriel by having a mistress like Ivy at the same time, the novel and film becoming a male fantasy on a "subverbal" level of consciousness.[13] This is brought out in the film when Jekyll receives word that Muriel will not be home for another month because her father and she are traveling in Europe. General Carew has purposely separated the two lovers so that they will not run headlong into marriage after only two months of courtship. Poole suggests that Jekyll take advantage of all the amusements London has to offer, but Jekyll, realizing his position in society, tells his butler: "A gentleman like me daren't take advantage of them, Poole. Gentlemen like me have to be very careful what they do and say." A series of close-ups follow showing Jekyll nervously tapping his hand on the desk with Muriel's letter and then tapping his feet, succeeded by a shot of a pot in the lab with flames leaping around it, then a shot of Jekyll's face puffing on his pipe with anger and finally the last close-up of the pot boiling over with a gush of milky thick fluid. The sexual connotation is obvious, and at this point the doctor takes the potion for the purpose of turning into Hyde so he can see Ivy.

The final form of montage to be covered is audial. The use of asynchronous sound has already been dealt with, but there is one important instance where the sound is not only asynchronous but symbolic. It is used as a type of filmic *parabiosis* fusing two distinct times and moods into one space, both being ironically juxtaposed. Similar occurrences exist in literature, to make a comparison between Mamoulian's style and such writers as Flaubert, Pound and Eliot. Flaubert had written about the famous incident of the "comices agricoles" in *Madame Bovary* by saying that "Everything should sound simultaneously; one should hear the bellowing of the cattle, the whisperings of the lovers and the rhetoric of the officials at the same time."[14] Simultaneity of sense impressions can be accomplished by breaking up the temporal sequence through dissolves in sound and image. Mamoulian in this sequence as well as in the first transformation of Jekyll into Hyde was able to carry out Flaubert's idea. The final meeting of Henry and Muriel is a much more simplified notion than the polyphonic sequence in *Madame Bovary*, for in the novel three different auditory intrusions upon the romantic scene are involved whereas in the film two different times are amalgamated within the same space through music. In the case cited in Flaubert, Joseph Frank proves this by using terminology appropriate to the film medium, saying that the French novelist "dissolves sequence by cutting back and forth between the various levels of action." Frank also speaks of Pound's *Cantos* and Eliot's *The Waste Land* in the same manner of the poet making use of "deliberate disconnectedness" and superimposing one time scheme upon another.[15] In the film Jekyll comes into the Carew living room, where he is no longer welcome by the General. The room is the same one in which Henry and Muriel were seen deeply in love and very happy. As Jekyll approaches Muriel, the music over the soundtrack is the same waltz they danced to on the last night of their love. Sound is employed here to convey a distinct time separate from the one in which the narrative is presently engaged. The contrast is ironic for the music recalls the happier times the lovers have spent together, and appropriately ends when Jekyll sets Muriel free from their mutual vows to wed.

These coding devices that have been presented enhance the characterization of the villain-hero and are stylistically bold and dramatically exciting. Mamoulian has taken the clichéd tools of the film trade and reworked them into multifaceted audio-visual signifiers extending the meaning of the word "technique" from a mere functionary vehicle for moving the plot forward to one which is both functional and conceptual.

The next film, *Mad Love*, Karl Freund's loosely based telling of *The Hands of Orlac*, also deals with a tormented villain-hero who is also the romantic lead. It is a film of the supernatural that does not attempt the more intricate rationalizations of the novel.

NOTES

1. Abraham Rothberg, "Introduction" to Robert Louis Stevenson's *Dr. Jekyll and Mr. Hyde* (New York: Bantam Books, 1973), pp. x, viii.

2. Arnold Hauser, cited in Devendra P. Varma, *The Gothic Flame* (New York: Russell and Russell, 1966), p. 67.

3. All the quotations have been taken from Robert Louis Stevenson's *Dr. Jekyll and Mr. Hyde*, pp. 27, 60, 64, 78, 79, 82, 93, 94.

4. Arthur Knight, "Rouben Mamoulian: The Artistic Innovator," in *The American Cinema*, ed. by Donald E. Staples (Voice of America: Forum Series, 1973), p. 281.

5. Dwight Macdonald, "Notes on Hollywood Directors," in *Introduction to the Art of the Movies*, ed. by Lewis Jacobs (New York: The Noonday Press, 1970), pp. 182–83.

6. James R. Silke, ed., *Rouben Mamoulian: Style is the Man*, Publication #2 (Washington, D.C.: American Film Institute Publication, 1971), p. 20.

7. Silke, p. 8.

8. Prawer, *Caligari's Children* (New York: Da Capo Press, 1980), p. 90.

9. The dialogue has been taken from a print of the restored version of the film. I have also used Richard J. Anobile's shot reconstruction of the film. There seem to be some minor inaccuracies in the dialogue he has recorded [Muriel Carew is not addressing her butler, Hudson, at the engagement party, it is Mr. Utterson, the lawyer]. See Richard J. Anobile, *Dr. Jekyll and Mr. Hyde* in *The Film Classics Library* (New York: Avon Books, 1975), p. 153.

10. William K. Everson, *Classics of the Horror Film* (Secaucus, N.J.: Citadel Press, 1974), p. 74. The restored version includes the opening subjective camera shot in its entirety, a scene in the "free ward" of the hospital where Jekyll's patient is a little girl who has to learn to walk again, a more complete scene of Ivy taking off her clothing so Jekyll can examine her, the cat attacking the bird in the tree which because of its violence causes a transformation in Jekyll to Hyde, and a more complete and highly melodramatic meeting between Muriel and Jekyll where he breaks off their engagement.

11. This has also been noticed by Roy Huss in James Whale's creation scene for *THE BRIDE OF FRANKENSTEIN* in an article entitled, "Almost Eve: The Creation Scene in *THE BRIDE OF FRANKENSTEIN*," in *Focus on the Horror Film* (Englewood Cliffs, N.J.: Prentice-Hall, 1972), p. 77.

12. Maya D. ren, "Cinema as an Art Form," in *Introduction to the Art of the Movies*, pp. 255–56.

13. Twitchell, *Dreadful Pleasures: An Anatomy of Modern Horror* (New York: Oxford University Press, 1985), p. 230.

14. Gustave Flaubert as quoted by Joseph Frank, ("Spatial Form in Modern Literature,") in *The Sewanee Review*, 53. (1945), p. 231; reprinted in Robert W. Stallman; ed., *Critiques and Essays in Criticism: 1920–1948* (New York: The Ronald Press Company, 1949), pp. 315–328.

15. Frank, p. 229.

CHAPTER 10

Mad Love: Torture by Obsession

. . . since that day, hasn't it been torture? What a terrible obsession, increased by the weakness of your brain . . . and by your natural nervousness.
—Maurice Renard, *The Hands of Orlac*

Mad Love (1935) is adapted from the 1929 novel, *The Hands of Orlac*, by Maurice Renard. All the names in the film with the exception of Stephen Orlac's have been changed, and more importantly, Renard's narrative is a crime thriller, rather than a supernatural tale, in which everything is rationally explained at the conclusion, like Clara Reeve's *The Old English Baron* (1778) which Walpole said was so "reduced to reason and probability . . . that any trial for murder at the Old Bailey would make a more interesting story."[1] Schiller's *The Ghost-See*[2] (1784), following in this tradition, is another piece of gothic fiction with a rationalistic twist in which a séance turns out to be a fraud. In a similar vein there is Radcliffe's *The Mysteries of Udolpho*, already spoken of, and in the nineteenth century Conan Doyle's *Hound of the Baskervilles* and *The Adventure of the Sussex Vampire*.

Renard delights in setting up subterfuges so that the reader constantly doubts the validity of the characters' actions and speech. For example, after Stephen is in a train accident, Rosine Orlac, escorted by a military doctor, drives him to the hospital of Professor Cerral who can save his hands from being amputated. Renard makes the surgeon's name and occupation something to be feared when he has the army doctor tell

Rosine: "I have heard of some experiments that he has tried—well, that are, to say the least—daring."³

Once Stephen is brought home from Cerral's clinic to his apartment he begins to "dream," while his wife also sees the surrealistic nightmare brought on by his torment.

> In the phosphorescence could be seen a grand piano on a platform—then a man in evening suit, Stephen. He bowed . . . then sat down and opened the piano . . . Of a sudden everything disappeared leaving only the keyboard . . . . Stephen's hands were placed on the notes, but the notes cannot be distinguished plainly. Then his right hand snatched up one of them—it was an ugly ring handled knife! The handle of the knife is marked with an X and covered with . . . a crimson liquid . . . . The gleaming knife . . . becomes a large square . . . . guillotine [with] a head [in it] . . . caught in the iron collar of the wood frame . . . . It is the grimacing face of Stephen.

On arriving at the apartment one day, Stephen and his wife discover a sinister sign that no one is able to explain: "There—in the door—. . . a knife, similar to the knife of Stephen's dream, was stuck . . . . [T]hat part of the blade which could be seen had blood on it . . . and . . . the handle of the knife was marked with an X. Stephen's face was like the face of a dead man."⁴ His mental condition deteriorates, and Rosine finds in his special room, called The Temple of Hands, a series of knives. When she discovers a knife like the one in his dream with blood on it imbedded in a door, she comes to the conclusion that he has become a somnambulist and "while freed from the control of his conscience, might . . . commit some foul deed for which he, nevertheless, would be responsible"⁵ After a series of knife murders in which Stephen's father and his father's close friend are killed, the detective, Cointre, discovers through fingerprints that the men were murdered by Vasseur (Rollo in the film), and thinks, "the manner of the stabbing is familiar to me. . . . I know the fingerprints . . . . This criminal, who was left-handed, was named Vasseur . . . whom I arrested . . . convicted, condemned, and guillotined."⁶ Stephen, meanwhile, comes into his father's inheritance and is blackmailed by a stranger who claims to be the guillotined Vasseur, explaining to Stephen the result of a grafting operation.

> Professor Cerral . . . amputates the hands of Orlac and replaces them with the hands of Vasseur . . . . You have a horror of them? They live on you with a personal life . . . . [I]t is Vasseur, who, thanks to you, lives again in those hands which are grafted on your flesh . . . . And you are afraid that this

vigorous growth will over-run you—that it will propagate its violent strength.

At this point in the novel we learn how Stephen's wife was able to see her husband's "nightmares": "a little hole in the wall, just large enough to admit a projector lens—a trichrome motion picture apparatus . . . . [A]ll that is needed to project real pictures into space is a set of lenses and curved mirrors."[7] To have this in the film might have been a nice play on the film-within-the-film idea but it would have taken the supernatural element out of Freund's picture, besides it seems to be a rather contrived plot device to explain the dreams.

Renard maintains his literary duplicity to the end. The supposed dead man in *Grand Guignol* style shows Stephen the result of Dr. Cerral's operation. Unlike the film, the resuscitated man and the doctor who performs the operation are not one and the same: "They were metal hands, managed by a harrowing orthopedic device. 'I am Vasseur,' announced the stranger. 'See!' And with an awkward gesture with his inert hands he drew aside his silk neckerchief, baring to Stephen's eyes a ghastly scar which encircled his neck."

In the end the supposed Vasseur is found out by the police to be Eusebio Nera, a moving-picture operator, a medium and even a hospital nurse. The severed hands are really metal gloves and the scar around the neck nothing more than sticking tape. Although Stephen does possess the hands of the dead Vasseur, Renard adds a new twist to the ending. The police inspector says, "The really guilty man, who should have died in Vasseur's place, is Eusebio Nera . . . . Vasseur was innocent, M. Orlac. Your hands have committed no crime."[8] The novel, unlike the film, leaves nothing unsettled. Hypnotism and autosuggestion account for Stephen's behavior, and even his new, grafted hands are not those of a murderer. On the other hand, *Mad Love* leaves much to the imagination and is startlingly different from Renard's work.

Mad Love has two Romantic leads, two tormented geniuses: the mad villain Professor Gogol (Peter Lorre) and Stephen Orlac (Colin Clive). The two main characters of *Mad Love* have schizoid conditions: a tormented pianist who has the tenderest feelings toward his wife and yet when provoked is ready to kill with a knife; a doctor who evinces a profound love for the infirm children of his clinic, saying to one woman, "I don't operate for money," attempts to murder the woman he insanely adores. Both men are geniuses in their own right: a composer-pianist and physician. But Stephen Orlac's original piano composition with its Chopin-like sounds of dark and melancholic dissonant chords is sinisterly suggestive of a troubled mind. While Stephen is associated musically with the figure of Chopin, Gogol is associated with Richard Wagner. In the operating room he has the nurse play a recording of Wagner's *Siegfried Idyll*. Siegfried is an archetype of Romantic love, the hero who overcomes all obstacles and wins the love of the sleeping beauty protected by a circle of sacred fire. There is a parallel. Professor Gogol delights in viewing every performance at *Le Théâtre des Horreurs*, where Yvonne is sadistically tortured on the rack and burned to reveal the name of her lover. Gogol views himself as the romantic hero, ready to take Yvonne away from the sordid life of the theater and keep her for his own as an object to worship. This too, forcibly indicates the disorder in the soul of the humanitarian Gogol.

The opening of the film, with the credits and cast printed on a glass window pane and the subsequent breaking of the glass by a human fist, sets up the expectation of violent action that is to come. The theme of physical violence is emphasized with the opening shot of a dummy hanging from the rafters. The camera then pans to a long shot of the sign *Le Théâtre des Horreurs*, with the face of a devil and his overly large eyes raised in stone under the lettering. As the camera dollies toward the face, there is a dissolve to a similar face worn by the ticket taker. Masks play on the theme of appearance and reality and find their paradigm in the Greek theater, not only changing the physiognomy but the voice of the actor as well, so that he could be heard in the open air. Yet there is a tradition in Eastern art incorporated into filmmaking which tends to minimize the distinction between appearance and reality. Bela Balazs, telling the story of the old Chinaman who painted such a beautiful picture that he walked into his own painting and never came back, concludes with the remark: "This was the Chinese belief: everything is what it seems, there is no difference between appearance and reality."[9] If one looks back upon the Guy Endore screen adapatation of Renard's *The Hands of Orlac,* the action that unfolds outside *Le Théâtre des Horreurs* is no less grotesque than what is performed within its walls, and Freund, its director, presents the theater as a microcosm of the drama that is to unfold in all its ghastliness. For if the hat-check girl in the theater can be made up to appear without a head, and in the context of where she works this costume does not seem strange, and in fact provides humor (a pun on all the "mindless" filmic hat-check girls), Professor Gogol can also make himself up in the part of the decapitated Rollo when he appears for his "performance" before Stephen Orlac. *Mad Love* becomes a convenient mirror to describe the tendency in fiction of reversing the images of the romance by reflecting a fictional world that is as ugly and absurd as the world of romance had been beautiful and coherent.[10] That is why the patrons at the theater can enjoy Yvonne's performance. Its *Grand Guignol* aesthetics of sadism have been turned into a beautiful and coherent narrative of evil husbands, women in distress, and romantic lovers who climb balconies to reach their beloved. But the reverse image of this might be seen in the true-to-life story the film unfolds: an impotent husband like Stephen, a lover like Gogol driven to madness and a heroine like Yvonne who attempts to use the professor's attraction for her to cure her spouse.

The viewer is introduced to Professor Gogol standing before the wax statue of Yvonne in a theater lobby. The intercutting of the statue with the real-life figure of Yvonne suggests a subjective state in which the statue is alive for the professor. In subsequent shots of the statue with other individuals who view it, also are inserted shots of the live actress to reinforce the theme: the professor's "mad love" infects other people, and Regan, the reporter (Ted Healy); Françoise, Gogol's housekeeper (Mary Beatty) and Yvonne herself see the transformation of the statue into a living being: Gogol *is* Pygmalion!

Yvonne's act parallels the insane jealousy of her lover, Gogol (rather than her husband, for this is the reverse mirror image). In the play within the film, Yvonne is tortured to death by her husband who wishes to discover the identity of her lover. When Yvonne is placed on the rack and screams in pain, there is a cut to the half-concealed masklike face of Gogol in the theater box, while the rest of the audience is either rapt in attention or, as in the case of some women, terrified. The cut to Gogol is repeated once again as Yvonne has a hot poker applied to her body, and Gogol lowers his eyes when in agony she cries out the name of her lover to her jealous husband. All the components of the play are inherent in the main drama: jealousy, love, lust and sadism; they foreshadow the attempted lust-murder at the film's conclusion. Gogol's psychosis, know as "algo-lagnia," is an abnormal activity where sexual pleasure results from the infliction or the experience of pain.

If there is a correlation between Gogol's unwholesome attraction to Yvonne and her act at *Le Théâtre des Horreurs,* there is an equally peculiar one between Stephen and the condemned criminal, Rollo (Edward Brophy). A friendly stranger on the train with whom Stephen shares his compartment eagerly announces to the pianist that an American criminal has stuck a knife in his father's back because of the murderer's involvement with a woman. When Stephen, after the operation on his hands, goes to his father's antique shop to request money, the latter antagonizes his son by maliciously suggesting that Stephen's wife "could supplement her earnings" through prostitution; Stephen almost kills his father with a knife in a fit of rage.

Five parallels are drawn between Rollo and Stephen. The first is on the train, the second when Stephen throws a fountain pen like a knife (as Rollo had done) at a bill collector who has come to remove the piano from the Orlac residence, and another, already mentioned, at the antique shop. On the second and third occasions, Stephen putting his hands up to his face to examine them in horror, unconsciously imitates Rollo's action who has performed the gesture with pride to show off his hands before his captors. The fourth parallel drawn between Rollo and Stephen is when Gogol, in disguise, attempts to drive Orlac insane by telling the pianist that his hands are those of the knife thrower now sitting before him. The fifth parallel occurs when Stephen saves his wife by throwing a knife at Gogol who is in a love-death embrace with Yvonne.

In a riveting scene toward the film's beginning, Gogol enters Yvonne's dressing room while she is listening to her husband give a piano recital on the radio. He is playing Chopin's *G Minor Ballade*. In close-ups of Gogol's face, the camera emphasizes his jealousy by dollying to him when Yvonnne innocently tells the doctor that she is married and is leaving the theater. The sound of Stephen's playing over the radio implies that the pianist is privy to the affair, making the audience sense a greater tension between Yvonne and Gogol. Stephen's gifted recital immediately brings to mind motifs in the film referring to hands: Gogol stresses his devotion by kissing Yvonne's several times; there is an obvious montage sequence of Orlac's hands in therapy after his train accident; Rollo, the knife thrower, examines his hands as does Stephen on many occasions; on the grand piano Stephen has a plaster cast of his hands with the legend, "Hands of Orlac," a nice narcissistic touch; Gogol, comforting a woman who professes to be poor, discovers, when he places his hand in hers, an expensive diamond ring that has been turned around so as not to be detected; Gogol disguises himself as Rollo and wears metal hands because he says his own have been taken from him and grafted to Stephen's. Again, in the conclusion, Gogol's hands are emphasized as he attempts to murder Yvonne by tying her braids of hair about her neck and strangling her.

Another prominent image is that of the guillotine and death by strangulation, or associated images dealing with the head. The attempted strangulation already mentioned at the film's conclusion parallels the opening scene of the manikin hanging from the rafters in *Le Théâtre des Horreurs*; there is Rollo who is to be guillotined, and a gruesome touch of the guillotine replica on Yvonne's anniversary cake which the actors of the theater have given her. This symbollically links Yvonne with the condemned Rollo and Gogol's psychological and physical experimentation on Stephen. Lastly, there is Gogol disguised as Rollo with a leather and metal brace supposedly holding his severed head grafted onto his neck after his execution.

As Gogol walks out from the alleyway of the theater, a man carries away the wax figure of Yvonne which is to be melted down. Gogol buys the statue, associating himself with Pygmalion and the statue with Galatea. The story told by Ovid has some parallels in *Mad Love*. Pygmalion is a gifted sculptor and a woman hater who resolves never to marry because his art is enough for him. In *Mad Love* Gogol is the gifted surgeon and subconsciously a woman hater who can only experience love when he is causing pain. He tells Yvonne: "Is there no room in your heart, even pity for a man who has never known the love of a woman but has worshiped you since the first day he has walked by that absurd little theater." This suggests Pygmalion's and Gogol's lack of association with and perhaps fear of the opposite sex. His mythological counterpart also dresses the statue he has made in rich clothes and brings her gifts of little birds and flowers.[11] This is hinted at in *Mad Love*. In the room with Yvonne's statue Gogol keeps a white cockatoo and a Venus Fly Trap fed by Françoise, the housekeeper, who complains that the negligees Gogol buys for the wax figure cost more than a month's wages. Added to this is his obsessional behavior about death that is enhanced by some of the dialogue. Françoise says over the telephone: "The professor isn't here. If you want to know he is visiting Madame Guillotine. He never misses one of those head choppings." At another time, while dressing the statue and feeding the Venus Fly Trap, she remarks that the professor "likes dead things." Likewise Gogol feeds his morbid love for Yvonne on late romantic poetry. He quotes from two of Elizabeth Browning's *Sonnets from the Portuguese* which prefigure his attempted murder of Yvonne, substituting the love embrace in the poems for necrophilic desires he has sublimated. He first recites a couple of lines from "Sonnet 7": "The face of all the world is changed, I think, / Since first I heard the footsteps of thy soul." He stops at this point; however the sonnet goes on with the speaker rescued from thoughts of death by love: "Move still, oh, still, beside me, as they stole / Betwixt me and the dreadful outer brink / Of obvious death, where I, who thought to sink / Was caught up into love, and taught the whole / Of a new rhythm." Once Yvonne rejects Gogol, he transfers these thoughts of death from himself to her. Immediately following this reading from "Sonnet 7" he recites two lines from "Sonnet 1": "Guess now who holds thee?—'Death', I said, but there / The silver answer rang . . . . "Not Death, but Love." Unfortunately Gogol's unrequited love turns to madness and he becomes the "death" that holds Yvonne in his grasp. The lines which come before these in the sonnet are violent in their sadistic imagery and suggest the manner in which the doctor plans to kill his unfaithful love: "a mystic shape did move / Behind me, and drew me backward by the hair / And a voice said in mastery while I strove . . . " This connection between love and death is also seen in his love for children and executions, which parallels the real-life situation of George Augustus Selwyn (1719–91) whose morbid attraction for sights of suffering and a pronounced affection for children are considered the prototypical case study of the algolagnic. "With . . . a kind heart, and a passionate fondness for children, he united a morbid interest in . . . witnessing criminal executions . . . . All the details of crime . . . were to Selwyn matters of the deepest and most extraordinary interest . . . and . . . afforded him a painful and unaccountable pleasure."[12]

There is a good expressionistic dream sequence in the film inspired by the one quoted earlier in Renard's novel in which Rosine sees her husband's "dream." The sequence in the film suggests the conflict Yvonne is experiencing by using Gogol's love for her to save her husband. The symbols of her struggle are present: the serenity of Stephen's erect figure superimposed over Yvonne as she sleeps (as though they were in bed together) gives place to views of sky and countryside with the piano played by Stephen's disembodied hands suggesting a type of castration. Depite the tranquility, the hands themselves disappear and eventually the tracks and onrushing train take on more ominous tones especially since the tracks replace the keys. Finally the face of Gogol is superimposed within the circular shape of the train wheels, suggesting Gogol's obsession with sexual domination of Yvonne; the speeding train serves as a phallic symbol of Gogol's desires.

Gogol's *doppelganger* is reflected in a mirror over the sink in the scrub room near the operating theater, where he conceives the idea to graft Rollo's hands onto Orlac's body. For a moment his face lights up with a maniacal smile, and he proclaims to his assistant, Dr. Wong (Keye Luke), that the operation is not impossible, for Napoleon said the word "impossible" was not French. After suddenly leaving the scene of an operation on a little girl, he returns to the scrubbing room and there in three different mirrors he meets with his double who presses him to kill Stephen's father, have the son blamed, and Stephen put away in an asylum so that he, Gogol, might be able to possess Yvonne. At this point the mirror image of the insane Gogol merges into his own persona.

Orlac, who can no longer play the piano with the hands he has, says to Yvonne: "Wonderful invention, the phonograph, keeps a man alive long after he's dead." The audience recognizes a grim irony: if the phonograph keeps a man's work alive after death, Rollo's hands and personality seem to have been kept alive through the transplant. Gogol gives the distraught Orlac little comfort with his pseudo-Freudian psychotherapy, saying: "After the shock of your accident came a second shock; your hands were altered by my knife. You could no longer play . . . your disturbed mind was ready for any phobia." He adds, "Your case is one of arrested wish fulfillment. It festered deep in your subconscious. If you could bring that forgotten memory . . . into consciousness, you would be cured instantly." When Dr. Wong asks Gogol if Orlac was told the truth about his operation, the professor replies: "I told him a lot of nonsense I don't believe myself. I wouldn't dare tell him those were the hands of a murderer. That would probably drive him [in a whisper] to commit murder himself." The dialogue, while contributing to the film's plot, ridicules the then increasing emphasis in American movies on Freudian analysis.[13]

Gogol pleads with Yvonne: "I a poor peasant have conquered science, why can't I conquer love? Don't you understand, you must be mine. You are not his." But Yvonne replies, "Liar, hypocrite. You disgust me." They are words that will come back to him before he attempts to strangle her. The fact, however, that Yvonne is a faithful wife is mitigated somewhat by her using Gogol's love to persuade him to operate on her husband. Of the three main characters in *Mad Love*, Gogol is not only the most prominent and forceful figure but the one who, in the final analysis, is the most sympathetic. His love, however perverted, is unfulfilled and drives him insane; Stephen, who seems to grow annoyingly neurotic, still has the love of his wife, but not of the audience. Gogol remains noble in his splendid isolation, but Stephen is pitiful in his narcissism. Two forces are working in the same direction: Gogol is being driven insane by love and Stephen is being driven insane through self-love, his growing breakdown due to his self-pity over the loss of his artistic talents.

The concluding reel and a half is beautifully handled to create suspense through a dramatic use of space and cutting. The scene opens with a shot of Gogol entering the door of his house, dressed in a grotesque costume of metal hands and a neck brace, laughing in a maniacal way. As this is taking place, Yvonne in Gogol's living room knocks over the wax statue of herself and Gogol's bird flutters about the room. The viewer next sees the broken statue and hears Gogol's laughter followed by a shot of Yvonne in consternation. The opening shots establish the two characters who must eventually meet and create the dramatic tension of the scene; however, Freund is careful to make sure that this happens only by degrees. The shots of Yvonne and the statue suggest a causal connection which now comes

to fruition when Yvonne becomes the "statue" to deceive Gogol. The bird's
piercing cries become an extension of the heroine's frenzy, and they
foreshadow the doctor's discovery of Yvonne as a flesh-and-blood "Galatea." Gogol in delight at the sight of what he believes is Yvonne's likeness
says to the "statue":"Triumph Galatea, triumph!" In the following subjective shot, the camera/Gogol begins to dolly in on the distressed Yvonne as
in voice-over he continues: "He thinks he murdered his father when it's I
who killed him!" At this point the camera has reached a close-up of the
terrfied Yvonne. Gogol's maniacal gaiety is counterpointed to the terror
on Yvonne's face in what Hugo Munsterberg called "aesthetic emotion."[14]
The effect of seeing one thing with our eyes and hearing another thing
with our ears becomes much more threatening than it would otherwise be
with synchronous sound and image. Gogol tells his "statue" that the real
Yvonne will now come to see him: "flesh and blood but not wax like
you . . . and he [Stephen] shall be shut up in the house where they keep
the mad. I, Gogol, will do that. He will be shut up when it is I who am
mad. But nobody knows that except you and me." Yvonne is in a state of
collapse, and Gogol laughing and gesticulating wildly moves to an organ
in the background as his white cockatoo flies toward him.

There is a quick fade to the police station where Stephen is being held
for the murder of his father. The discovery that the fingerprints on the
knives are those of Rollo, however, cause Stephen to explain the story of
his transplant, and the police decide to go to Professor Gogol's house.
These slowly paced scenes involving the police and Stephen retard the
main action and constitute three separate locations. (1) at headquarters, (2)
in the police car and (3) before Gogol's house. The scenes become
increasingly shorter to bring the main sequence to a climax.

When the main sequence resumes, more emphasis is given to the scene
by Yvonne moving toward Gogol while the bird brushes past her face.
Gogol turns around from the organ saying: "There's blood on your cheek,
Galatea. So it seems that wax can bleed." Yvone screams and Gogol grabs
her violently: "Galatea! I am Pygmalion! You were wax but you came to
life in my arms." As soon as Yvonne says, "Let me go!" the ancient myth
becomes a reality to Gogol. He responds in wonder: "You speak to me,
my love. I have made you live, Galatea. Give me your lips!" She repeats
her injunction to let her go, but Gogol, still uncomprehending, believes
Yvonne to be the wax statue turned to flesh: "Why are you afraid of me, I
love you, I love you. You came to life [he fondles her hands] for me. Don't
you know me, Galatea?" The distraught Yvonne pleads to be released with
a promise to come back. Gogol vehemently says: "You are lying. You
won't come back. You hate me. You despise me." Yvonne's voice is heard

over this as Gogol recalls her previous words: "Liar, hypocrite! You disgust me!" When Gogol protests his lover to her, he hears in his mind "Each man kills the thing he loves," and repeats it to himself. The phrase from Oscar Wilde's poem "The Ballad of Reading Goal" (1898) foreshadows Gogol's attempted murder of Yvonne as did Elizabeth Browning's poems earlier: "Yet each man kills the thing he loves, / By each let this be heard, / Some do it with a bitter look, / Some with a flattering word. / The coward does it with a kiss, / The brave man with a sword!"

The blocking of the shots is quite effective in emphasizing the power of Gogol over the heroine, even where Yvonne takes most of the screen space and lighting. At this point the police are outside the house where the wax figure has been thrown by Yvonne. Gogol has pinned Yvonne close to the wall, and an insane look appears on his face. He starts to strangle Yvonne, but she faints. The police now in the house rush up the stairs while Gogol places Yvonne on a couch and bending over her ties her hair about her neck, quoting Robert Browning's "Porphyria's Lover": "And so I found / a thing to do, and all her hair / In one long string I wound / three times her little throat around." There is a shot of Gogol tying Yvonne's hair about her neck as pounding on the door is heard from without. Gogol continues: "and strangled her . . . no pain feels she." On the other side of the door Stephen starts prying open the panel within the door. There is a shot of Gogol, who continues reciting the Browning poem as he strangles Yvonne with her own hair: "I am quite sure she feels no pain," with more cutting between Gogol, Yvonne, Stephen and the police. Stephen, throwing a knife through the panel, determinedly tells the officers to get out of his way. There is a front view of Gogol as the knife goes into his back, a cut to the police opening the door, a rear-view shot of Gogol and then another shot of him falling; the men rush in and Stephen greets his wife, a shot of the dying Gogol with the voice-over of Yvonne and Stephen uttering each other's names followed by a two-shot of Stephen and Yvonne. Gogol falls over slowly and then a fade to black with music from Brahms's *Symphony No. 1*.

Freund has left nothing out in his reading of Browning's "Porphyria's Lover," which the mad Gogol quotes to Yvonne. The poet writes: "As a shut bud that holds a bee / I warily oped her lids." In the poem the madman has just strangled the woman he loves, but the simile that Browning presents parallels Freund's showing the Venus Fly Trap feeding on insects as Gogol watches with curious interest. By extension Gogol is the Venus plant (symbolic of the love-death interest he has in Yvonne) and Yvonne the fly, just as in the poem the lover is the bud which has trapped the bee (Porphyria) in its death embrace. The poem is an excursion into abnormal psychology; the monologue, originally published under the title *Madhouse Cells*, might have given the scriptwriters an idea for the title of the film.[15]

This final sequence is longer due to the necessity of bringing the parallel actions together. At first the crosscutting between the police and Stephen on one hand and Gogol and Yvonne on the other is minimal. It soon quickens, however, until there is a rapid alternation of shots between the two actions to increase the suspense at the point when Gogol strangles Yvonne as the police attempt to break in. The final bit of dialogue between husband and wife is ironic in its juxtaposition of sound and picture; while Stephen and Yvonne are in an off-screen love-embrace, the camera focuses on Gogol in his death throes. Surely this is a pathetic shot, and the impact of viewer sympathy rests neither with Yvonne nor Stephen but with Gogol.

If Yvonne is not the most sympathetic or enobling character, she remains one of the many persecuted women in the gothic film. This convention in literature was "refurbished in the eighteenth century by Richardson with his celebrated heroine Clarissa Harlow," which was a more refined depiction of de Sade's sexual perversity. Gothic romances of the late eighteenth and early nineteenth centuries contain numerous examples of this convention in the English language. Antonia in *The Monk,* "seduced by the perverted monk Ambrosio (who turns out to be her brother) . . . awakes . . . in a fearful crypt among decayed corpses . . . is made the object of a loathsome love among these emblems of death, and is finally stabbed." Ann Radcliffe's heroines are also emblems of the persecuted woman: Marchesa di Mazzini in the *Sicilian Romance* (1790) is imprisoned by her evil husband in a horrifying dungeon; Emily de Saint-Aubert is a virtuous woman detained against her will in the sinister Castle of Udolpho. The same fate holds true for Adeline in *The Romance of the Forest* (1791) and for Ellena in *The Italian, or the Confessional of the Black Penitents* (1791). In Miss Wilkinson's *The Priory of St. Clair* (1811), Julietta is forced into a convent, is drugged and conveyed to the sinister gothic castle of the Count of Valve and comes to life only to be slain on the high altar. She avenges herself after death by haunting the Count.[16] And of course there is Beatrice in Shelly's drama, *The Cenci* (1819), who is sexually molested by her father. Although the women in the horror films do not experience the degradation that the heroines of Romantic literature do because of the Production Code, much is implied rather than stated by the somnambulistic stance they are made to take. Only in a film like Rouben Mamoulian's *Dr. Jekyll and Mr. Hyde*, or *Le Théâtre des Horreurs* in *Mad Love* do the women become victims of a lust-murder. Yet they too submit, much like their sleepwalking sisters in many films already discussed. Parker Tyler brings this out when he says that "the somnambule's myth essentially signifies the ritual readying of woman for sex by depriving her of her conscious powers through hypnotism."[17] For Tyler the defenseless somnambule appears as an object of desire to the subconscious minds of the male audience, for in becoming hypnotized she is rendered utterly passive and obedient.

Yvonne in *Mad Love* is what might be termed in Tyler's language the "canary" type, that is, the agitated woman in fear of her virtue. But Tyler adds: "the more active a frail woman is, *the more effectively she displays her inviting fragility.*"[18] The final part of the sentence has been emphasized because Yvonne, more than most heroines of the horror film in the thirties, might be considered more active: she is a sexually desirable woman appearing in sado-masochistic acts at the theater. She uses Gogol's desire for her to save Stephen; she rushes to Gogol's house at night in a negligee with the intention of persuading Gogol to help her husband once more. Yet toward the close of the film, Yvonne is struggling for her life and Stephen, with the grafted hands of a convicted murderer, is able to save her. It is not through the pianist's skill then, that Yvonne is saved. When they finally embrace it is because the villain-hero's death has left them free to perform this act. It is significant that after his accident Stephen awkwardly and unsuccessfully attempts to embrace Yvonne while both his hands are bandaged; the two can only envy lovers in a passing boat. Their love-embrace at the film's conclusion now becomes a prelude to their own active life.

The final film to be analyzed deals with the *femme fatale* as vampire. This vampire not only combines the destructiveness of the woman who can ruin her victim's physical well-being by luring him into a life of dissipation, that is, the "vamp" as portrayed in the silent films: the Theda Baras, the Lyla de Puttis, and the Pola Negris, but also the "vampire" who after killing the body has the power to damn the soul. Gloria Holden's Countess Zeleska in *Dracula's Daughter* is a composite of Keats's "La Belle Dame sans Merci," Kipling's "The Vampire" and LeFanu's *Carmilla.* She is part "vamp" and part "vampire."

NOTES

1. Horace Walpole, *The Letters of Horace Walpole*, Vol. X, ed. by Mrs. Paget Toynbee (Oxford: Oxford Press, 1904), pp. 216–17.
2. Johann Friedrich von Schiller, *The Ghost-Seer or the Apparitionist*, in *Gothic Tales of Terror,* Vol.2, edited by Peter Haining (Baltimore, Maryland: Penguin Books, Inc., 1972), p. 56.

3. Maurice Renard, *The Hands of Orlac,* trans. and adapted by Florence Crew-Jones (New York: E. P. Dutton and Co., Inc., 1929), p. 21.

4. Renard, pp. 70–73, 81–82.

5. Renard, p. 191.

6. Renard, pp.260–61.

7. Renard, pp. 281–85.

8. Renard, pp. 290–93, 337.

9. Bela Balazs, *Theory of Film,* trans. by Edith Bone (New York: Dover Publications, 1970), p. 191. For Western mentality the movie screen, according to psychoanalyst J. B. Pontalis, is not only a surface for projection but a surface for protection, a screening and a screening-off. See Dennis Giles in "Conditions of Pleasure in Horror Cinema," in *Planks of Reason,* edited by Barry Keith Grant (Metuchen, N.J.: Scarecrow Press, Inc., 1984), p. 39.

10. See Robert Scholes and Robert Kellogg, *The Nature of Narrative* (New York: Oxford University Press, 1968), p. 153.

11. Edith Hamilton, *Mythology* (New York: Mentor Books, 1961), pp. 108–10.

12. J. H. Jesse, *George Selwyn and His Contemporaries* (Bentley Publishing Co., 1843), pp. 4–5.

13. In *Dracula's Daughter*, the psychoanalyst, Dr. Garth, is a smug, priggish man responsible for giving the Countess unsound medical advice, and indirectly causing the death of a patient under the vampire's spell when through hypnotism, he tries to elicit information from her. See also after World War II: *Lady in the Dark, Spellbound, The Dark Mirror, Possessed* and in the fifties *Harvey.*

14. Hugo Munsterberg, *The Film: A Psychological Study* (New York: Dover Publications, 1970), pp. 57 and ff.

15. Park Honan, *Browning's Characters: A Study in Poetic Technique* (New Haven: Yale University Press, 1962), pp. 30–31.

16. Mario Praz, *The Romantic Agony*, translated by Angus Davidson (New York: Oxford University Press, 1970), pp. 95, 111, and 113.

17. Parker Tyler, *The Hollywood Hallucination* (New York: Simon and Schuster 1970), pp. 75–76.

18. Tyler, p. 77.

CHAPTER 11

Dracula's Daughter: Vampirism as Psychosis

You must come with me, loving me to death; or else hate me, and still come with me and hating me through death and after.
—J. Sheridan LeFanu, *Carmilla*

While this book on horror films contains movies that deal with the *homme fatal* as first observed in *Dracula*, the notion of a fatal woman, particularly as vampire, is relatively modern to Western literature and continued into the twentieth century with a more urbane connotation of one who "sets out to charm or captivate men . . . by an unscrupulous use of sexual attractiveness."[1] This more modern definition comprises part of the character played by Gloria Holden in Lambert Hillyer's *Dracula's Daughter* (1936); the other half is the supernatural creature that subsists on the blood of the living.

In literature the traditional vampire was essentially a male figure, and only in the second half of the nineteenth century did the vampire become a woman, but there was no established type the way there is of the Byronic hero.[2] The several pieces from literature discussed here by no means exhaust the fictional output dealing with the fatal woman.

A picture of the *femme fatale* may be seen in Coleridge's uncompleted poem, "Christabel"(1797–1801). Geraldine, a malign spirit who is as pale as death, has Christabel's father, Sir Leoline, in her spell with her serpentlike eyes. Not only is Geraldine associated with the serpent in the archetypical Biblical story of Adam's temptation, but she is connected with the Byronic hero in the description of her eyes, which express mystery and torment, "full of wonder and full of grief," with a hint of the modern vamp as "she rolled her large bright eyes divine." In Keats's poem entitled "Lamia" (1819), a serpent woman persuades Apollo to transform her back into a woman so she can marry a young man of Corinth. At the wedding feast, his eyes are opened by his instructor and he dies while Lamia vanishes. The most unusual story of such a serpent woman, however, is to be found in Stoker's novel *The Lair of the White Worm* (1911). In it Lady Arabella March, a "vamp" in the "flapper" sense of the word and a serpent in mortal guise, waits for the hero, Edgar Caswall, to visit her: "She tore off her clothes, with feverish fingers, and in full enjoyment of her natural freedom, stretched her slim figure in animal delight. Then she lay down on the sofa—to await her victim! Edgar Caswall's life blood would more than satisfy her for some time to come."[3]

Keats's "La Belle Dame sans Merci" (1819) presents the fatal woman as vampire in a medieval setting. A knight falls prey to the charms of a woman who causes him to dream of a parade of her "death-pale" lovers uttering a "horrid warning" from mouths that "gaped wide." The female vampire in *Varney the Vampire* (1847) is a minor character not as fully elaborated upon as the one in *Carmilla* or the sensual creatures in *Dracula*. Prest paints his female vampires in such broad terms that much of the horrific element is lost. When his female vampire attacks a sixteen-year-old girl, Prest is reluctant to portray the actual event, which is audially described by the girl's mother as "a strange sucking sound as if an animal was drinking with labour and difficulty."[4] LeFanu's *Carmilla* (1871) is perhaps the best female vampire story; it is as sophisticated as *Varney the Vampire* is crude. The novella is rich in sensuality and decadence: the heroine, Laura, properly demure, the vampire, Carmilla, appropriately voluptuous. The story is narrated in the first person by the heroine, to whom the vampire speaks in explicitly amorous tones: "she would press me more closely in her trembling embrace, . . . breathing so fast that her dress rose and fell with the tumultuous respiration. It was like the ardour of a lover; . . . her hot lips travelled along my cheek in kisses."[5] Although Stoker's novel *The Lady of the Shroud* (1909) has a contrived rationalistic explanation for its female vampire, like Todd Browning's *Mark of the Vampire*, it is part of the tradition of the *femme fatale*. The vamp tells her lover, Rupert Sent Leger, "Some [say] . . . that I am one of those unhappy Un-dead whom men call Vampires—who live on the blood of the living, and bring eternal damnation as well as death with the poison of their dreadful kisses."[6] She, always seen in a shroud and sleeping in a coffin, has a lover who is enamored of her whether she be dead or alive; in fact, he is half in love with the idea of possessing the dead. She in turn gives him a fragment of her shroud as a love token. The novel indulges heavily in necrophilia and the seduction of an all-too-willing young man.

Lambert Hillyer's female vampire in *Dracula's Daughter*, however, is more sympathetic and realistic than these fatal women of Romantic and Victorian literature and begins where *Dracula* ended five years earlier, making use of the set design of Whale's *Frankenstein*. The film credits state the script was based on Bram Stoker's "Dracula's Guest," and suggested by Oliver Jeffries with screenplay and story credited to Garrett Fort. Stoker's short story originally had been a part of *Dracula* but had to be deleted because the publishers wished to make it a financial success.[7] Yet the credit given Bram Stoker in the opening film titles might just as well have said "inspired by a story of Bram Stoker" instead of "based," which suggests a much closer adherence to the original.

John L. Balderston (coauthor of the play *Dracula* and scriptwriter of the film *The Mummy*) was first asked to write a treatment for *Dracula's Daughter* which he loaded with gruesome details saying: "Why should Cecil B. DeMille have a monopoly on the great box office values of torture and cruelty . . . . I want to see her [Dracula's daughter] loathsome deaf mute servants carry into her boudoir savage-looking whips, chains, straps, etc. and hear the cries of the tortured victims."[8] The treatment seemed quite brutal and was turned down by Universal, but according to Michael Brunas it was closer to Stoker's story. Balderston's treatment opens with the final scene from *Dracula*. Van Helsing puts a stake through Dracula's heart but realizes his work is not finished and goes to Transylvania to destroy the wives of Dracula. He misses, however, the tomb of Dracula's daughter, and she in turn goes to London, under the name of Countess Szkekeley, enthralling a young aristocrat, Edward "Ned" Wadhurst, who falls under her spell. Both Van Helsing and Dr. Seward, together with the young man's friends, confront the vampire, and Ned, nearly a vampire himself, drives the stake through her heart.[9] The final script by Garrett Fort, however, bore little resemblance to Balderston's treatment or the original short story. There is a section in the short story where the protagonist [Jonathan Harker, it is presumed] comes across the mausoleum of Countess Dolingen of Gratz in a storm. The door of the mausoleum is unlocked so the protagonist walks in for protection. The lightning reveals the inside of the tomb:

> I saw . . . a beautiful woman with rounded cheeks and red lips, seemingly sleeping on a bier. As the thunder broke overhead I was grasped as by the hand of a giant and hurled out into the storm . . . . Just then there came another blinding flash, which seemed to strike the iron stake that surmounted the tomb and to pour through the earth . . . as in a burst of flame.

The dead woman rose for a moment of agony, while she was lapped in the flame, and her bitter scream of pain was drowned in the thundercrash.

This is all that directly deals with Harker's encounter with the vampire Countess. In the short story he is protected from other vampires ("a vague white, moving mass, as if all the graves around me had sent out the phantoms of their sheeted-dead,")[10] by Dracula in both the form of a physical force ("hand of a giant") and a wolf.

Dracula had kept the delicate balance between the natural and supernatural, and *Dracula's Daughter* does much the same, but with a specific difference: the discrepancies are not strictly between objectifiable personifications of good (human love and the science of medicine) and evil (satanic love and the supernatural), but between the inner and outer consciousness of the antagonist, Countess Zeleska (Gloria Holden) and the science of psychoanalysis. Yet the director, in juxtaposing these polarities, creates a tension equal to that of *Dracula*. Although the Countess is possessed by the curse of the Draculas, she believes that assistance from Dr. Jeffrey Garth (Otto Kruger) will transform her to normalcy. Zeleska becomes a tragic heroine in the modern sense, realizing the evil influence over her, appealing for help and being unable to obtain it. The only solution for her mental anguish is either to accept the fact of what she is and live with it or die. She chooses to live with her affliction, and because of her choice she must die, for the outcome of the film is preordained to fit 1930s conventions. The paradox presented is basic to the tragic form. Tragedy's intense occupation is with evil in the universe, but it also discovers a principle of goodness that coexists with the evil. This same principle is embodied in Countess Zeleska.

The film's dialogue is similar to *Dracula*'s, since both screenplays were written by Fort, and while some of it is hackneyed or sententious, some of the dialogue is also quite good, having a "sacramental" tone about it, especially in the sequence where the Countess exorcises the body of her father, and an antiphonal quality in the exchanges between the Countess and her servant, Sandor (Irving Pichel).

For the most part the film eschews the gothic and uses Carfax Abbey and Castle Dracula respectively as a framing device for the deaths of the Count and his daughter, thrusting its modernity upon the viewer to press home the anomaly of the vampire with a neurosis that can be cured. Essentially the action is little different from *Dracula*, but the motif has changed. Its superficial stance at psychoanalysis is meant to reinforce the reality of the supernatural. The action, however, basically remains the same: the Countess's servant is analogous to Renfield in his asking for eternal life; Van Helsing must persuade Dr. Seward and John of the vampire's existence the way he must persuade Sir Humphrey and Garth in *Dracula's Daughter*; John becomes jealous of the Count's attentions to Mina in *Dracula* as Janet becomes of Garth's attentions to the Countess in *Dracula's Daughter*; the corpse of the man that the Countess has drained of blood in *Dracula's Daughter* is shown in the operating theater at the same camera angle as Lucy's body in *Dracula*, and the eventual union of the Count with Mina at Carfax Abbey is parallel to that of the Countess with Jeffrey at her Carpathian castle. Hillyer's film also contains less comic relief than *Dracula* because its screenplay is not a stage derivative whose conventions required humorous interludes but attempts, by psychoanalytical trappings, to add greater depth of character to the Countess.[11]

Psychosis is part of the film's romanticism, for in presenting a tortured villain-hero who desires to be so much like other humans, Zeleska echoes the words of Frankenstein's monster: "I was wretched, helpless and alone. Many times I considered Satan as a fitter emblem of my condition."[12] Goethe makes an interesting observation on romantic literature by connecting it with the "morbid and sickly," even "pathological."[13] Carlos Clarens has said that "to Dreyer, vampirism is a sickness of the soul."[14] For Lambert Hillyer one might say that vampirism becomes a sign of contemporary *angst*. The veneer of psychoanalysis only brings out the inherent romanticism of a tragic situation.

The Countess and Garth represent two distinct ideologies: she at the outset is the embodiment of Romantic melancholy, filled with inhibitions, tormented by the past and fearful of the present; Garth, the embodiment of the scientific mind, is the symbol of the integrating force. He speaks for the control of impulse and the ordering of the emotions as the mark of growth. Hillyer's figures nevertheless are not ideational, that is, they are not a sounding board for a thesis but are characterizational in that their personalities are developed for their own sake.

If David Manners and Helen Chandler in *Dracula* represent the typical romantic couple, she under the influence of the Count, and slightly aloof, he her humble servant, in *Dracula's Daughter*, Janet Blake (Marguerite Churchill) and Garth represent a comradeship that disregards the conventional roles of lover and mistress. Yet both are not particularly sympathetic characters. But where the romantic leads in the Browning film are trapped as if by fate, those in Hillyer's film throughout most of the narrative remain coolly untouched and, on a minor level, their constant battles are amusing.

It is little wonder that the countess is the real tragic heroine. She is like a goddess among very foolish mortals. The archetype of the tragic hero, according to Nietzsche is the god Dionysus. He is presented as an erring, striving, suffering individual—a god experiencing in himself the anguish of individuation,[15] and for this reason too, *Dracula's Daughter* is a progression in the development of the vampire on film. *Dracula* places the nightmare in an existing reality even though the figure of the vampire remains shrouded in mystery, while Browning's *Mark of the Vampire* denies the existence of the reality described in *Dracula*. *Dracula's Daughter*, on the other hand, toys with the idea that although vampires do exist, it is a sickness of the soul which can be cured, and in so doing opens up the figure of the vampire as tragic hero.

To begin with, it must be stated that there is no one formula to which all tragedies conform. Aristotle based his definition of tragedy on the works of the Greek dramatists, but over three thousand years have intervened since his statement that tragedy is the "imitation of an action that is serious and also, as having magnitude . . . with incidents arousing pity and fear wherewith to accomplish its catharsis of such emotions." New types of serious plots with unhappy endings have been developed which Aristotle could not foresee.[16] During the Middle Ages, tragedy was conceived simply as the story of an eminent person who, deservedly or not, is brought from prosperity to wretchedness by an unpredictable turn of Fortune's wheel. By the end of the nineteenth century and on into the twentieth, plays like Arthur Miller's *Death of a Salesman* were considered tragedies; Willy Loman, an ordinary salesman, belongs to the "aristocracy of passionate souls" of tragic temperament. He has misjudged reality and his error destroys him.[17]

The above definitions will be used to analyze *Dracula's Daughter* as a modern "middle" tragedy. To call the film high tragedy would be to overestimate the Countess's sense of values and to overlook her failure to achieve any true understanding of herself and of reality. The dialogue does not contain a sufficient indication of absolute striving for tragic effect, although this type of language in the horror film is uncalled for. In the statements just presented above there is a similarity. The eminent person involved in the medieval definition can be compared to the Aristotelian definition where "magnitude" is the constituent part of the genre, while the individual brought from prosperity to wretchedness is similar to the concept of *hamartia* (tragic flaw). This term is closely allied with two others, *hubris* and *catharsis*, and it might be useful to explain these three in relation to *Dracula's Daughter* as essential ingredients for tragedy.

The misfortunes of tragedy do not simply happen nor are they sent; they proceed mainly from human actions producing exceptional calamity and frequently ending in the death of the tragic hero. Therefore, to turn to the center of the tragedy, one must turn to the character from where the action issues. It is there that the major difficulty lies. For Aristotle the tragic *catharsis* is to evoke pity and fear, and thus purge such emotions from the spectator. The reason for this is that tragedy is a social art form and reconciliation must take place within the audience and not within the actors. Countess Zeleska's death may serve to affirm the feeling of moral order (especially for men like Garth, Von Helsing[18] and the police inspector) in a purposeful universe upon which tragic reconciliation depends. In spite of the fate of the tragic heroine, society, at the end of tragedy must undergo, as Irving Ribner maintains, [19] a symbolic rebirth: there is always a Garth and a Janet Blake to begin life with a renewed hope in the future, and the viewer participates in this. This sense of final reconciliation is perhaps what Aristotle meant by *catharsis*. But if pity and fear are to be evoked through the Countess's tragic flaw stemming from ambition (she wishes to make Garth her lover) and overconfidence (through psychoanalysis she might lift the curse of Dracula) known as *hubris*, it is then necessary to illustrate how, in the tragic heroine's breaking of moral law, pity or sympathy can still be elicited.

Although the Countess retains some token of our admiration and sympathy, as will be shown, she thoroughly deserves her destruction. From the very beginning signs are given that the Countess possesses a great nobility: she performs the burial rites for her father so that his soul is at rest; she attempts to free herself from the curse of vampirism; she reluctantly is forced to seek human blood, begs help from a psychoanalyst when she no longer is able to overcome her drives and continues to seek his aid after her first attempt to follow his instructions has failed. From this point on Lambert Hillyer had the task of trying to keep contradictory currents moving simultaneously, that is, the events portraying the Countess's growing deceit and the tide of our mounting sympathy. This is even more difficult especially since Dr. Garth is not only a passive protagonist, but an unsympathetic one at that. There is an opposition of persistent forces that characterize a tragic event thus producing a strong tension. The murders of two gentlemen and Lili (Nan Grey), a destitute girl, by Zeleska become more intense in portrayal, but so does the audience's sympathy for the vampire; the attacks are followed almost immediately by scenes of suffering and self-torture on the part of the Countess. She knows what she is doing, yet she does not understand the two forces working upon her from the outside: the curse of the Draculas and Dr. Garth's inciting and confusing power which causes her to fall in love with him. Countess Zeleska is the typical tragic heroine, a paradox and mystery. She is not the plaything of fate but is not entirely free. The essence of her nature is brought out by suffering (the Countess tells Garth: "I need you to save my soul.")". The principle source of suffering is her sense of consciousness, both her guilt and guiltlessness. A tragic heroine, like the Countess, is placed in a universe of irreconcilables, acting in a situation where she is both innocent and guilty and, sensitive to her condition, suffers. Now if the catharsis is to be complete, the viewer must be made to feel that Zeleska is being killed in a just cause, and that her state of mind and the circumstances of her death are such as befit a woman who, for all her crimes, has not altogether lost our pity. The action of this film is disciplinary, then, insofar as the protagonists indirectly bring about the Countess's death not only for punitive reasons, but also for the sake of the woman herself. The conclusion brings relief that the conflict has played itself out. Zeleska realizes that it had to be. Garth tells her that it is "too late for experiments." She simply replies that she believes he is correct in his diagnosis.[20] With this portrait of the tragic heroine, an analysis of the picture is now in order to illustrate the theories thus offered.

The first eight minutes of the film are a recapitulation of the proceedings that took place in Browning's 1931 *Dracula*. There is a theory for the repetition of events in *Dracula's Daughter* that is found in *Dracula*. Taylor Stoehr, writing about the gothic novel and its structure, states

> repetition produces . . . an ambivalence toward history: events repeat themselves in succeeding generations, thus undercutting ideas of duration, sequence, temporal cause and effect. The typical formula is the family curse, which is worked out over long periods of time as if in a single moment. Theoretically the novel could continue forever repeating this moment; in fact, the family usually dies out.[21]

The section quoted is particularly apt to *Dracula's Daughter*. Hollywood usually never allows the family simply to die out. Dracula and his initiates, as well as the Frankenstein offspring, have died and risen countless times, although a film with a Countess Dracula does not reappear as a distinct title until Peter Sasdy's *Countess Dracula* (1972).[22]

Primarily, *Dracula's Daughter* is interesting for its concepts, however banal they might seem to modern audiences, rather than its visual aspect, but the important sustained visual sections will be analyzed; they include the cremation of Count Dracula, the Countess's attack on a man, her attack on the girl who models for her and the final sequence in Transylvania.

The opening, with the police descending the stone staircase (the tower set from Whale's *Frankenstein*), starts with the music of a cello followed by a second cello or perhaps a viola, creating a singularly eerie effect. The police, who are comic foils throughout, find Renfield's body and hear Professor Von Helsing destroy Dracula. After the constable has examined the Count's body, he asks the professor, when did Dracula die? The professor solemnly replies that it was about 500 years ago. This first sequence, which has taken place in Carfax Abbey, is a partial recapitulation of the 1931 film, just as *The Bride of Frankenstein* (1935) opens with scenes from the 1931 *Frankenstein*. Its tone mixes humor with the ghastly business of death by the stake.

Sir Basil Humphrey (Gilbert Emery), commissioner of Scotland Yard, remains a skeptic as does Jeffrey Garth, the psychologist whom Von Helsing (Edward Van Sloan) calls upon as a defense attorney. Part of the problem in many of these films is to convince the man of science about the supernatural. A catechistical format is used here to familiarize the viewer with past events so that this scene in the commissioner's office is a further recapitulation on a verbal level of the Browning film.

The first appearance of Countess Zeleska is done quite well. A policeman in a jailhouse walks to the room where the bodies of Dracula and Renfield are being kept. He hears an off-screen sound as if a door were creaking open, and he turns slowly around in that direction. The camera quickly pans to screen left and tilts downward slightly to the figure of a woman clothed completely in black; only her eyes are showing. There is a shot of the policeman staring at her, and a cut to the Countess looking at the officer. She advances. As the policeman moves to screen left, the camera pans in that direction and dollies in with the Countess moving in a circular direction (counterclockwise). She is mostly out of the frame and remains to the left of it. With her back to the camera, she asks if the policeman is the officer in charge. The camera continues to pan slowly about until the policeman sits down in his chair behind the desk. There is a cut to the Countess looking off screen toward the officer, saying that she has come to see Dracula's body. She proceeds to hypnotize him with a jeweled ring on her finger. As the sequence continues, the camera work illustrates three concepts:

1. The tilting downward of the camera reveals the Countess, who looks deceptively tall despite the slightly high camera angle; she is monolithic in her black garb.

2. The off-centered blocking of the Countess, her image partially out of the frame and her back to the camera, signals to the viewer the strangeness of the situation. When she does speak only her eyes can be seen.

3. The camera movement at the end of the shots described above has a sinister quality in that it seems to enmesh the officer; she now appears to dominate

the frame as the officer sits at the desk. Even more menacing and threatening
is the icy cold voice accompanying Zeleska's eyes which gives the impression
of a voiced-over image.

At the conclusion of these shots the Countess's face is partially seen, and
the synchronization of voice and image made somewhat manifest.

The cremation of Dracula is an impressive sequence for its mystic and
gothic grace, and for the light it sheds on the character of the Countess. It
is wonderfully atmospheric especially with the low camera angles, the
panning and tilting of the camera through the fog-enshrouded woods, and
the figure of the Countess framed by the trees. For the first time her face
is seen with its pale alabaster skin set off by high cheekbones in a regal,
even haughty demeanor. Throughout this melancholy sequence a Brahms-
ian woodwind choir of flutes, oboes, clarinets and finally bassoons is
heard which adds to the dreariness. Her exorcism is filled with melodic
sounds of assonance and alliteration, with its archaism and periphrasis
especially when she begins to invoke the evil powers: "Unto Adoni and
Azeril, into the keeping of the lords of the flame and the lower pits, I
consign this body to be forevermore consumed in this purging fire." This
exorcism is temporally elongated through the use of various shots interspersed with the prayer: Sandor on the hill, the Countess throwing salt on
the pyre, pulling a veil over her face, and reaching out for the wooden
cross. Her torment has only momentarily departed for Sandor quickly
instills the old fear in her. The Countess extols the fact that she is now
free to live as any mortal woman and assume a place in the daylight world
of the living instead of the shadowy world of the dead. So overjoyed is
she that Zeleska repeats the word "free" three times. But Sandor is
skeptical of her new-found happiness and questions what the day will
bring.

The next sequence opens with an anachronistic but atmospherically
suitable, establishing shot of the Chelsea District of London where a man
is seen lighting the street lamps. Zeleska has an art studio here and once
inside, while playing the Chopin *Nocturne in F Sharple Major*, defiantly
informs her servant: "Dracula is destroyed, his body is in ashes, the spell
is broken. I can live a normal life now, think normal things, even play
normal music again. Listen . . . [she sits down to play the piano]." The
repetition (as a rhetorical device) of the word "normal" parallels the
repetition of her last jubilant remarks with the word "free" But in the end
it is the same result, a build-up and a let-down for the Countess. As she
plays a nocturne an antiphonal conversation ensues. Zeleska as if remem-
bering says, "My cradle song, the song my mother once sang to me long,

long ago, rocking me to sleep as she sang in the twilight." Sandor's single word in reply, "Twilight" is menacingly delivered in Irving Pichel's base voice. Zeleska rebukes him with, "Quiet! Quiet, you disturb me! Twilight, long shadows on the hill side." To which Sandor irritatingly replies, "Evil Shadows!" But the Countess, fearful of what her servant is implying, hastens to stop his troubling thoughts: "No! No! Peaceful shadows, the flutter of wings in the tree tops." As though not hearing her, he answers, "The wings of bats!" Once again Zeleska tries to change the mood by replying, "No, no, the wings of birds. From far off the barking of a dog," but the servant continues, "Barking because there are wolves about!" The Countess attempts to silence Sandor, and he knowingly answers, "Why are you afraid?" She starts to play more wildly and passionately at the piano and nervously interjects "I'm not! I'm not, I've found release!" Sandor answers back, "The music doesn't speak of release," and regretfully Zeleska says, "No, no, you're right!" The servant now analyses the performance with the words: "That music tells of the dark, evil things, shadowy places." Zeleska rising from the piano cannot bear what Sandor says and cries out: "Stop! Stop! Stop! Sandor, look at me. What do you see in my eyes?" He simply responds "Death." As a chant that takes place between the two, Zeleska always uses a double imperative, "Quiet," "No," "I'm not," and finally, "Stop" repeated three times, hinting at her grim determination at normalcy. Even the music is interpreted by Sandor programmatically,[23] and as Zeleska plays, he counteracts all the images of light, goodness and restfulness with "evil shadows," "wings of bats" and "wolves." The antiphony concludes with Sandor's nihilistic utterance, "Death," as he hands the Countess her cape and ring.

The first of her attacks in a deserted street on a man of pleasure is portrayed at a slow, deliberate pace with constant intercutting between the Countess's face and the victim. The street set produced by Universal has that ersatz Germanic look about it which negates any specific time period, although in well-lit rooms or during the day in a speeding automobile the ambiance is that of 1930s England. The first attack by Zeleska is short, devoid of most sexual connotations associated with a vampire's kiss, but the sequence is prolonged by the many camera set-ups. The victim is seen in a long shot from various angles, all of which, with the exception of one shot, contain the presence of the Countess. There are no screams, no struggling; the action is so muted as to be only suggested. Back in her studio, after the attack, Zeleska rushes to the coffin, seen just enough at the right of the frame to prepare the viewer for a shot of the Countess inside it where only her arm is seen as she lowers the creaking lid. The action is restrained and reminiscent of *Dracula*. Once Sandor has exited from the frame, an emptiness as well as a felt presence is produced, for the camera which dollies back reveals the coffin at full length, metaphorically becoming an extension of the Countess herself. There is a dissolve to an operating theater with tiers of medical men over the body of the Countess's victim. These shots have been copied directly from *Dracula* with the exception that it uses three shots for the operating theater room instead of two as in *Dracula's Daughter*.

When Dr. Garth first meets Von Helsing the more than familiar conversation parallels that between the professor and Sir Basil Humphrey. Both criminology and psychiatry are skeptical about vampires. Von Helsing's words to Garth, "who can define the boundary line between the superstition of yesterday and the scientific fact of tomorrow?" are almost a direct quote from *Dracula*. The conflict, then, not only rests between the protagonists and antagonists in these films, but between the protagonists themselves. Garth's condescending attitude toward the professor makes for a very unsympathetic character. His intellect has superseded his human passion for love, either for Von Helsing or the opposite sex.

Garth first meets Zeleska at Lady Esme Hammond's (Hedda Hopper) party. This party recalls a scene from *Dracula*. When John asks Van Helsing what produced the marks on Mina's throat, a maid immediately announces "Count Dracula" as she ushers him into the room. At Lady Hammond's party, Garth looks at a painting of a woman amid a desolate landscape and asks his hostess the painter's name. The butler in an officious voice announces the arrival of "Countess Marya Zeleska." Not only does the scene recall *Dracula*, but the Countess's painting foreshadows by its very likeness Zeleska's next victim, Lili. The choosing of the victim is actually brought about by Garth, with his rather dubious psychological advice to the Countess. As in *Dracula*, there is the classic statement with the same dramatic pause made by the vampire at Lady Esme's dinner party: "Thank you, I never drink [pause] wine." After dinner Garth speaks about the Von Helsing case, saying that the professor believes in the existence of vampires. The Countess replies, "Why not, possibly there are more things in heaven and on earth than are dreamed of in your psychiatry, Mr. Garth." This paraphrase from Shakespeare's *Hamlet* has been the recurrent theme, implicit and explicit, in most thirties' horror films, and appears in Browning's *Dracula* in a somewhat altered form. But it is this very scene that proves to be a major plot point, for the Countess solicits Garth's aid to help her overcome her "affliction" without actually specifying what it is. Garth, urged by his guests to give a medical explanation for vampirism, diagnoses it as an "obsession" that, like any mental disorder, can be treated in a sympathetic manner thereby releasing the mind from the obsession. At the word "release" Zeleska looks wonderfully hopeful and asks to see Garth one evening. This pseudopsychological jargon fills much of the film, and although one can criticize it because it is not profound, it is one of the main ingredients that keep *Dracula's Daughter* a fresh entry in the field of the vampire film. In 1936 it was an odd and unexpected approach.

With the fade-in Garth is in Zeleska's apartment fidgeting with his tie and looking around for a mirror. There is a running joke about Garth not being able to tie his bow tie which, in a film that is superficially Freudian, has Freudian overtones. [24] The lack of a mirror is a perfect way to introduce the vampire's aversion for reflecting surfaces. Garth innocently remarks that for a woman's apartment it is the first he has ever been in that did not have at least twenty mirrors. Zeleska not so innocently replies that Professor Von Helsing would immediately recognize occult reasons why there are no mirrors. In fact she is bold enough to add that Hungarian legends claim that vampires are not reflected in mirrors. For once it would seem that we have a vampire who wishes to be caught by the psychiatrist. Garth, close to Zeleska, is interrupted by a telephone call from his jealous secretary, Janet, an interruption that has come at a moment of intimacy (an example of coitus interruptus?), so that both the sexuality connected with the role of vampire and the sexual symbolism of the tie are sustained. And when Zeleska implores Garth for help, he asks if it is in his professional capacity that she requires his assistance. The Countess significantly answers that she seeks his help as a courageous and strong man. Garth answers, again suggesting the impotence of the romantic lead, that her request places him at a disadvantage. When she begs for help saying that someone is controlling her will, Garth's assertive rejoinder is that her strength should come from within and the next time that she experiences this urge the secret is to fight it head on, not to avoid it. Not only is Garth's advice glib (he compares this to a test given to alcoholics with a bottle of liquor before them), it makes the practice of psychiatry seem like a simple home remedy. It appears that the doctor is not only figuratively impotent (and this includes his capacity for deep human relations with a woman), he is also impotent to save Zeleska and to save Janet from her.

Zeleska, because of her infatuation for Garth, does attempt to carry out his instructions by turning to painting and obtaining a female model to pose for her. She tells the model, Lili, picked up off the streets by Sandor, that her beautiful hands are "so white and bloodless." After the young woman has partially undressed to pose, Zeleska says, "Finish your wine, it'll warm you," adding, "Stand by the fire for a moment, you mustn't catch cold." The perverse intentions of Zeleska become apparent. Suspense is created in several ways. While the attack of the vampire is off-screen, the victim's screams can be heard. As the shots of Zeleska's presence on-screen progressively lengthen there is a proportionate decrease in the length of time Lili and Zeleska are on screen together. Thus for the first half of the sequence, the Countess's on-screen presence is important because the viewer wishes to know her reaction to the temptation for blood. But once the light of the Countess's jewel ring shines into Lili's eyes, the viewer realizes that Zeleska has given in, and it is the off-screen presence of the Countess that creates the stress. For this reason there are no more "two shots." As the young woman's strength fails, the length of time her image is shown on the screen decreases, while the Countess's screen presence once again begins to rise imperceptively. As soon as Lili screams, the camera quickly tilts up to a satanic mask over the fireplace which suggests the tone of the off-screen action.

The turning point in Garth's attraction toward the Countess comes in Zeleska's confrontation with Janet outside his office. The shots of the Countess are taken at a low angle giving her a majestic presence, while those of Janet are on a flat angle. Zeleska in her final attempt to be cured comes to Garth because she is suffering and cannot make it without him. In fact Zeleska extravagantly claims that Garth is the only one who can save her from being destroyed. Garth gives her a cold stare, and she responds pitifully that she is leaving London for good and that nothing remains for her but horror. When he attempts to quiet her through a hypnotizing machine that works by mirrors,25 she, of course, refuses, but wants him to come with her to the continent; he is coldly indifferent. This dialogue further illustrates her torment caused by the family curse yet paradoxically suggests that it is not that the Countess is not evil, but that those who represent good are so righteous.

Garth accuses Zeleska of Lili's death and tells her that she is coming with him to Scotland Yard. Her reply is disarming: "You're no longer the sympathetic Samaritan. No, you're a policeman. There isn't anything I won't do now to enlist your aid in freeing me of the curse of the Draculas. I am Dracula's daughter." The rebuke epitomizes the woman's desperation and relates back to the statement on the ambivalence of temporal duration in the gothic story since *Dracula's Daughter* picks up immediately where its predecessor left off five years earlier without hint of a time lapse, and as Dracula has moved from Transylvania to London for "fresh" victims, so too does his daughter, repeating the act and, in essence, the story.

The concluding sequence takes place in Transylvania where, in desperation, Zeleska has Janet kidnapped so that Garth will follow. A wedding festival is in progress; music is played reminding one of Whale's festive villagers in *Frankenstein* or the customers at The Lion's Head in *The Invisible Man*. The scene is a favorite convention of horror filming that is meant to contrast the terror instilled in natural man (the happy rural villagers in celebration) by evil supernatural forces. Lambert Hillyer starts off slowly and alternates between the frenzied activity of the villagers and their fear once they suspect the vampire's presence at Castle Dracula and the deadly calm inside the castle and the ominous use of continuous establishing shots of it to retard the action. Inside the castle, the camera work is reminiscent of Freund's in *Dracula*: the slow dollying in to the coffin, the hand emerging, and the reticence of the camera to show the vampire as the camera pans smoothly to a window, while the off-screen sound of the closing coffin lid is heard. Then, in a reverse pan back to the coffin, is the full figure of the vampire seen. Janet, in a trance and reclining on a couch, is most seductive and passive as Sandor's words to the Countess imply: "Beautiful and helpless." While Janet is being used as a lure to ensnare Garth, Zeleska is also attracted to the beauty of the woman in repose.

Sandor is attracted both to Janet and to Zeleska and wishes to become a vampire so that he can live throughout eternity. Eternal life is one of the reasons for the myth of the vampire, associated with the drinking of human blood to ensure an existence after death.[26] Twitchell sees the Roman Catholic Church as continuing the myth of the vampire in the West because of its promulgation of the dogma of transubstantiation. He reports that as the vampire drank blood and captured the spirit of the individual so does the Christian drink the blood and eat the body of Christ to possess His divinity.[27] In *Dracula's Daughter* Sandor seeks this communion with the vampire, and if not obtained he threatens that he will kill Garth if he comes to the castle and insinuates that the Countess will also be destroyed. At the same time Zeleska provides the film with its denouement by no longer caring for release from Dracula's curse but desiring Garth's life.

While Garth is seen before the castle, there are shots of the Countess moving closer to the recumbent Janet to drink her blood. The temporality of this action is protracted to increase suspense by crosscutting shots of Garth climbing the spider-webbed staircase of the castle (as in *Dracula*) with other shots involving Garth and Sandor. As Zeleska is about to strike her entranced victim, Garth fires a gun at the fleeing Sandor, the sound stopping the Countess from her attack. When Garth finally meets Zeleska, she offers him eternal life in exchange for the life of Janet about whom Garth is now deeply concerned because he is powerless to bring her out of her trance. The low angles reserved for Zeleska not only place her in the position of authority, but also, in spite of her pleading, give her physiognomy a noble and powerful look. Garth capitulates and intends to sacrifice his life for Janet's; however, as Zeleska begins to hypnotize Garth, she is shot through the heart by Sandor's arrow, the phallic symbol that ultimately penetrates the woman he once loved. The police now arrive with Von Helsing, and as Zeleska falls on the balcony outside, her spell is broken as in a fairy tale: Garth is freed from her power; Janet, like Mina in *Dracula*, stirs in pain on the couch as though she herself received the shaft wound; and Sandor is felled by police bullets. Only now does Jeffrey take Janet in his arms and embrace her, coming to potency after the villain-heroine is done away with. The film's cyclic progression is completed. A close-up of the face of the dead Countess is seen and Sir Basil's voice is heard praising her beauty while Von Helsing replies that indeed she was beautiful a hundred years ago when she died. With the fade-out, the family curse has come to an end and the viewer is reminded of the Count's death and Von Helsing's words that open the film.

It is appropriate to conclude this study with the death of *Dracula's Daughter* for it marks the end of the first tide of horror films to reach the public with the coming of sound and completes the genre's cycle by returning to the plot and theme begun in 1931 with *Dracula*. Seen by today's younger viewers, these eleven films might seem almost as old as some of the literary works on which they were based, but despite the technological gap that exists between them and the modern horror film, they continue to be shown on television and in revival houses, indicating that they still attract audiences of various ages and interests. On a more profound level they persist in possessing the power to "massage the psyche, stimulating its growth and development in order that it might better see itself and find its place in the . . . fullness of human reality."[28] This burden placed on the horror film by Telotte seems eminently reasonable in light of the persistence of the genre. Nevertheless, as the moviegoer must walk out into the world of reality after the lights go on, so too is it time to return to a brighter world, and recognize what is at work behind the moving images which have stimulated our psyches not quite free from the shadows cast by celluloid illusions.

NOTES

1. *The Oxford Universal Dictionary*, 1918. colloq.

2. Mario Praz, *The Romantic Agony*, translated by Angus Davidson (New York: Oxford University Press, 1970), pp. 77–78, 191.

3. Bram Stoker, *The Lair of the White Worm* (London: Jarrolds Publishers, 1966), p. 179.

4. Thomas Preskett Prest, *Varney the Vampyre or the Feast of Blood*, Vol 3 (New York: Arno Press, 1970), p. 828.

5. Sheridan LeFanu, *Carmilla*, in *Best Ghost Stories of J. S. LeFanu*, (New York: Dover Publications, 1964), pp. 291–92.

6. Bram Stoker, *The Lady of the Shroud* (London: Arrow Books Ltd., 1974), p. 119.

7. Peter Haining, *The Ghouls* (New York: Pocket Books, 1972), p. 167.

8. Michael Brunas, John Brunas, and Tom Weaver, *Universal Horrors: The Studio's Classic Films, 1931–1946* (North Carolina: McFarland & Company, Inc., 1990), p. 158.

9. Brunas, *Universal Horrors*, p. 158.

10. Stoker as cited in Haining, *The Ghouls*, pp. 173–75.

11. Although John L. Balderston wrote the original screenplay, which was considered "a rather humorless affair" based on Bram Stoker's short story, "Dracula's Guest," Fort rewrote the script, and according to Brunas, "the prolonged stretches of comedy relief are a distracting nuisance." I cannot agree with this statement. In fact most of the humor between Garth and Janet is quite sophisticated and modern. Brunas, *Universal Horrors*, p. 162.

12. Mary Shelly, *Frankenstein or the Modern Prometheus* (New York: New American Library, 1965), p. 124.

13. J. P. Eckermann, *Conversations of Goethe in the Last Years of his Life*, trans. by John Oxendord, in *Criticism: The Major Texts* edited by Walter Jackson Bate (New York: Harcourt, Brace and Company, 1952), pp. 402–03.

14. Carlos Clarens, *An Illustrated History of the Horror Film* (New York: Capricorn Books, 1968), p. 108. For an analysis of forensic pathology of vampirism see Paul Barber, "The Real Vampire," in *Natural History* (October 1990), pp. 74–82.

15. Friedrich Nietzsche, *The Birth of Tragedy from the Spirit of Music*, trans. by William A. Hausmann, in *Modern Continental Literary Criticism*, ed. by O. B. Hardison, Jr. (New York: Appleton-Century-Crofts, 1962), p. 231.

16. M. H. Abrams, *A Glossary of Literary Terms* (New York: Rinehart and Company, Inc., 1958), p. 98. See Aristotle, *Poetics* in *The Rhetoric and the Poetics of Aristotle*. Translated by Ingram Bywater. New York: The Modern Library, 1984, chap. 6, 1441. b 21–31.

17. John Gassner, *Masters of the Drama* (New York: Dover Publications, 1954), p. 744.

18. Van Helsing's name has been changed in *Dracula's Daughter* to "Von Helsing" and will be spelled throughout this chapter as such.

19. Irving Ribner, *Patterns in Shakespearean Tragedy* (New York: Barnes and Noble, Inc., 1960), p. 10.

20. Although Andrew Tudor places the film in his "External Autonomous" category in that the Countess is an "outside" threat to the characters and is not dependent on anyone for her actions, I disagree that she is an autonomous creature. When her father dies she transfers her dependence to Dr. Garth. Only when he cannot help her does her jealous love for the doctor reduce her to fight

on a purely human level. Her lack of autonomy is what makes her so sympathetic. See Andrew Tudor, *Monsters and Mad Scientists: A Cultural History of the Horror Movies* (Cambridge: Basil Blackwell, Inc., 1989), pp. 8, 9–10, 31.

21. Taylor Stoehr, "Pornography, Masturbation, and the Novel," in *Salmagundi* (Fall 1967-Winter 1968), pp. 28–56.

22. For information on the real vampire countess, Elizabeth Bathroy, see: Gabriel Ronay, *Exploding the Bloody Myths of Dracula and Vampires* (London: Golbancz, 1972) and Raymond T. McNally and Radu Florescu, *In Search of Dracula* (New York: Warner Paperback Library, 1973), p. 225. Also see the segment in Valerian Borowczyk's film *Immoral Tales* (1976) on Countess Elizabeth Bathroy.

23. Joseph Machlis, *The Enjoyment of Music* (New York: W. W. Norton and Company, Inc., 3rd edition, 1970), chap. 22: "The Nature of Program Music," pp. 101–37. Romantic music many times was accredited with literary or pictorial associations (Romantic Synesthesia).

24. Freud in his book *On Dreams* states that a tie may represent the male organ and rooms represent women, their entrances and exits the openings of the body. Given the context of the psychoanalytic ambiance of the film, here is another impotent romantic lead. Sigmund Freud, *On Dreams*, trans. by James Strachey (New York: W. W. Norton and Company, Inc., 1952), pp. 108–09.

25. In *Burn Witch Burn!* the device called a Luys Mirror is also used.

26. Dracula, paraphrasing Deuteronomy, says in the 1931 film (with its intended double entendre), "The blood is the life, Mr. Renfield." Jesus stated that eternal life was gained through the drinking of blood: see Matthew 26:27–29; Mark 14:22–26; Luke 22:15–20; 1 Cor. 11:23–25. No wonder Sandor is jealous of Garth's position as a rival for the gift of everlasting life.

27. James B. Twitchell, *Dreadful Pleasures: An Anatomy of Modern Horror* (New York: Oxford University Press, 1985), pp. 108–09.

28. J. P. Telotte, *Dreams of Darkness: Fantasy and the Films of Val Lewton* (Chicago: University of Illinois Press, 1985), p. 5.

Conclusion

I can do with my pencil what I know,
What I see. . . . Yourself are judge.
                    —Robert Browning, "Andrea del Sarto"

Christian Metz has said *"Fantastic art is fantastic only as it convinces . . . and* the power of unreality in films derives from the fact that *the unreal seems to have been realized,* unfolding before our eyes as if it were *the flow of common occurrence—not the plausible illustration of some extraordinary process only conceived in the mind."*[1] The italics above point toward the use of conventions which are utilarian vehicles for portraying the artifice of particular genres, so that the viewer accepts the tenor of the piece. The longevity of these horror films from the 1930s rests in their ability to convince, to invest the supernatural with a "semblance of truth." All Metz has done is to paraphrase Coleridge's method of composing the *Lyrical Ballads.* In the *Biographia Literaria* he writes that his efforts were "directed to persons and characters supernatural . . . yet so as to transform from our inward nature a human interest and a semblance of truth sufficient to procure . . . that willing suspension of disbelief . . . which constitutes poetic faith."[2] We can trace the pleasure derived from horror back to gothic conventions.

Noel Carroll's keen insight into the horror film locates the focus of pleasure in the genre on the narrative itself, saying that horror films revolve around the existence of the abnormal and the importance of the narrative is the confirmation of the monster's existence.[3] I would like to add that what makes the confirmation of the monster's existence and the narrative around which this confirmation takes place appealing are the conventions within the genre which have evolved through the decades. Conventions bring with them a certain amount of familiarity that the viewing audience appreciates and comes to expect. Those conventions rooted in the gothic and listed below are found in the films that have appeared in this study and might be more easily identified if arranged under four major headings of Plot, Characterization, Technique, and *Mise-en-scène*.

Plot

1. The first and basic quality of horror films is that they attempt to frighten the viewer principally through situations and characters, and through other aesthetic qualities available to the director.

2. Strong overtones of necrophilia prevail.

3. The main thrust of the film is to present the supernatural as real, not as a dream or something that can be explained away.

4. The majority of the films are repetitious and are basically centered on the rise and fall of the villain-hero, a *de causibus* theme of Elizabethan drama.

5. The plot demands that virtue be triumphant and evil destroyed. The horror film takes place in a closed universe; there is always a restoration of moral and physical order at the end.

6. In some films the ending is unhappy although closed because the heroine cannot be united to the hero since he is also the villain: *Dr. Jekyll and Mr. Hyde, The Invisible Man.*

7. The films moralize in general terms; they usually attack the pride of a man who would make himself like God. The message for the villain-heroes is that they must not tamper with things that are beyond their knowledge.

8. An often-repeated phrase in the films, "There are more things in heaven and on earth than are dreamed of in your philosophies," becomes a call to orthodoxy over the Romantic image of man as the center of the universe; but this is also ambivalent because at times it is spoken by the villain-heroes who hold supernatural power over others while setting themselves up as the center of the universe.

9. Another quotation echoed in these films, "The superstition of yesterday is the scientific reality of today," is usually spoken by the benign wizards to separate those who believe in the supernatural from those who do not. It is similar in meaning to the quotation above.

10. The films play on distortions of religious myths, for example, the vampire is a symbol of eternal life and incarnate evil.

11. Many of the horror films deal with primordial images: death-rebirth, the Devil, God, and Paradise-Hades.

12. Many of the actions are in the form of a quest, whether scientific or romantic on the part of the romantic lead, the villain-hero or the benign wizard/scientist: *White Zombie, The Mummy, Mad Love, Island of Lost Souls*.

13. Narratives are mirror images of romantic stories reflecting the ugly and abnormal instead of the beautiful and the utopic: *Mad Love, Dracula, Frankenstein, Dr. Jekyll and Mr. Hyde*.

14. Science is either presented as outright evil or only as chimerical good; orthodoxy wins out over experimentation. At other times science is satirized: *Mad Love, Dracula's Daughter, Frankenstein, The Bride of Frankenstein*.

15. Eroticism and sadism are mixed together: *Island of Lost Souls, Mad Love, Dr. Jekyll and Mr. Hyde, Dracula's Daughter, Frankenstein*.

16. The films employ a surrogate voyeuristic audience who watches the experiments and reacts appropriately: *Frankenstein, The Bride of Frankenstein, The Invisible Man*.

17. Actions take place at night or during storms. Darkness of the film space acts as an extension of the darkness of the theater.

18. Use is made of classical or semiclassical music to set a tone either in the opening credits or within the films as characters listen to or play music (usually a piano or organ): *Dracula, The Mummy, Dr. Jekyll and Mr. Hyde, Mad Love, White Zombie, The Bride of Frankenstein*.

19. Sometimes the area of morality (at least in the beginning of the film) is neither black nor white but gray.

Characterization

(VILLAIN-HERO)

1. The films follow literary gothic conventions by dealing with characterization over action.

2. The majority of villain-heroes are males, the *homme fatal*, and come from the upper class.

3. Films deal with characters grotesque in body or in spirit.

4. The scientist of gothic horror attempts to reach toward the mystical and spiritual with pure scientific reasoning.

5. The villain-hero has his archetype in biblical literature and ancient myths: he is a Satanlike character whose main purpose is to tempt and to taunt.

6. The villain-hero is usually referred to as "mad."

7. For the villain-hero there is a transformation in his position that is cyclic; he moves from the state of death (a literal one as in *The Mummy* or a figurative one as in *The Devil Doll*) to life and back again.

8.   The villain-hero's intentions are good to begin with but are subverted and turn toward evil.

9.   The villain-hero is a destiny symbol; he tends to govern, control or influence the lives of those around him.

10. As a symbol of destiny, the villain-hero is motivated by revenge; this places him on the side of evil and becomes the motivation for the actions he performs.

11. The villain-hero usually believes in perfectible man, although the plot demands that his creations are the opposite in form.

12. The villain-hero's belief is in unlimited freedom, usually for evil.

13. The villain-hero's creature is an extension of his evil and an expression of his power.

14. The villain-hero is usually a seer, a mystic, but he is many times unappreciated.

15. The villain-hero's ideas are reflected in the eccentricity of his life, the abnormality of his behavior and the architectonics of the places he inhabits.

16. The villain-hero is unpredictable, unorthodox; of necessity he is devious and crafty.

17. The villain-hero is presented as a tormented individual isolated from his fellow man. The torment is expressed as a conflict between the inner self and the external world.

18. Villain-heroes are the principle of destruction not only for others but for themselves.

19. Villain-heroes employ deformed assistants (either physically or mentally). This deformity parallels the spiritual deformity of the villain: *Dracula, Frankenstein, The Bride of Frankenstein, White Zombie, Dracula's Daughter.*

20. The villain-heroes are the figures with the greatest depth of character; the others are basically flat.

21. Many times the villain-hero is an extension of the romantic lead, the uninhibited alter ego (*Dracula, The Mummy, Frankenstein*) or part of a split in the personality of the villain-hero (*Dr. Jekyll and Mr. Hyde*).

22. The villain-hero as scientist is a Promethean figure.

23. Villain-heroes many times are characterized through their eyes, which become a reflection of their souls.

24. The villain-hero excites the viewer's sympathy.

25. The villain-heroes are either first seen as godlike, and therefore part of a myth (Dracula, the mummy, and the Frankenstein monster are "immortal"), or are seen performing marvelous actions and therefore part of a romance (the scientists of many of these films).

26. The villain-heroes are gods capable of bestowing eternal life, yet they are also identified as human beings.

27. The villain-hero moves in a world in which the ordinary laws of human nature are suspended.

28. The villain-hero is superior in kind and degree to other men and to man's environment through most of the narrative, yet ceases to be as the film unfolds.

29. To bring the narrative to a conclusion, the villain-hero reaches the level of being inferior in power or intelligence to the protagonists of the films, so that the protagonists have the sense of looking down on a scene of frustration. Dracula, for all his immortality, can die; the mummy is destroyed by the prayers of a young maiden.

30. Many villain-heroes, having died in one film, appear again in others, or appear in a different persona but in a similar narrative: *Dr. Jekyll and Mr. Hyde*, for example, is a story about the bestial or fallen-nature side of man that parallels stories of werewolves. The Frankenstein monster makes his return in *The Bride of Frankenstein*, Dracula's daughter repeats her father's quest for victims.

Characterization

(ROMANTIC LEADS)

1. Romantic leads believe in rules of conduct conformable to society and the authority it represents.

2. Romantic leads are materialists, skeptical of the supernatural, coming from upper-class society. They are there to give credibility to the supernatural by their very disbelief.

3. Romantic leads do not elicit much sympathy but are part of the plot device to create conflict in the narrative.

4. Romantic leads are passive, and their passivity renders them impotent. Their active sexual side is mirrored in the villain-hero, who represents the romantic lead's suppressed self.

5. There is a change in appearance when the heroine falls under the spell of the villain-hero; she is more sexually active and attractive; this begins her initiation into evil.

6. The heroine is menaced when she is most vulnerable, that is, when isolated and, in many cases, in the dark, both literally and figuratively.

7. The heroine is sometimes a somnambule and quite passive.

8. Somnambules usually dress in white flowing garments, a sign of their virginity.

9.   If two women vie for the affection of a man, the darker one is more passionate, the lighter one more virtuous: *Island of Lost Souls, Dracula's Daughter*. One exception, however, is *Dr. Jekyll and Mr. Hyde*.

Characterization
(BENIGN WIZARD)

1.   The benign wizard practices white magic and triumphs over the black magic of the evil wizard/villain-hero: *Dracula, The Mummy, White Zombie, Frankenstein*.

2.   Benign wizards believe in rules, authority and conformity.

3.   The benign wizard shares the midground in belief between the skeptical romantic leads and the mystic-wise villain-hero.

4.   The benign wizard is more intellectually active in his fight against the villain-hero than the romantic leads, but the benign wizard does not necessarily destroy the evil force at the conclusion of the film: Dr. Muller in *The Mummy*, Dr. Lanyon in *Dr. Jekyll and Mr. Hyde*, the priest in *White Zombie*

5.   The benign wizard, although sometimes a seer in his own right, bases his notion of experimentation on imitation of previous models: Waldman in *Frankenstein*, Lanyon in *Dr. Jekyll and Mr. Hyde*, Dr. Kemp in *The Invisible Man*, Dr. Garth in *Dracula's Daughter*.

6.   The benign wizard holds to the notion that human beings are imperfect or sinful and not equal to God.

7.   The benign wizards praise intellect when accompanied by careful judgment.

8.   The benign wizard is predictable in his opinions about the villain-hero, science and the moral and social law.

9.   The benign wizard is, at times, a father figure for the romantic leads.

10.   With the exception of the villain-hero, the benign wizard usually is the most interesting figure in the film.

11.   The benign wizard's ideas are reflected in the unity of his life, the normality of his behavior and the orderliness of his place of work.

Characterization
(OTHERS)

1.   Intentional humor in the horror films comes from the lower-class characters.

2.   Creatures turn against their creator.

3.   Faithful assistants sometimes turn on their masters and cause the death of the villain-hero.

4. A contrast between the social classes is evident either between the peasants and upper class, who are the main characters, or the tradespeople and the romantic leads and villain-hero.

5. The films are peopled with stock figures that represent various virtues and vices.

6. Villagers in remote country places are usually presented as happy individuals who are superstitious; the actions of the villain-hero turn them into fearful people: *Dracula, Dracula's Daughter, Frankenstein.*

Film Technique

1. Certain conventions related to shooting techniques in laboratory sequences in the horror films are observed:

    a. Repetition of similar shots (instruments and electrical objects).

    b. Percussive use of a montage of shots when the experiment reaches a climax.

    c. Dutch angles and objects to divide the screen and destroy harmony of composition in the frame.

    d. Extremes in key lighting or in juxtaposition of camera placement, and extremes in uniting various focal distances.

    e. Certain reaction shots of various characters to the work being performed on the subject in the lab.

2. Off-screen space is used to create tension.

3. Space is undefined to create suspense or a feeling of the unknown; heroine runs through passages that do not seem to be contiguous with each other. This undefined screen space serves as a means of dramatic conflict.

4. Prologues create moral parameters for the narrative.

5. Diction is stylized, not realistic as in other genres: *White Zombie, The Mummy, Dr. Jekyll and Mr. Hyde, Dracula.*

6. Certain shots are expressionistic and mirror the inner conflict of the situation or a character's state of mind:

    a. Dutch angles and percussive editing of *Frankenstein* and *The Bride of Frankenstein* denote madness or the frenzy of creative forces and the danger involved.

    b. Balanced shots are used to represent Jekyll, and wild camera movement to represent Hyde.

    c. Low angles give a consistent powerful image to the presence of the villain-hero.

    d. Flat angles are used for romantic leads.

    e. Crosscutting is extensively used toward the end of the films to prolong narrative suspense.

    f. Subjective camera enforces suspense as it explores a space that is predetermined, through convention, to terminate in conflict.

7. Shadows play an important part to define character: *The Bride of Franken-stein, Dr. Jekyll and Mr. Hyde, White Zombie, Island of Lost Souls.*

8. The vampire's emergence from the coffin is stylized: dollying into the object, a hand emerging, and a panning away from the coffin by the camera as vampire emerges off screen, followed by a reverse pan to reveal the full figure of the vampire: *Dracula, Dracula's Daughter.*

Mise-en-Scène

1. Landscapes act as objective correlatives to represent the situation at hand; this includes the architecture of rooms and buildings.

2. The landscape has, many times, a dreamlike quality about it: *White Zombie, Dracula, Dracula's Daughter.*

3. Mansions or castles are inhabited by the villain; either its size, exotic locale or dilapidated condition is emphasized.

4. Staircases have dramatic value in these films; action takes place on them: *Dracula, White Zombie, Dracula's Daughter.*

5. Films rely on expressionistic sets to define a tone that makes a judgment on the action and describes psychological states; *Frankenstein, The Bride of Frankenstein, White Zombie.*

6. Love of the exotic is usually exemplified in the settings and sometimes in the costumes: *Dracula, Island of Lost souls, Mad Love, White Zombie.*

7. Films take place in an atemporal setting, that is, they do not offer any indication that they occur at a time that is relevant to the action.

8. Anachronistic style of films shows nineteenth-century atmosphere intruded upon by modern-day reality: *Dracula, Frankenstein, The Bride of Frankenstein, Dracula's Daughter.*

9. Most of the action takes place in remote villages or in magnificent houses that are still isolated from urban dwellers or in obscure corners of the city: *Dracula's Daughter.*

10. Because the action in these horror films is localized, the film has a closed-ended atmosphere of a self-contained world. In this sense they are opposed to "action" films whose boundaries encompass a wider range of locale.

11. The local tavern serves several functions: meeting halls as well as places of entertainment that define the atmosphere of the village. It is also a neutral territory where the natural and preternatural meet: *Dracula, The Invisible Man, Dracula's Daughter.*

12. Fire is used as a means to purge evil from the land: *Frankenstein, The Bride of Frankenstein, Island of Lost Souls, The Devil Doll.*

These conventions are one of the main reasons for the unity in the films, and they transform the real world into the world of artistic reality. But this transformation does not end at escapism after all, for art, according to Schiller, raises man from reality to appearance and through appearance to the knowledge of the real. This liberating force is provided by the horror films of the 1930s which allowed for a free play of people's imagination with the world of appearance on screen, resulting in an aesthetic response, a purified form of joy which is an expression of man's humanity.[4]

The horror film genre of the Great Depression, with its roots in popular Romantic fiction, was favored by the masses and still is today, presenting a world where the impossible was possible, where chaos could be controlled and happy endings were likely even under the most dire circumstances. It became the wish fulfillment of depression-age America for apparently all sorts of manifest and covert reasons. It also pointed toward a darker side of the movie-going public which found enjoyment not only in Shirley Temple, Tim Holt and Edward G. Robinson, but also in such unlikely figures as the living dead and man-made monsters.

NOTES

1. Christian Metz, *Film Language: A Semiotics of the Cinema*, trans. by Michael Taylor (New York: Oxford University Press, 1974), p. 5.

2. Samuel Taylor Coleridge, *Biographia Literaria* in *Criticism: the Major Texts*, ed. by Walter Jackson Bate (New York: Harcourt, Brace and Company, 1952), p. 376.

3. Noel Carroll, *The Philosophy of Horror or Paradoxes of the Heart* (New York: Routlege, 1990), pp. 190–92.

4. Johann Friedrich von Schiller, *Letters on the Aesthetic Education of Man*, ed. by O. B. Hardison, Jr., in *Modern Continental Literary Criticism* (New York: Appleton-Century-Crofts, 1962), p. 42.

Bibliography

FILMS

Listed here are the original companies that produced the films. Many of them no longer hold the rights to the films. Turner Entertainment Company now has the rights to *Dr. Jekyll and Mr. Hyde, Mad Love* and *The Devil Doll*. Universal owns *Island of Lost Souls* besides the others listed here. As of this time it is uncertain if anyone holds the rights to *White Zombie*.

Director	Film	Company
Browning, Tod	*Dracula* (1931)	Universal
	The Devil Doll (1936)	MGM
Freund, Karl	*The Mummy* (1932)	Universal
	Mad Love (1935)	MGM
Halperin, Victor	*White Zombie* (1932)	Amusement Securities
Hillyer, Lambert	*Dracula's Daughter* (1936)	Universal
Kenton, Erle	*Island of Lost Souls* (1933)	Paramount
Mamoulian, Rouben	*Dr. Jekyll and Mr. Hyde* (1932)	Paramount
Whale, James	*Frankenstein* (1931)	Universal
	The Invisible Man (1933)	Universal
	The Bride of Frankenstein (1935)	Universal

MAJOR NONFICTION TEXTS

Abrams, M. H. *A Glossary of Literary Terms*. New York: Rinehart and Company, Inc., 1958.

_____. *The Mirror and the Lamp*. New York: W. W. Norton and Company, Inc. 1958.

Aristotle, *Poetics. The Rhetoric and The Poetics of Aristotle*. Translated by Ingram Bywater. New York: The Modern Library, 1984.

Balazs, Bela. *Theory of Film*. Translated by Edith Bone. New York; Dover Publications, 1970.

Bate, Walter Jackson ed. *Criticism: The Major Texts*. New York; Harcourt, Brace and Company, 1952.

Beck, Calvin Thomas. *Heroes of the Horrors*. New York: Collier Books, 1975.

The Bible [Revised Standard Version]. New York: Meridian Books, 1964.

Bojarski, Richard. *The Films of Bela Lugosi*. Secaucus, N.J.: Citadel Press, 1980.

Brunas, Michael, John Brunas, and Tom Weaver. *Universal Horrors: The Studio's Classic Films, 1931–1946*. North Carolina: McFarland & Company, Inc., 1990.

Butler, Ivan. *Horror in the Cinema*. New York: A. S. Barnes and Co., 1970.

Butler, Kathleen T. *A History of French Literature*. Vol. I. New York: E. P. Dutton and Co., Inc., 1923.

Carroll, Noel. *The Philosophy of Horror or Paradoxes of the Heart*. New York: Routlege, 1990.

Clarens, Carlos. *An Illustrated History of the Horror Film*. New York: Capricorn Books, 1968.

Curtis, James. *James Whale*. Metuchen, N.J.: Scarecrow Press Inc., 1982.

Daniels, Les. *Living in Fear: A History of Horror in the Mass Media*. New York: Charles Scribner's Sons, 1975.

Dickson, Lovat. *H. G. Wells: His Turbulent Life and Times*. New York: Atheneum, 1969.

Eisner, Lotte H. *The Haunted Screen*. California: University of California Press at Berkeley, 1969.

Eliade, Mircea. *The Sacred and the Profane*. Translated by Willard R. Trask. New York: Harcourt, Brace and World, Inc., 1959.

Everson, William K. *Classics of the Horror Film*. New Jersey: Citadel Press, 1974.

Fiedler, Leslie F. *Love and Death in the American Novel*. New York: Dell Publishing Co., Inc., 1967.

Forry, Steven Earl. *Hideous Progenies: Dramatizations of Frankenstein from Mary Shelley to the Present*. Philadelphia: University of Pennsylvania Press, 1990.

Frank, Alan G. *Horror Movies*. London: Octopus Books Ltd., 1975.

Freud, Sigmund. *On Dreams*. Translated by James Strachey. New York: W. W. Norton and Company, Inc., 1952.

Frye, Northrop. *Anatomy of Criticism*. Princeton: Princeton University Press, 1973.

Fulton, A. R. *Motion Pictures: The Development of an Art from Silent Films to the Age of Television*. Norman: University of Oklahoma Press, 1960.

Gassner, John. *Masters of the Drama*. New York: Dover Publications, 1954.

Hamilton, Edith. *Mythology*. New York: Mentor Books, 1961.

Hardy, Phil, Tom Milne, and Paul Willemen, eds. *The Encyclopedia of Horror Movies*. New York: Harper and Row, 1986.

Honan, Park. *Browning's Characters: A Study in Poetic Technique*. New Haven: Yale University Press, 1962.

Horace. *The Art of Poetry. Criticism: The Major Texts*. Edited by Walter Jackson Bate. New York: Harcourt, Brace and Company, 1952.

Jesse, J. H. *George Selwyn and His Contemporaries*. London: Bentley Publishing Co., 1843.

Kendrick, Walter. *The Thrill of Fear*. New York: Grove Weidenfeld, 1991.

Ketterer, David. *Frankenstein's Creation: The Book, the Monster and Human Reality*. Canada: University of Victoria, 1979.

Kracauer, Siegfried. *Theory of Film*. New York: Oxford University Press, 1960.

Levine, George and U. C. Knoepflmacher, eds. *The Endurance of Frankenstein: Essays on Mary Shelley's Novel*. Los Angeles: University of California Press, 1979.

Lindsay, Vachel. *The Art of the Moving Picture*. New York: Liveright Publishing Corporation, 1970.

Losano, Wayne A. *The Horror Film and the Gothic Narrative Tradition*. Ph.D. Diss. Troy: Rensselaer Polytechnic Institute, 1973.

Lovecraft, Howard Phillips. *Supernatural Horror in Literature*. New York: Dover Publications, 1973.

Machlis, Joseph. *The Enjoyment of Music*. 3rd ed. New York: W. W. Norton and Company, Inc., 1970.

McNally, Raymond T., and Radu Florescu. *In Search of Dracula*. New York: Warner Paperback Library, 1973.

Mank, Gregory William. *It's Alive!: The Classic Cinema Saga of Frankenstein*. New York: A. S. Barnes and Co., Inc. 1981.

Metz, Christian. *Film Language: A Semiotics of the Cinema*. Translated by Michael Taylor. New York: Oxford University Press, 1974.

Munsterberg, Hugo. *The Film: A Psychological Study*. New York: Dover Publications, 1970.

Nietzsche, Friedrich. *The Birth of Tragedy from the Spirit of Music*. Translated by William A. Hausmann. *Modern Continental Literary Criticism*. Edited by O. B. Hardison, Jr. New York: Appleton-Century-Crofts, 1962.

Nye, Russel. *The Unembarrassed Muse: The Popular Arts in America*. New York: The Dial Press, 1970.

Panofsky, Erwin. *Meaning in the Visual Arts*. New York: Doubleday, 1955.

Prawer, S. S. *Caligari's Children: The Film as Tale of Terror*. New York: Da Capo Press, 1980.

Praz, Mario. *The Romantic Agony*. Translated by Angus Davidson, New York: Oxford University Press, 1970.

Pritchett, V. S. *The Living Novel*. London: Chatto and Windus, 1954.

Ribner, Irving. *Patterns in Shakespearean Tragedy*. New York: Barnes and Noble, Inc., 1960.

Riley, Philip J., ed. *Dracula [Original 1931 Shooting Script]* Atlantic City: MagicImage Filmbooks, 1990.

Roffman, Peter and Jim Purdy, *The Hollywood Social Problem Film*. Bloomington: Indiana University Press, 1981.

Ronay, Gabriel. *Exploding the Bloody Myths of Dracula and Vampires*. London: Golbancz, 1972.

Rothberg, Abraham. "Introduction." In Stevenson's *Dr. Jekyll and My. Hyde*. New York: Bantam Books, 1973.

Scholes, Robert, and Robert Kellogg. *The Nature of Narrative*. New York: Oxford University Press, 1968.

Seabrook, W. B. *The Magic Island*. New York: Harcourt, Brace and Company, 1929.

Sidney, Philip. *An Apology for Poetry. Criticism: The Major Texts*. Edited by Walter Jackson Bate. New York: Harcourt, Brace and Company, 1952.

Silke, James R. ed. *Rouben Mamoulian: Style is the Man*. Publication #2. Washington, D.C., American Film Institute Publication, 1971.

Skal, David J. *Hollywood Gothic*. New York: W. W. Norton and Company, Inc., 1990.

Sontag, Susan. *Against Interpretation*. New York: Dell Publishing Co., Inc., 1966.

Stallman, Ronald W., ed. *Critiques and Essays in Criticism: 1920–1949*. New York: The Ronald Press Company, 1949.

Sypher, Wylie. *Loss of Self in Modern Literature and Art*. New York: Vintage Books, 1962.

Telotte, J. P. *Dreams of Darkness: Fantasy and the Films of Val Lewton*. Chicago: University of Illinois Press, 1985.

Tropp, Martin. *Mary Shelley's Monster*. Boston: Houghton Mifflin Company, 1977.

Tudor, Andrew. *Monsters and Mad Scientists: A Cultural History of the Horror Movie*. Cambridge: Basil Blackwell, Inc., 1989.

Twichell, James B. *Dreadful Pleasures; An Anatomy of Modern Horror*. New York: Oxford University Press, 1985.

Tyler, Parker. *The Hollywood Hallucination*. New York: Simon and Schuster, 1970.

_____. *Magic and Myth in the Movies*. New York: Simon and Schuster, 1970.

Varma, Devendra P. *The Gothic Flame*. New York; Russell and Russell, 1966.

Walpole, Horace. *The Letters of Horace Walpole*. Vol. X. Edited by Mrs. Paget Toynbee. Oxford: Oxford Press, 1904.

PROSE FICTION

Ainsworth, William Harrison. "The Spectre Bride." Vol. 1 of *Gothic Tales of Terror*. Baltimore: Penguin Books, Inc., 1972.

Anne of Swansea [Mrs. Julia Anne Curtis]. *The Unknown*. Vol. 1 of *Gothic Tales of Terror*. Edited by Peter Haining. Baltimore, Maryland: Penguin Books, 1973.

Anobile, Richard J. *Dr. Jekyll and Mr. Hyde*. Script. New York: Avon Books, 1975.

Austen, Jane. *Northanger Abbey*. New York: Holt, Rinehart & Winston, 1965.

Beale, Charles Willing. *The Ghost of Guir House. Five Victorian Ghost Novels.* Edited by E. F. Bleiler. New York: Dover Publications, 1971.

Bierce, Ambrose. *Some Haunted Houses. Ghost and Horror Stories of Ambrose Bierce*. Edited by E. F. Bleiler. New York: Dover Publications, 1964.

The Black Spider Vol. 1 of *Gothic Tales of Terror*. Edited by Peter Haining. Baltimore, Maryland: Penguin Books, 1973.

Brown, Charles Brockden. *Wieland, or the Transformation*. New York: Harcourt, Brace and World, Inc., 1926.

Bulwer-Lytton, Sir Edward. *The Haunted and the Haunters. Classic Ghost Stories*. New York: Dover Publications, 1975.

Chambers, Robert W. *The Yellow Sign. The King in Yellow and Other Stories* New York; Dover Publications, 1970.

Collins, Wilkie. *The Dream Woman. Tales of Terror and the Supernatural*. Edited by Herbert van Thal. New York; Dover Publications, 1972.
_____ . *Mad Monkton. Tales of Terror and the Supernatural*.

Corelli, Marie. *The Sorrows of Satan*. Illinois: Palmer Publications, Spring 1965.

Crawford, F. Marion. *The Upper Berth. Classic Ghost Stories*, New York: Dover Publications, 1975.

Deane, Hamilton, and John L. Balderston. *Dracula*. New York: Samuel French, 1960.

Doyle, Sir Arthur Conan. *The Adventure of the Sussex Vampire. The Complete Sherlock Holmes*. New York: Doubleday and Company, Inc., 1930.

Fort, Garrett. *Dracula [1931 Shooting Script]* Vol. 13. Atlantic City: Magic-Image Filmbooks, 1990.

Haggard, H. Rider. *She*. New York: Dover Publications, 1951.

Haining, Peter, ed. *The Ghouls*. New York: Pocket Books, 1972.

Hunt, Leigh. *A Tale of a Chimney Corner*. Vol. 1 of *Gothic Tales of Terror*. Edited by Peter Haining. Baltimore Maryland: Penguin Books, 1973.

Huysmans, J. K. *La-Bas*. Translated by Keene Wallace. New York: Dover Publications, 1972.

Irving, Washington. *Adventure of the German Student*. Vol. 2 of *Gothic Tales of Terror*. Edited by Peter Haining. Baltimore, Maryland: Penguin Books, 1973.

LeFanu, J. S. *Carmilla. Best Ghost Stories of J. S. LeFanu*. New York: Dover Publications, 1964.

_____ . *A Chapter in the History of A Tyrone Famile. Ghost Stories and Mysteries.* Edited by E. F. Bleiler. New York: Dover Publications, 1975.

_____ . *The Murdered Cousin. Ghost Stories and Mysteries.*

_____ . *The Mysterious Lodger. Ghost Stories and Mysteries.*

_____ . *The Room in the Dragon Volant. Ghost Stories and Mysteries.*

_____ . *Sir Dominic Sarsfield. Classic Ghost Stories.* New York: Dover Publications, 1975.

_____ . *Uncle Silas.* New York: Dover Publications, 1966.

Lewis, M. G. *The Bravo of Venice.* New York: McGrath Publishing Co., 1972.

_____ . *Mistrust or Blanche and Osbright. Seven Masterpieces of Gothic Horror.* Edited by Robert Donald Spector. New York: Bantam Books, 1971.

_____ . *The Monk.* New York: Grove Press, 1959.

_____ . *Louise or the Living Spectre.* Vol. 2 of *Gothic Tales of Terror.* Edited by Peter Haining. Baltimore, Maryland: Penguin Books, Inc. 1973.

Marryat, Frederic. *The Werewolf. Classic Ghost Stories.* New York: Dover Publications, 1975.

Maturin, Charles Robert. *Melmoth the Wanderer.* Lincoln: University of Nebraska Press, 1972.

_____ . *Melmoth the Wanderer.* London: R. Bentley and Son, 1892.

Maugham, W. Somerset. *The Magician.* New York: Penguin Books, 1980.

Menzies, Sutherland. *Huges, The Wer-Wolf.* Vol. 2 of *Gothic Tales of Terror.* Edited by Peter Haining. Baltimore, Maryland: Penguin Books, Inc., 1973.

Merritt, A. *Burn Witch Burn!* New York: Liveright Publishing Corporation, 1952.

_____ . *Seven Footprints to Satan.* New York: Liveright Publishing Corporation, 1952.

O'Brien, Fitz James. *Wondersmith. Terror By Gaslight: More Victorian Tales of Terror.* Edited by Hugh Lamb. New York: Taplinger Publishing Company, 1976.

Oliphant, Margaret. *The Open Door. Classic Ghost Stories.* New York: Dover Publications, 1975.

Pigault-Lebrun, Charles. *The Unholy Compact Abjured.* Vol. 2 of *Gothic Tales of Terror.*

Poe, Edgar Allan. *Berenice. Collected Works of Edgar Allan Poe.* Edited by Thomas Ollive Mabbott. Cambridge: Belknap Press, 1978.

_____ . *Fall of the House of Usher. Fall of the House of Usher and Other Tales.* New York: New American Library, 1962.

_____ . *Ligeia. American Poetry and Prose.* 4th ed. Edited by Norman Foerster. Boston: Houghton Mifflin Company, 1962.

_____ . *The Thousand-and-Second Tale of Scheherazade. The Complete Works.* New York: Desmond Publishing Company, 1908.

Polidori, John William. *The Vampyre*. Vol. 1 of *Gothic Tales of Terror*. Edited by Peter Haining. Baltimore, Maryland: Penguin Books, Inc., 1973.

Prest, Thomas Preskett. *Varney the Vampyre or the Feast of Blood*. 3 Vols. New York: Arno Press, 1970.

Radcliffe, Ann. *Gaston De Blondeville or the Court of Henry III Keeping Festival in Ardenne*. 2 vols. New York; McGrath Publishing Co., 1972.

_____ . *The Italian or the Confessional of the Black Penitents*. New York: Oxford University Press, 1971.

_____ . *The Mysteries of Udolpho*. London: Oxford University Press, 1966.

Radcliffe, Mary-Anne. *Manfrone or the One-Handed Monk*, Vol. 1. New York: Arno Press, 1972.

Reeve, Clara. *The Old English Baron*. *Seven Masterpieces of Gothic Horror*. Edited by Robert Donald Spector. New York: Bantam Books, 1971.

Renard, Maurice. *The Hands of Orlac*. Translated by Florence Crew-Jones. New York: E. P. Dutton and Co., Inc., 1929.

Reynolds, G. W. M. *Wagner, the Wehr-Wolf*. New York: Dover Publications, 1975.

Riddell, Mrs. J. H. *Old Mrs. Jones*. *The Collected Ghost Stories of Mrs. J. H. Riddell*. Edited by E. F. Bleiler. New York; Dover Publications, 1977.

Schiller, Johann Friedrich von. *The Ghost-Seer or the Apparitionist*. Vol. 2 of *Gothic Tales of Terror*. Edited by Peter Haining. Baltimore, Maryland: Penguin Books, Inc., 1973.

Schreiber, Alois Wilhelm. *The Devil's Ladder*. Vol. 2 of *Gothic Tales of Terror*.

Shelley, Mary. *Frankenstein or the Modern Prometheus*. New York: New American Library, 1965.

_____ . *The Heir of Mondolfo*. *Seven Masterpieces of Gothic Horror*. Edited by Robert Donald Spector. New York; Bantam Books, 1971.

_____ . *The Mortal Immortal*. *Classic Ghost Stories*. New York; Dover Publications, 1975.

The Spectre Barber. Vol. 2 of *Gothic Tales of Terror*. Edited by Peter Haining. Baltimore, Maryland: Penguin Books, Inc., 1973.

Stevenson, Burton E. *A King in Babylon*. Boston: Small, Maynard and Co., 1917.

Stevenson, Robert Louis. *Dr. Jekyll and Mr. Hyde*. New York: Bantam Books, 1973.

Stoker, Bram. *Dracula*. New York: New American Library, 1965.

_____ . *The Jewel of Seven Stars*. London: Jarrolds Publishers, 1966.

_____ . *The Lady of the Shroud*. London: Arrow Books Ltd., 1974.

_____ . *The Lair of the White Worm*. London: Jarrolds Publishers, 1966.

Sue, Eugene. *The Wandering Jew*. New York: The Modern Library, 1940.

_____ . *The Wandering Jew*. Vol. 2 of *Gothic Tales of Terror*. Edited by Peter Haining. Baltimore, Maryland: Penguin Books, Inc., 1973.

Tieck, Johann Ludwig. *The Bride of the Grave*. Vol. 2 of *Gothic Tales of Terror*. Edited by Peter Haining. Baltimore, Maryland: Penguin Books, Inc., 1973.

Tolstoy, Alexis. *The Family of a Vourdalak. Vampires: Stories of the Supernatural.* Translated by Fedor Nikanov. New York: Hawthorn Books, Inc., 1969.

_____ . *The Vampire. Vampires: Stories of the Supernatural.*

Walpole, Horace. *The Castle of Otranto.* New York: Holt, Rinehart and Winston, 1965.

Wells, H. G. *The Invisible Man. Seven Science Fiction Novels of H. G. Wells.* New York: Dover Publications, 1934.

_____ . *The Island of Doctor Moreau. Seven Science Fiction Novels of H. G. Wells.* New York: Dover Publications, 1934.

Whitlatch, James. *The Mummy. The Mummy [original shooting script].* Atlantic City: MagicImage Filmbooks, 1989.

ARTICLES

Ackerman, Forrest J. "Forward" *The Bride of Frankenstein.* Script. Edited by Philip J. Riley. Vol. 2. Atlantic City: MagicImage Filmbooks, 1989.

Bloom, Harold. "Afterward," *Frankenstein.* New York: New American Library, 1965.

Bunnell, Charlene. "The Gothic: A Literary Genre's Transition to Film." *Planks of Reason: Essays on the Horror Film.* Edited by Barry Keith Grant. Metuchen, N. J.: Scarecrow Press, Inc., 1984.

Carter, Margaret L. "A Preface from Polidori to Prest." In *Varney the Vampire or the Feast of Blood* by Thomas Preskett Prest. New York: Arno Press, 1970.

Dadoun, Roger. "Fetishism in the Horror Film." *Fantasy and the Cinema.* Edited by James Donald. London: British Film Institute Press, 1989.

Deren, Maya. "Cinema as an Art Form." *Introduction to the Art of the Movies.*

Dillard, R. H. W. "Even a Man Who is Pure at Heart." *Man and the Movies.* Edited by W. R. Robinson. Baton Rouge: Louisiana State University Press, 1967.

Eckermann, J. P. *Conversations of Goethe in the Last Years of His Life. Criticism: The Major Texts.* Edited by Walter Jackson Bate. New York: Harcourt, Brace and Company, 1952.

Evans, Walter. "Monster Movies: A Sexual Theory." *Sexuality in the Movies.* Edited by Thomas R. Atkins. New York: Da Capo Press, 1975.

_____ . "Monster Movies and Rites of Initiation." *Journal of Popular Film.* Vol. 4 No. 2. (1975): 124–142.

Forster, E. M. "The Challenge of Our Time." *Two Cheers for Democracy.* New York: Harcourt, Brace & Company, 1951.

Frank, Joseph. "Spatial Form in Modern Literature." *The Sewanee Review.* LIII. Nos 2, 3 and 4. (1945).

Giles, Dennis. "Conditions of Pleasure in Horror Cinema." *Planks of Reason*. Edited by Barry Keith Grant. Metuchen, N.J.: Scarecrow Press, Inc., 1984.

Hume, Robert D. "Gothic versus Romantic: A Revaluation of the Gothic Novel." *PMLA* 84, (1969).

Huss, Roy. "Almost Eve: The Creation Scene in *The Bride of Frankenstein*." *Focus on the Horror Film*. Edited by Roy Huss and T. J. Ross. Englewood Cliffs, N.J.: Prentice-Hall, 1972.

————. "Vampire's Progress: Dracula from Novel to Film via Broadway." *Focus on the Horror Film*.

Jensen, Paul. "*The Invisible Man*, A Retrospective." *Photon* 23: 10–23.

Jones, Ernest. "On the Nightmare of Bloodsucking." *Focus on the Horror Film*.

Kawin, Bruce. "The Mummy's Pool." *Planks of Reason: Essays on the Horror Film*.

Knight, Arthur. "Rouben Mamoulian: The Artistic Innovator." *The American Cinema*. Edited by Donald E. Staples. Voice of America: Forum Series, 1973.

Lowry, Richard and Richard deCordova. "Enunciation and the Production of Horror in *White Zombie*." *Planks of Reason: Essays on the Horror Film*.

Macdonald, Dwight. "Notes on Hollywood Directors." *Introduction to the Art of the Movies*. Edited by Lewis Jacobs. New York: The Noonday Press, 1970.

Rothberg, Abraham. "Introduction." *Dr. Jekyll and Mr. Hyde*. New York: Bantam Books, (1973): vii–xix.

Shipley, Joseph T., ed. "Romanticism." *Dictionary of World Literature*. New Jersey: Littlefield, Adams & Co., 1960.

Stoehr, Taylor. "Pornography, Masturbation, and the Novel," *Art of the Essay*. Edited by Leslie Fielder. New York: Thomas Y. Crowell Company, 1969.

————. "Pornography, Masturbation, and the Novel." *Salmagundi* (Fall 1967-Winter 1968): 28–56.

Telotte, J. P. "Faith and Idolatry in the Horror Film." *Planks of Reason: Essays on the Horror Film*.

Tyrer, Thomas. "Tales from the Tube: Why TV is Afraid of Scary Series." *Electronic Media*. October 28, 1991: 1, 32.

Weight, Harold. *Hollywood Filmograph* (April 4, 1931).

Welsch, Janice R. and Syndy M. Conger. "The Comic and the Grotesque in James Whale's Frankenstein Films." *Planks of Reason*.

West, Robert H. "Supernatural." *Dictionary of World Literature*.

Wood, Robin, "An Introduction to the American Horror Film." *Movies and Methods Vol. II*. Edited by Bill Nichols. Berkeley: University of California Press, 1985.

Wright, Andrew. "Introduction." *The Castle of Otranto*. New York: Holt, Rinehart & Winston, 1965.

MAJOR POETRY

Coleridge, Samuel Taylor. "Christabel," and "Rime of the Ancient Mariner." *Norton Anthology of English Literature*. Vol. 2. New York: W. W. Norton and Company, 1986.

Gordon, George, [Lord Byron]. *Manfred. Types of Philosophic Drama*. New York; Prentice-Hall, 1928.

Keats, John. "La Belle Dame Sans Merci" and "Lamia." *Norton Anthology of English Literature*. Vol. 2.

Percy, Thomas. *Reliques of Ancient English Poetry*. Philadelphia: Porter and Coates, 1890.

Scott, Sir Walter. *The Complete Poetical Works of Sir Walter Scott*. New York: Houghton, Mifflin and Company, 1900.

Shelley, Percy Bysshe. *The Cinci. The Complete Works of Percy Bysshe Shelley*. Edited by Roger Ingsin and Walter E. Peck. New York; Scribner, 1926–28.

Stagg, John. "The Vampyre." "The Vampire in Legend, Lore and Literature," by Davendra P. Varma. *Varney the Vampyre*. Vol. 1. New York: Arno Press, 1970.

Index

Daughter and, 165–68, 170, 171,
174, 176, 177, 178; Dracula's
emergence from tomb and, 11–
12; entrapment symbolism and,
13, 16; eroticism in, 9–10;
Frankenstein compared with, 60;
gothic conventions in, 5, 11; London setting and, 15; Lucy's death
and, 16; *The Mummy* compared
with, 27, 28, 31–32, 34–35, 36;
music in, 15; play compared
with, 19–22; power of action theory and, 38; religious symbolism
in, 13–14, 17, 18–19; romanticism in, 10–11, 38; seduction of
Mina and, 16; somnambulism in,
14, 17; supernatural and, 16–17;
verbal versus visual images and,
17, 18, 19; viewer alliance and,
7–8; *White Zombie* and, 48
Dracula (novel), 5–6, 7, 8–9, 17–18
Dracula (stage version), 19–22
Dracula's Daughter: antiphonal sequence in, 172–73; attack sequences in, 173, 175–76;
Balderston and, 165; *Burn Witch
Burn!* and, 118; concluding sequence of, 176–78; cremation sequence and, 172; dialogue in,
166, 168; *Dracula* and, 165–68,
170, 171, 174, 176, 177, 178;
heroine's first appearance and,
171–72; humor and, 167; music
in, 170, 172, 176–77; opening of,
170–71; polarities in, 166; romanticism in, 167; science and, 175;
sexuality in, 175; Stoker and,
165; supernatural and, 166; tragic
elements of, 168–70; viewer sympathy and, 169; villain-hero
image in, 166, 167, 169–70

Edeson, Arthur, 67, 108
Edore, Guy, 115

Egyptology, 28
Eliot, T. S., 147
Emery, Gilbert, 171
Endore, Guy, 152
Everson, William K., 134
Evolution and Ethics, 75–76
Exodus, 17

The Fall of the House of Usher, 46–
47
The Family of a Vourdalak, 4
Faragoh, Francis Edwards, 65
Fitzgerald, Edward, 26
Flaubert, Gustave, 146–47
Florey, Robert, 65
Ford, Grace, 115
Fort, Garrett, 7, 13, 65, 115, 118,
165, 166
Frank, Joseph, 147
Frankenstein (film): authenticity
and, 64–65; black humor in, 60,
71; *The Bride of Frankenstein*
and, 96, 98; conclusion of, 54;
conflicts in, 68; creation sequence in, 68–70; destruction of
monster sequence in, 71–72; dialogue in, 67, 69–70; *Dracula*
compared with, 60; eroticism in,
68; expressionistic devices in, 67,
71; eyes and, 67; framing devices
for, 63; graveyard sequence of,
66–67; *Island of Dr. Moreau*
compared with, 78; monster-cre-
ator relationship in, 60–61, 62;
monster's first appearance and,
70–71; moralistic stance of, 62;
necrophilia in, 68; Prometheus
myth and, 28; romanticism in,
59–60, 62–63, 66, 67; science
and, 60; stage version compared
with, 65–66
Frankenstein (novel), 61–62, 63–
65, 66, 76, 104

About the Author

MICHAEL SEVASTAKIS is Associate Professor of Communications at the College of Mt. St. Vincent.